Ancient And Modern Celebrated Freethinkers

by
Charles Bradlaugh
Anthony Collins
John Watts

Double9
BOOKS

Ancient And Modern Celebrated Freethinkers

by Charles Bradlaugh
Anthony Collins
John Watts

ISBN: 978-93-61159-08-4

Published by

DOUBLE 9 BOOKS

2/13-B, Ansari Road
Daryaganj, New Delhi – 110002
info@double9books.com
www.double9books.com
Tel. 011-40042856

ABOUT THE AUTHOR

Charles Bradlaugh was an English political activist and atheist. He founded the National Secular Society in 1866, 15 years after George Holyoake coined the term "secularism" in 1851. In 1880, Bradlaugh was elected Liberal Member of Parliament for Northampton. Bradlaugh's attempt to confirm as an atheist culminated in a temporary prison sentence, fines for fraudulent voting in the House of Commons, and a series of by-elections in which he regained his place. He was eventually allowed to take an oath in 1886. In 1888, a parliamentary bill he introduced was passed, allowing members of both Houses of Parliament to affirm when sworn in. Anthony Collins and John Watts co-wrote the seminal book "Ancient and Modern Celebrated Freethinkers." Anthony Collins (1676-1729) was a well-known English philosopher who helped to shape the Enlightenment and advocated for free thought. John Watts, whose material is less widely available, most certainly worked with Collins on this compilation. The book, released in 1733, contains biographical portraits of famous figures who opposed traditional religious beliefs, preaching rationality and skepticism. It is still a crucial document in the history of freethought, demonstrating the intellectual fortitude of those who have challenged established religious norms throughout history.

CONTENTS

EDITORS' PREFACE

In these pages, appearing under the title of "Half-Hours with the Freethinkers," are collected in a readable form an abstract of the lives and doctrines of some of those who have stood foremost in the ranks of Freethought in all countries and in all ages; and we trust that our efforts to place in the hands of the poorest of our party a knowledge of works and workers—some of which and whom would otherwise be out of their reach—will be received by all in a favorable light. We shall, in the course of our publication, have to deal with many writers whose opinions widely differ from our own, and it shall be our care to deal with them *justly* and in all cases to allow them to utter in their own words their essential thinkings.

We lay no claim to originality in the mode of treatment—we will endeavor to cull the choicest flowers from the garden, and if others can make a brighter or better bouquet, we shall be glad to have their assistance. We have only one object in view, and that is, the presenting of free and manly thoughts to our readers, hoping to induce like thinking in them, and trust-ing that noble work may follow noble thoughts. The Freethinkers we intend treating of have also been Free Workers, endeavoring to raise men's minds from superstition and bigotry, and place before them a knowledge of the real.

We have been the more inclined to issue the "Half-Hours with the Freethinkers" in consequence, not only of the difficulty which many have in obtaining the works of the Old Freethinkers, but also as an effective answer to some remarks which have lately appeared in certain religious publications, implying a dearth of thought and thinkers beyond the pale of the Church. We wish all men to know that great minds and good men *have* sought truth apart from faith for many ages, and that it is because few were prepared to receive them, and many united to *crush* them, their works are so difficult of access to the general mass at the present day.

THOMAS HOBBES

This distinguished Freethinker was born on the 5th of April, 1588, at Malmesbury; hence his cognomen of "the philosopher of Malmesbury." In connection with his birth, we are told that his mother, being a loyal Protestant, was so terrified at the rumored approach of the Spanish Armada, that the birth of her son was hastened in consequence. The subsequent timidity of Hobbes is therefore easily accounted for. The foundation of his education was laid in the grammar school of his native town, where most probably his father (being a clergyman) would officiate as tutor. At the age of fifteen he was sent to Oxford. Five years of assiduous study made him proficient as a tutor; this, combined with his amiability and profound views of society, gained him the respect of the Earl of Devonshire, and he was appointed tutor to the Earl's son, Lord Cavendish. From 1610 to 1628, he was constantly in the society of this nobleman, in the capacity of secretary. In the interval of this time he travelled in France, Germany, and Italy; cultivating in each capital the society of the leading statesmen and philosophers. Lord Herbert, of Cherbury, the first great English Deist, and Ben Jonson, the dramatist, were each his boon companions. In the year 1628, Hobbes again made the tour of the Continent for three years with another pupil, and became acquainted at Pisa with Galileo. In 1631 he was entrusted with the education of another youth of the Devonshire family, and for near five years remained at Paris with his pupil.

Hobbes returned to England in 1636. The troublous politics of this age, with its strong party prejudices, made England the reverse of a pleasant retirement, for either Hobbes or his patrons; so, perceiving the outbreak of the Revolution, he emigrated to Paris. There in the enjoyment of the company of Gassendi and Descartes, with the *elite* of Parisian genius, he was for awhile contented and happy. Here he engaged in a series of mathematical quarrels, which were prolonged throughout the whole of his life, on the quadrature of the circle. Seven years after, he was appointed mathematical tutor to the Prince of Wales, afterwards Charles II. In 1642, Hobbes published the first of his principal works, "De Cive, or Philosophical Rudiments Concerning Government and Society." It was written to curb the spirit of anarchy, then so rampant in England, by exposing the inevitable results which must of necessity spring from the want of a coherent government amongst a people disunited and uneducated. The principles inculcated in this work were reproduced in the year 1651, in the "Leviathan, or the Matter, Form, and Power of a Commonwealth, Ecclesiastical and Civil;" this, along with a "Treatise on Human Nature," and a small work on "The Body Politic," form the groundwork of the "selfish schools" of moral philosophy. As soon as they were published, they were attacked by the clergy of every country in Europe. They were interdicted by the Pontiffs of the Roman and Greek Church, along with the Protestants scattered over Europe, and the Episcopal authorities of England. Indeed, to such an extent did this persecution rise, that even the royalist exiles received warning that there was no chance for their ostracism being removed, unless "the unclean thing (Hobbes) was put away from their midst." The young prince, intimidated by those ebullitions of vengeance against his tutor? was obliged to withdraw his protection from him, and the old man, then near seventy years of age, was compelled to escape from Paris by night, pursued by his enemies, who, according to Lord Clarendon, tracked his footsteps from France. Fortunately for Hobbes, he took refuge with his old protectors, the Devonshire family, who were too powerful to be wantonly insulted. While residing at Chatsworth, he would no doubt acutely feel the loss of Descartes, the Cardinal de Richelieu, and Gassendi; in the place of those men he entered into a warm friendship with Cowley, the poet, Selden, Harvey, the discoverer of the circulation of the blood, Charles Blount, and the witty Sir Thomas Brown.

In 1654, he published a "Letter upon Liberty and Necessity;" this brief tractate is unsurpassed in Free-thought literature for its clear, concise, subtle, and demonstrative proofs of the self-determining power of the will, and the truth of philosophical necessity. All subsequent writers on this question have largely availed themselves of Hobbes's arguments, particularly the pamphleteers of Socialism. It is a fact no less true than strange, that Communism is derived from the system of Hobbes, which has always been classed along with that of Machiavelli, as an apology for despotism. The grand peculiarity of Hobbes is his method. Instead of taking speculation and reasoning upon theories, he carried out the inductive system of Bacon in its entirety, reasoning from separate generic facts, instead of analogically. By this means he narrowed the compass of knowledge, and made everything demonstrative that was capable of proof. Belief was consequently placed upon its proper basis, and a rigid analysis separated the boundaries of Knowing and Being. Hobbes looked at the great end of existence and embodied it in a double axiom. 1st. The desire for self-preservation. 2nd. To render ourselves happy. From those duplex principles which are inherent in all animals, a modern politician has perpetrated a platitude which represents in a sentence the end and aim of all legislation, "the greatest happiness for the greatest number." This is the *ultimatum* of Hobbes's philosophy. Its method of accomplishment was by treating society as one large family, with the educated and skilled as governors, having under their care the training of the nation. All acting from one impulse (self-preservation,) and by the conjoint experience of all, deriving the greatest amount of happiness from this activity. Hobbes opposed the Revolution, because it degenerated into a faction; and supported Charles Stuart because there were more elements of cohesion within his own party, than amongst his enemies. It was here where the cry of despotism arose; the "Round-heads" seeing they could not detach the ablest men from the King's party, denounced their literary opponents as "lovers of Belial, and of tyranny." This was their most effective answer to the "Leviathan." In after years, when the Episcopal party no longer stood in need of the services of Hobbes, they heaped upon him the stigma of heresy, until his *ci-devant* friends and enemies were united in the condemnation of the man they most feared. Mr. Owen, in his schema of Socialism, took his leading idea on non-responsibility from Hobbes's explanation of necessity, and the freedom of the will. The old divines had inculcated a doctrine to the effect that the "will" was a separate entity of the human mind, which swayed the whole disposition, and was of itself essentially corrupt. Ample testimony from the Bible substantiated this position. But in the method of Hobbes, he lays down the facts that we can have no knowledge without experience, and no experience without sensation. The mind therefore is composed of classified sensations, united together by the law of an association of ideas. This law was first discovered by Hobbes, who makes the human will to consist in the strongest motive which sways the balance on any side. This is the simplest explanation which can be given on a subject more mystified than any other in theology.

A long controversy betwixt Bishop Bramhall, of Londonderry, followed the publication of Hobbes's views on Liberty and Necessity. Charles II. on his restoration, bestowed an annual pension of £100 on Hobbes, but this did not prevent the parliament, in 1666, censuring the "De Cive" and "Leviathan," besides his other works. Hobbes also translated the Greek historian, Thucydides, Homer's Odyssey, and the Illiad. The last years of his life were spent in composing "Behemoth; or, a History of the Civil Wars from 1640 to 1660," which was finished in the year he died, but not published until after his death. At the close of the year 1679, he was taken seriously ill. At the urgent request of some Christians, they were permitted to intrude their opinions upon his dying bed, telling him gravely that his illness would end in death, and unless he repented, he would go straight to hell. Hobbes calmly replied, "I shall be glad then to find a hole to creep out of the world." For seventy years he had been a persecuted man, but during that time his enemies had paid him that tribute of respect which genius always extorts from society. He was a man who was hated and dreaded. He had reached the age of ninety-two when he died. His words were pregnant with meaning; and he never used an unnecessary sentence. A collection of moral apothegms might be gathered from his table-talk. When asked why he did not read every new book which appeared, he said, "If I had read as much as other men, I should have been as ignorant." His habits were simple; he rose early in the morning, took a long walk through the grounds of Chatsworth, and cultivated healthful recreation. The after part of the day was devoted to study and composition. Like Sir Walter Raleigh, he was a devoted admirer of the "fragrant herb." Charles II.'s constant witticism, styled Hobbes as "a bear against whom the Church played their young dogs, in order to exercise them."

If there had been a few more similar "bears," the priestly "dogs" would long since have been exterminated, for none of them escaped unhurt from their encounters with the "grizzly" of Malmesbury, except it was in the mathematical disputes with Dr. Wallis.

He was naturally of a timid disposition: this was the result of the accident which caused his premature birth, and being besides of a reserved character, he was ill-fitted to meet the physical rebuffs of the world. It is said that he was so afraid of his personal safety, that he objected to be left alone in an empty house; this charge is to some extent true, but we must look to the mitigating circumstances of the case. He was a feeble man, turned the age of three-score and ten, with all the clergy of England hounding on their dupes to murder an old philosopher because he had exposed their dogmas. It was but a few years before, that Protestants and Papists had complimented each other's religion by burning those who were the weakest, and long after Hobbes's death, Protestants murdered, ruined, disgraced, and placed in the pillory Dissenters and Catholics alike, and Thomas Hobbes had positive proof that it was the intention of the Church of England to *burn him alive*, on the stake, a martyr for his opinions. This, then, is a sufficient justification for Hobbes feeling afraid, and instead of it being thrown as a taunt at this illustrious Freethinker, it is a standing stigma on those who would re-enact the tragedy of persecution, if public opinion would allow it.

Sir James Mackintosh says: * "The style of Hobbes is the very perfection of didactic language. Short, clear, precise, pithy, his language never has more than one meaning, which never requires a second thought to find. By the help of his exact method, it takes so firm a hold on the mind, that it will not allow attention to slacken. His little tract on human nature has scarcely an ambiguous or a needless word. He has so great a power of always choosing the most significant term, that he never is reduced to the poor expedient of using many in its stead. He had so thoroughly studied the genius of the language, and knew so well how to steer between pedantry and vulgarity, that two centuries have not superannuated probably more than a dozen of his words."

* Second Dissertation: Encyclopaedia Brit., p. 318.

Lord Clarendon describes the personal character of Hobbes as "one for whom he always had a great esteem as a man, who besides his eminent parts of learning and knowledge, hath been always looked upon as a man of probity, and a life free from scandal."

We now proceed to make a selection of quotations from the works of this writer, commencing with those on the "Necessity of the Will," in reply to Bishop Bramhall.

"The question is not whether a man be a free agent—that is to say, whether he can write, or forbear, speak, or be silent, according to his will; but whether the will to write, and the will to forbear, come upon him according to his will, or according to anything else in his own power. I acknowledge this liberty, that I can *do*, if I *will*, but to say, I can *will* if I *will*, I take to be an absurd speech." Further replying to Bramhall's argument, that we do not learn the "idea of the freedom of the will" from our tutors, but we know it intuitively, Hobbes says, "It is true very few have learned from tutors that a man is not free to will; nor do they find it much in books. That they and in books that which the poets chaunt in the theatres, and the shepherds on the mountains, that which the pastors teach in the churches, and the doctors in the universities; and that which the common people in the markets, and all the people do assent unto, is the same that I assent unto; namely, that a man hath freedom to do if he will; but whether he hath freedom to will, is a question which it seems neither the Bishop nor they ever thought of.... A wooden top that is lashed by the boys, and runs about, sometimes to one wall, sometimes to another, sometimes spinning, sometimes hitting men on the shins, if it were sensible of its own motion, would think it proceeded from its own will, unless it felt what lashed it. And is a man any wiser when he runs to one place for a benifice, to another for a bargain, and troubles the world with writing errors, and requiring answers, because he thinks he does it without other cause than his own will, and seeth not what are the lashings which cause that will?"

Hobbes casually mentions the subject of "praise or dispraise," in reference to the will; those who are old enough will remember this was one of the most frequent subjects of discussion amongst the earlier Socialists. "These depend not at all in the necessity of the action praised or dispraised. For what is it else to praise, but to say *a thing is good?* Good, I say, for me, or for somebody else, or for the State and Commonwealth. And what is it to say an action is good, but to say it is as I would wish, or as another would have it, or according to the will of the State—that is to say, according to the law! Does my lord think that no action could please me, or the commonwealth, that should proceed from necessity! Things may be therefore necessary, and yet praiseworthy, as also necessary, and yet dispraised, and neither of them both in vain; because praise and dispraise, and likewise reward and punishment, do, by example, make and conform the will to good or evil. It was a very great praise, in my opinion, that Vellerius Paterculus gives Cato, where he says that he was good by nature, '*et quia aliter esse non potuit.*'' — 'And because he could not do otherwise.''' This able treatise was reprinted, and extensively read about twenty years ago; but, like many other of our standard works, it is at present out of print.

The "Leviathan" is still readable, a bold masculine book. It treats everything in a cool, analytic style. The knife of the Socialist is sheathed in vain; no rhapsody can overturn its impassioned teachings. Rhetoric is not needed to embellish the truths he has to portray, for the wild flowers of genius but too frequently hide the yawning chasms in the garden of Logic. It is not to be expected that this book will be read now with the interest with which it was perused two centuries ago; then every statement was impugned, every argument denied, and the very tone of the book called forth an interference from parliament to stop the progress of its heresies. Now the case is widely different, and the general tenor of the treatise is the rule in which are illustrated alike the works of the philosophers and the dreams of the sophists (priests.) We give part of the introduction. "Nature (the art whereby God hath made and governs the world) is, by the art of man, as in many other things, so in this also, imitated, that it can make an artificial animal. For seeing life is but a motion of limbs, the beginning whereof is in some principal part within; why may we not say that all automata (engines that move themselves by springs and wheels, as doth a watch) have an artificial life? For what is the heart but a spring; and the nerves but so many strings; and the joints but so many wheels, giving motion to the whole body, such as was intended by the Artificer? Art goes yet further, imitating that rational and most excellent work of nature, man. For by art is created that great leviathan, called a Commonwealth, or State, which is but an artificial man though of greater stature and strength than the natural, for whose protection and defence it was intended, and the sovereignty of which is an artificial soul, as giving life and motion to the whole body. To describe the nature of this artificial man, I will consider,

"1st. The *matter* thereof, and the *artificer*, both which is man.

"2nd. *How,* and by what *covenants* it is made, what are the *rights* and *just* power or authority of a sovereign; and what it is that *preserveth* and dissolveth it.

"3rd. What is a Christian Commonwealth.

"Lastly, what is the kingdom of darkness.

"The first chapter treats of 'Senses.' Concerning the thoughts of man, I will consider them first singly, and afterwards in train, or dependence upon one another. Singly, they are every one a representation, or appearance, of some quality or accident of a body without us, which is commonly called an object. Which object worketh on the eyes, ears, and other parts of a man's body, and by diversity of working, produceth diversity of appearances. The original of them all is that which we call sense, for there is no conception in a man's mind, which hath not at first totally or by parts been begotten upon the organs of sense; the rest are derived from that original."

Speaking of "Imagination," Hobbes says, "That when a thing lies still, unless somewhat else stir it, it will lie still forever, is a truth no one doubts of. But that when a thing is in motion, it will eternally be in motion, unless somewhat else stay it, though the reason be the same—namely, that nothing can change itself—is not so easily assented to. For men measure not only other men, but all other things, by themselves; and because they find themselves subject after motion to pain and lassitude, think everything else grows weary of motion, and seeks repose of its own accord—little considering whether it be not some other motion, wherein that desire of rest they find in themselves consisteth.... When a body is once in motion, it moveth (unless something else hinder it) eternally, and whatsoever hindereth it, cannot in an instant, but in time, and by degrees, quite extinguish it; and as we see in the water, though the wind cease, the waves give not over rolling for a long time after; so also it happeneth in that motion which is made in the internal parts of man, then, when he sees, dreams, etc. For after the object is removed, or the eye shut, we still retain an image of the thing seen, though more obscure than when we see it.... The decay of sense in men waking, is not the decay of the motion made in sense, but an obscuring of it, in such manner as the light of the sun obscureth the light of the stars; which stars do no less exercise their virtue, by which they are visible in the day, than in the night. But because amongst many strokes which our eyes, ears and other organs receive from external bodies, the predominant only is sensible; therefore the light of the sun being only predominant, we are not affected with the actions of the stars.... This decaying sense, when we would express the thing itself (I mean fancy itself), we call imagination, as I said before, but when we would express the Decay, and signify the sense is fading, old and past, it is called Memory: so that imagination and memory are but one thing, which, for divers considerations, hath divers names." *

Such is the commencement of this celebrated book, it is based upon materialism; every argument must stand this test upon Hobbes's principles, and characteristically are they elaborated. Hobbes ("De Cive") says of the immortality of the soul, "It is a belief grounded upon other men's sayings, that they knew it supernaturally; or that they knew those who knew them, that knew others, that knew it supernaturally." A sparkling sneer, and perhaps the truest answer to so universal an error. Dugald Stewart, in his analysis of the works of Hobbes, says, ** The fundamental doctrines inculcated in the political works of Hobbes, are contained in the following propositions:—All men are by nature equal, and, prior to government, they had all an equal right to enjoy the good things of this world. Man, too, is by nature, a solitary and purely selfish animal; the social union being entirely an interested league, suggested by prudential views of personal advantage. The necessary consequence is, that a state of nature must be a state of perpetual warfare, in which no individual has any other means of safety than his own strength or ingenuity; and in which there is no room for regular industry, because no secure enjoyment of its fruits. In confirmation of this view of the origin of society, Hobbes appeals to facts falling daily within the cycle of our experience. "Does not a man, (he asks) when taking a journey, arm himself, and seek to go well accompanied? When going to sleep, does he not lock his doors? Nay, even in his own house, does he not lock his chests? Does he not there accuse mankind by his action, as I do by my words?" For the sake of peace and security, it is necessary that each individual should surrender a part of his natural right, and be contented with such a share of liberty as he is willing to allow to others; or, to use Hobbes's own language, "every man must divest himself of the right he has to all things by nature; the right of all men to all things, being in effect no better than if no man had a right to anything." In consequence of this transference of natural rights to an individual, or to a body of individuals, the multitude become one person, under the name of a State, or Republic, by which person the common will and power are exercised for the common defence. The ruling power cannot be withdrawn from those to whom it has been committed; nor can they be punished for misgovern-ment. The interpretation of the laws is to be sought, not from the comments of philosophers, but from the authority of the ruler; otherwise society would every moment be in danger of resolving itself into the discordant elements of which it was at first composed.—The will of the magistrate, therefore, is to be regarded as the ultimate standard of right and wrong, and his voice to be listened to by every citizen as the voice of conscience."

* *Leviathan. Ed. 1651.*

** *Dissertation on the Progress of Ethical Science, p. 41.*

Such are the words of one of Hobbes's most powerful opponents. Dr. Warburton says, "The philosopher of Malmesbury was the terror of the last age, as Tin-dal and Collins are of this. The press sweats with controversy; and every young churchman militant would try his arms in thundering on Hobbes's steel cap." This is a modest acknowledgment of the power of Hobbes, from the most turbulent divine of the eighteenth century.

Victor Comyin gives the following as his view of the philosophy of Hobbes:—"There is no other certain evidence than that of the senses. The evidence of the senses attests only the existence of bodies; then there is no existence save that of bodies, and philosophy is only the science of bodies.

"There are two sorts of bodies: 1st, Natural bodies, which are the theatre of a multitude of regular phenomena, because they take place by virtue of fixed laws, as the bodies with which physics are occupied; 2nd, Moral and political bodies, societies which constantly change and are subject to variable laws.

"Hobbes's system of physics is that of Democritus, the atomistic and corpuscular of the Ionic school.

"His metaphysics are its corollary; all the phenomena which pass in the consciousness have their source in the organization, of which the consciousness in itself is simply a result. All the ideas come from the senses. To think, is to calculate; and intelligence is nothing else than an arithmetic. As we do not calculate with out signs, we do not think without words; the truth of the thought is in the relation of the words among themselves, and metaphysics are reduced to a perfect language. Hobbes is completely a nominalist. With Hobbes there are no other than contingent ideas; the finite alone can be conceived; the infinite is only a negation of the finite; beyond that it is a mere word invented to honor a being whom faith alone can reach. The idea of good and evil has no other foundation than agreeable or disagreeable sensations; to agreeable or disagreeable sensation it is impossible to apply any. other law than escape from the one and search after the other; hence the morality of Hobbes, which is the foundation of his politics. Man is capable of enjoying and of suffering; his only law is to suffer as little, and enjoy as much, as possible. Since such is his only law, he has all the rights that this law confers upon him; he may do anything for his preservation and his happiness; he has the right to sacrifice everything to himself. Behold? then, men upon this earth, where the objects of desire are not superabundant, all possessing equal rights to whatever may be agreeable or useful to them, by virtue of the same capacity for enjoyment and suffering. This is a state of nature, which is nothing less than a state of war, the anarchy of the passions, a combat in which every man is arrayed against his neighbor. But this state being opposed to the happiness of the majority of individuals who share it, utility, the offspring of egotism itself, demands its exchange for another, to wit, the social state. The social state is the institution of a public power, stronger than all individuals, capable of making peace succeed war, and imposing on all the accomplishment of whatever it shall have judged to be useful, that is, just."

Before we dismiss the father of Freethought from our notice, there remains a tribute of respect to be paid to one whom it is our duty to associate with the author of the "Leviathan," and who has but just passed away—one man amongst the British aristocracy with the disposition of a tribune of the people, coupled with thoughts at once elevated and free, and a position which rendered him of essential service to struggling opinion. This man saw the greatness, the profound depth, the attic style, and the immense importance of the works of Hobbes, along with their systematic depreciation by those whose duty it should be to explain them, especially at a time when those works were not reprinted, and the public were obliged to glean their character from the refutations (so called) by mangled quotations, and a distorted meaning. Impelled by this thought, and anxious to protect the memory of a philosopher, his devoted disciple, at a cost of £10,000, translated the Latin, and edited the English works of Hobbes, in a manner worthy alike of the genius of the author, and the discernment of his editor. For this kindness, a seat in Parliament was lost by the organization of the clergy in Cornwall. The name of this man was Sir William Molesworth. Let Freethinkers cherish the memory of their benefactor.

We now take our leave of Thomas Hobbes. He had not the chivalry of Herbert; the vivacity of Raleigh; the cumulative power of Bacon; or the winning policy of Locke. If his physical deformities prevented him from being as daring as Vane, he was as bold in thought and expression as either Descartes, or his young friend Blount. He gave birth to the brilliant constellation of genius in the time of Queen Anne. He did not live to see his system extensively promulgated; but his principles moulded the character of the men who formed the revolution of 1688, equally as much as Hume established the Scotch and German schools of philosophy; and Voltaire laid the train by which the French Revolution was proclaimed. Peace to his memory! It was a stormy struggle during his life; its frowns cannot hurt him now. Could we believe in the idea of a future life, we should invoke his blessings on our cause. That cause which for near two hundred years has successfully struggled into birth, to youth, and maturity. Striking down in its onward course superstitions which hath grown with centuries, and where it does not exterminate them, it supplies a purer atmosphere, and extracts the upas-sting which has laid low so many, and which must yet be finally exterminated. The day is rapidly dawning when our only deities will be the works of genius, and our only prayer the remembrance of our most illustrious chiefs.

A.C.

LORD BOLINGBROKE

Henry St. John, Lord Bolingbroke, was born in his family seat at Battersea, on the 1st of October 1672, and died there on November 15th, 1751, in his 79th year. He was educated by a clergyman in an unnatural manner, and speedily developed himself accordingly. When he left Oxford, he was one of the handsomest men of the day—his majestic figure, refined address, dazzling wit, and classic eloquence, made him irresistibly the "first gentleman in Europe." Until his twenty-fourth year, he was renowned more for the graces of his person, and the fascination of his wild exploits, rather than possessing a due regard to his rank and abilities. His conduct, however, was completely changed when he became a Member of Parliament. The hopes of his friends were resuscitated when they discovered the aptitude for business—the ready eloquence, and the sound reasoning of the once wild St. John. He soon became the hardest worker and the leader of the House of Commons. The expectations of the nation rose high when night after night he spoke with the vivacity of a poet, and the profundity of a veteran statesman on public affairs. In 1704, he received the seals as Secretary-of-War, and was mainly instrumental in gaining Marlborough's victories, by the activity with which he supplied the English General with munitions of war. On the ascendency of the Whigs, St. John resigned his office, and retired into privacy for two years, when the Whig administration was destroyed, and St. John re-appeared as Secretary for Foreign Affairs. His greatest work now was the negotiation of the treaty of Utrecht. This treaty was signed by St. John (then Lord Bolingbroke,) he being sent to Paris as the British Plenipotentiary, and was hailed by the Parisians as a guardian angel. To such an extent was this feeling manifested, that when he visited the theatres every one *rose* to welcome him. So long as Queen Anne lived, Bolingbroke's influence was paramount, but associated with him was the Earl of Oxford, in opposition to the Whig party, and serious differences had arisen between the rivals. Oxford-was dismissed four days before the Queen's death, and Bolingbroke officiated in his place, until Oxford's vacancy was filled, which all expected would be given to himself. A stormy debate in the Privy Council so agitated the Queen, that it shortened her life, and the Council recommended the Earl of Shrewsbury as Premier, and with him the Whigs.

With the accession of George, came the impeachment of Bolingbroke by the victorious Whigs. Knowing that it was their intention to sacrifice him to party revenge, and that his accusers would likewise act as his judges, he wisely withdrew himself to France. The Pretender held a mimic court at Avignon, and a debating society at Lorraine, entitled a Parliament. He offered Bolingbroke the office of Secretary of State, which was accepted by him; and it was only at this time that the emanations of the exiled Stuart's cabinet possessed either a solidity of aim, or a definite purpose. If Louis XIV. had lived longer, he might have assisted the Pretender, but with his death expired the hopes of that ill-fated dynasty. Bolingbroke strove to husband the means which the Chevalier's friends had collected, but the advice of the Duke of Ormond was listened to in preference to Bolingbroke's. The results which Bolingbroke foretold—proceeding rashly and failing ignominiously—both occurred. The insurrection broke out, and failed—no other end could have been anticipated. Intrigues were fast coiling themselves around the secretary; he was openly blamed for the reverses in Scotland—but he was alike careless of their wrath or its issue. One morning Ormond waited upon him with two slips of paper from the Pretender, informing him that his services were no longer required. After his dismissal he was impeached by the lackeys of the Pretender under seven heads, which were widely distributed throughout Europe. There is this anomaly in the life of Bolingbroke, witnessed in no other Englishman: In one year he was the most powerful man in England—Secretary of State—an exile—and then in the same year he occupied a similar office to one who aimed at the English throne, and was impeached by both parties.

For several years he occupied himself in France with philosophical pursuits—until the year 1723—when he received a pardon, which allowed him to return to England, but still his sequestered estates were not returned, and this apology for a pardon was negotiated by a bribe of £11,000 to the German Duchess of Kendal—one of the king's mistresses.

Alexander Pope was Bolingbroke's constant correspondent. Pope had won the applause of England by his poems, and was then considered the arbiter of genius. Voltaire occupied a similar position in France. Since Pope first laid the copy of his greatest epic at the feet of Bolingbroke, and begged of him to correct its errors, he had gradually won himself that renown which prosperity has endorsed. But what a unity in divergence did those philosophers present! The calm moralism of Pope, his sweet and polished rhyme, contrasted with the fiery wit and hissing sarcasm of the Frenchman, more trenchant than Pope's, yet wanting his sparkling epigrams. The keen discernment of both these men saw in Bolingbroke a master, and they ranked by his side as twin apostles of a new and living faith. It was the penetration of true greatness which discerned in the English peer that sublimity of intellect they possessed themselves, without the egotism of an imbecile rival. Bolingbroke had cherished the ethics of one, and restrained the rancor of the other—and both men yielded to him whose system they worshipped; and this trinity of Deists affords the noblest example which can be evoked to prove the Harmony of Reason amidst the most varied accomplishments. Although Pope's name occurs but seldom in the history of Freethought—while that of Bolingbroke is emblazoned in all its glory, and Voltaire is enshrined as its only Deity—yet we must not forget that what is now known as the only collection of St. John's works (the edition in five volumes by Mallet,) were written for the instruction of Pope—sent to him in letters—discussed and agreed to by him—so that the great essayist is as much implicated in them as the author of the Dictionary. It is said, "In his society these two illustrious men felt and acknowledged a superior genius; and if he had no claim to excellence in poetry—the art in which they were so pre-eminent—he surpassed them both in the philosophy they so much admired."

For ten years after this period, he devoted himself to various political writings, which were widely circulated; but we must waive the pleasure at present of analyzing those, and confine our attention to the alliance between Pope and Bolingbroke, in the new school of philosophy.

Bolingbroke's principal friends were Pope, Swift, Mallet, Wyndam, and Atterbury. The first three were most in his confidence in regard to religion: and although Pope was educated a Roman Catholic, and occasionally conformed to that hierarchy (and like Voltaire, for peace, died in it,) yet the philosophical letters which passed between Pope and St. John, fully established him as a consistent Deist—an honor to which Swift also attained, although being a dignitary of the Church: but if doubts arise on the subject, they can easily be dispelled. General Grimouard, in his "Essai sur Bolingbroke," says that "he was intimate with the widow of Mallet, the poet, who was a lady of much talent and learning, and had lived upon terms of friendship with Bolingbroke, Swift, Pope, and many other distinguished characters of the day, who frequently met at her house." The General adds, that the lady has been frequently heard to declare, that these men were all equally deistical in their sentiments (*que c'était une société de purs déistes;*) that Swift from his clerical character was a little more reserved than the others, but he was evidently of the same sentiments at bottom.

There is a remarkable passage in one of Pope's letters to Swift, which seems rather corroborative of the General's. He is inviting Swift to come and visit him. "The day is come," he says, "which I have often wished, but never thought to see, when every mortal I esteem is of the same sentiments in politics and religion." Dr. Warton remarks upon this paragraph "At this time therefore (1733) he (Pope and Bolingbroke were of the same sentiment in religion as well as politics);" * and Pope writing to Swift is proof sufficient that Bolingbroke, Swift, and himself, were united in opinions. Wherever Swift's name is known, it is associated with his spleen on account of his not being elevated to the Episcopal Bench, when he was promised a vacancy, which was reserved for him; but Queen Anne absolutely refused to confer such a dignity upon the author of "Gulliver's Travels" — that profound satire upon society and religion; and this occurring at a time when his energetic services were so much needed in defence of the government he so assisted by pamphleteering, satire, and wholesale lampoons. Mr. Cooke says, "The Earl of Nottingham, in the debate upon the Dissenters' Bill, chiefly founded his objection to the provision that the Bishops should have the only power of licensing tutors, upon the likelihood there was that a man who was in a fair way for becoming a Bishop, was hardly suspected of being a Christian." This pointed allusion to Swift passed without comment or reply in a public assembly, composed in a great measure of his private friends and associates. This seems to intimate that the opinion of his contemporaries was not very strong in favor of Swift's religious principles. This may suffice to prove the unanimity of sentiment existing among this brilliant coterie — one a political Churchman — another the greatest poet of his age — the third, the most accomplished statesman of his country. Although they were united in religious conviction, it would have been certain ruin to any of the confederates if the extent of their thoughts had reached the public ear. The Dean wrote for the present — the poet for his age — and the peer for the immediate benefit of his friends and a record for the future. But they were all agreed that some code of ethics should be promulgated, which should embody the positive speculations of Bolingbroke, with the easy grace of Pope — the elaborate research of the philosopher with the rhetoric of the poet. Swift coalesced in this idea, but was, to a certain extent, ignorant of its subsequent history. It was not thought prudent to trust Mallet and others with the secret. For this purpose the "Essay of Man" was designed on the principles elaborated by Bolingbroke in his private letters to Pope. It was Bolingbroke who drew up the scheme, mapped out the arguments, and sketched the similes — it was Pope who embellished its beauties, and turned it into rhyme. Doctor Warton, the editor of Pope, also proves this: — "Lord Bathurst told the Doctor that he had read the whole of the 'Essay on Man' in *the handwriting of Bolingbroke*, and drawn up in a series of propositions which Pope was to amplify, versify, and to illustrate." If further proofs are required, that Bolingbroke was not only a co-partner but coadjutor with Pope, it is found in the opening of the poem, where the poet uses the plural in speaking of Bolingbroke —

"Awake, my St. John, leave all meaner things
To low ambition, and the pride of kings.
Laugh when we must, be candid when you can,
And vindicate the ways of God to man."

* Cook's Life of Bolingbroke, 2nd vol., p. 97..

This is sufficient to prove the partnership in the poem, and from the generally acknowledged fact of his connection, we have no hesitation in declaring that this poem is the grand epic of Deism, and is as much the offspring of Bolingbroke, as his own ideas when enunciated by others. There is not a single argument in the Essay but what is much more elaborated in the works of Bolingbroke, while every positive argument is reduced to a few poetic maxims in the Essay. We may as well look here for Bolingbroke's creed, rather than amongst his prose works. There is, however, this difference, that in the Essay there is laid down an ethical scheme of positivism — *i.e.*, of everything in morals which can be duly tested and nothing more: while in the prose writings of Bolingbroke, the negative side of theology is discussed with an amount of erudition which has never been surpassed by any of the great leaders of Freethought. The first proposition of the Essay is based on a postulate, upon which the whole reasoning is built. Overthrow this substratum, and the philosophy of the Essay is overturned — admit it, and its truth is evident; it is —

"What can we reason but from what we know?"

This is equivalent to saying that we can only reason concerning man as a finite part of an infinite existence, and we can only predicate respecting what comes under the *category of positive knowledge* ; we are therefore disabled from speculating in any theories which have for a basis opposition to the collected experience of mankind. This was a position laid down by Bolingbroke to escape all the historical arguments which some men deduce from alleged miraculous agency in the past, or problematical prophecy in the future. It *likewise* shows the untenable nature of all analogy, which presumes to trace an hypothetical first cause or personal intelligence, to account for a supposed origin of primeval existence, by which nature was caused, or forms of being first evolved. Although it may be deemed inconsistent with the philosophy of Bolingbroke to admit a God in the same argument as the above, we must not forget that in all speculative reasoning there must be an assumption of some kind, which ought to be demonstrated by proof, or a suitable equivalent in the form of universal consent. Yet in the case of the God of the Essay, we look in vain for the attributes with which Theists love to clothe their God, and we can but perceive inexorable necessity in the shape of rigid and unswerving laws, collected in one focus by Pope, and dignified with the name of God; so that the difference betwixt a Deist of the old, and an Atheist of the modern school, is one of mere words—they both commence with an assumption, the Atheist only defining his terms more strictly, the subject-matter in both instances being the same. The only difference being, the one deceives himself with a meaningless word, the other is speechless on what he cannot comprehend. The Essay shows a scheme of universal gradation, composed of a series of links, which are one entwined within the other—every rock being placed in its necessitated position—every plant amidst its growth bearing an exoteric similitude to itself—every animal, from the lowest quadruped to the highest race of man, occupying a range of climate adapted to its requirements. The Essay here is scientifically correct, and agrees with the ablest writers on necessity. A German philosopher renowned alike for rigid analysis and transcendent abilities as a successful theorist, observes, "When I contemplate all things as a whole, I perceive one *nature* one *force* : when I regard them as individuals, many forces which develop themselves according to their inward laws, and pass through all the forms of which they are capable, and all the objects in nature are but those forces under certain limitations. Every manifestation of every individual power of nature is determined partly by itself, partly by its own preceding manifestations, and partly by the manifestations of all other powers of nature with which it is connected; but it is connected with all, for nature is one connected whole. Its manifestations are, therefore, strictly necessary, and it is absolutely impossible to be other than as it is. In every moment of her duration nature is one connected whole, in every moment must every individual be what it is because all others are what they are, and a single grain of sand could not be moved from its place, without, however imperceptibly to us, changing something throughout all parts of the immeasurable whole. Every moment of duration is determined by all past moments, and will determine all future movements, and even the position of a grain of sand cannot be conceived other than it is, without supposing other changes to an indefinite extent. Let us imagine that grain of sand to be lying some few feet further inland than it actually does; then must the storm-wind that drove it in from the sea-shore have been stronger than it actually was; then must the preceding state of the atmosphere, by which this wind was occasioned, and its degree of strength being determined, have been different from what it actually was, and the preceding changes which gave rise to this particular weather, and so on. We must suppose a different temperature from that which really existed—a different constitution of bodies which influenced that temperature. How can we know that in such a state of weather we have been supposing, in order to carry this grain of sand a few yards further, some ancestors of yours might not have perished from hunger, cold, or heat, long before the birth of that son from whom you are descended, and thus you might never have been at all, and all that you have done, and all that you ever hope to do, must have been hindered, in order that a grain of sand might lie in a different place." * The whole of the first book is devoted to the necessitated condition of man in relation to the universe. In one portion there is a succession of beautiful similes, portraying the blissful state we are in, instead of being gifted with finer sensibilities, or a prescience, which would be a curse.

Fichte's "Destination of Man," pp. 8, 9

Pope, although an ardent disciple of Bolingbroke, did not entirely forsake the prejudices of childhood; he still indulged in a bare hope of a future life, which his master, with more consistency, suppressed. So that when the poet rhymed the propositions of St. John, he pointed them with "hope" in an eternal future; for that speculation which was still *probability* in his day, is now nearly silenced by modern science. But we must not confound the ideas of futurity, which some of the Deists expressed, with those of Christianity. They were as different as the dreams of Christ and Plato were dissimilar. Pope "hoped" for a future life of intellectual enjoyment devoid of evil, but the heaven of the gospel is equally as necessary to be counterbalanced by a hell, as the existence of a God requires the balancing support of a devil. We therefore can sympathise with the description of a heaven, the poor Indian looked for:—

"Some safer world in depths of woods embraced,
Some happier island in the watery waste;
Where slaves once more their native land behold,
Nor fiends torment, nor Christians thirst for gold.
To be—contents his natural desires,
He asks no angels' wings, no seraphs' fires,
But thinks, admitted to that equal sky,
His faithful dog should bear him company."

Pope durst not emphatically deny the future-life theory, so he attacked it by elaborating a physical instead of a spiritual heaven. So heterodox a notion of the Indian's future sports, is not to be found in theology, especially as he pictures the Indian's sports with his dog. Here was a double blow aimed at Christianity by evolving a "positive" idea of future pleasures, and the promulgation of sentiments anti-Christian.—Again he attacks them for unwarrantable speculation in theology, when he says—

"In pride, in reasoning pride our error lies."

This is a corollary to the first proposition, "What can we reason but from what we know?" The only predicate we can draw from this is, the undoubted fact we have no right to profess to hold opinions of that, upon which we cannot have any positive proof. The last line of the first book has been generally thought open to attack. It relates to necessity—"Whatever is, is right"—and is not to be viewed in relation to society as at present constituted, but to the physical universe.

The second book deals with man in relation to himself as an individual; the third as a member of society, and the last in respect to happiness. Throughout the whole Essay the distinctions arising from nature and instinct are defined and defended with vigor and acuteness. Both are proved to be equally great in degree, in spite of the hints constantly thrown out in reference to "God-like Reason *versus* Blind Instinct." We confess our inability to discern the vaunted superiority of the powers of reason over those of its blinder sister. We see in the one matchless wisdom—profound decision—unfailing resource—a happy contentment as unfeigned as it is natural. On the other hand, we see temerity allied with cowardice—a man seeking wisdom on a watery plank, when every footmark may serve him for a funeral effigy; political duplicity arising from his confined generalization of facts; a desire to do right, but checked by accident and cunning—everywhere uneasy—always fatal. If the Christians' fables were true, we might say that Adam and Eve were originally in possession of Instinct and Reason, and fell by listening to the promptings of volition, instead of the unswerving powers of the brutes, and for a hereditary punishment was cursed with a superabundance of reason. For with all our intellectual prerogatives, we have yet failed to arrive at a definite course of action which should influence our conduct. The Essay, speaking of Government by Christianity, says:—

> *"Force first made conquest, and that conquest law,*
> *Till superstition taught the tyrant awe.*
>
> *She taught the weak to bend, the proud to pray,*
> *To power unseen, and mightier far than they:*
> *She, from the rending earth and bursting skies,*
> *Saw Gods descend and fiends infernal rise.*
> *Here fixed the dreadful, there the blessed abodes,*
> *Here made her devils, and weak hope her Gods.*
> *Gods partial, changeful, passionate, unjust,*

Whose attributes were rage, revenge, or lust.

Such as the souls of cowards might conceive,

And formed like tyrants; tyrants would believe.

Zeal then, not charity, became the guide,

And Hell was built in spite, and Heaven in pride."

And again—

"For modes of faith let graceless zealots fight,

His can't be wrong whose life is in the right."

The Essay concludes with an invocation to Bolingbroke—whom Pope styles, "my guide, philosopher, and friend." Such is the conclusion of the most remarkable ethical poem in any language. It is the Iliad of English Deism. Not a single allusion to Christ—a future state of existence given only as a faint probability—the whole artificial state of society satirized—prayer ridiculed, and government of every kind denounced which does not bring happiness to the people. The first principle laid down is the corner-stone of materialism—"What can we reason but from what we know?"—which is stated, explained, and defended with an axiomatic brevity rarely equalled, never surpassed—with a number of illustrations comprising the *chef d'oeuvre* of poetic grace, and synthical melody combined with arguments as cogent as the examples are perfect.

It stands alone in its impregnability—a pile of literary architecture like the "Novum Organan" of Bacon, the "Principia" of Newton, or the Essay of Locke. The facades of its noble colonnades are seen extending their wings through the whole sweep of history, constituting a pantheon of morals, where every nation sends its devotees to admire and worship.

Let us now turn to the philosophical works of Bolingbroke. By the will of Bolingbroke he devised this portion of his manuscripts to David Mallet, the poet, for publication. The noble Lord's choice is open to censure here. He knew the character of Mallet, and could expect little justice from him who should have been his biographer. The MSS. were all prepared for the press long before Bolingbroke died. In this original state, they were addressed to Pope. When published they appeared as "Letters or Essays addressed to Alexander Pope, Esq." The political friends of St. John wished their suppression, fearing that they would injure his reputation by being anti-Christian. A large bribe was offered by Lord Cornbur if Mallet would destroy the works. He, no doubt, thinking more money could be made by their publication, issued them to the world in 1754, but without giving a biography or notes to the books, his work being simply correcting the errors of the press. True, there existed no stipulation that he should write the Life of Bolingbroke, but no one can doubt that such was the intention of the statesman, when he bequeathed to him property which realized £10,000 in value. Every one knows the huge witticism of Dr. Johnson, who accused Bolingbroke of cowardice, under the simile of loading a blunderbuss, and then leaving a Scotchman half-a-crown to fire it when he was out of the way. When those posthumous works appeared, the grand jury of Westminster presented them to the judicial authorities as subversive of religion, morality, and government. They were burnt by the common hangman.

With difficulty we give a quotation from Boling-broke's ideas of a Future Life. In vol. IV., p. 348, he says, "I do not say, that to believe in a future state is to believe in a vulgar error; but this I say, it cannot be demonstrated by reason: it is not in the nature of it capable of demonstration, and no one ever returned that irremediable way to give us an assurance of the fact."

Again, he speaks personally in reference to himself, Pope, and Wollaston, whom he had been opposing:—

> "He alone is happy, and he 'is truly so, who can say,
> Welcome life whatever it brings!
> Welcome death whatever it is!
> If the former,—we change our state.

That you, or I, or even Wollaston himself, should return to the earth from whence we came, to the dirt under our feet, or be mingled with the ashes of those herbs and plants from which we drew nutrition whilst we lived, does not seem any indignity offered to our nature, since it is common to all the animal kind: and he who complains of it as such, does not seem to have been set, by his reasoning faculties, so far above them in life; as to deserve not to be levelled with them at death. We were like them before our birth, that is nothing. So we shall be on this hypothesis, like them too after our death, that is nothing. What hardship is done us? Unless it be a hardship, that we are not immortal because we wish to be so, and flatter ourselves with that expectation.

"If this hypothesis were true, which I am far from assuming, I should have no reason to complain, though having tasted existence, I might abhor non-entity. Since, then, the first cannot be demonstrated by reason, nor the second be reconciled to my inward sentiment, let me take refuge in resignation at the last, as in every other act of my life: let others be solicitous about their future state, and frighten or flatter themselves as prejudice, imaginative bad health—nay, a lowering day, or a clear sunshine shall inspire them to do: let the tranquillity of my mind rest on this immovable rock, that my future, as well as my present state, are ordered by an Almighty Creator, and that they are equally foolish, and presumptuous, who make imaginary excursions into futurity, and who complain of the present."

Lord Bolingbroke died in the year 1751, after a long and painful illness, occasioned by the ignorance of a quack. While lying on his death-bed he composed a discourse, entitled "Considerations on the State of the Nation." He died in peace—in the knowledge of the truth of the principles he had advocated, and with that calm serenity of mind, which no one can more fully experience than the honest Freethinker. He was buried in the church at Battersea. He was a man of the highest rank of genius, far from being immaculate in his youth, brave, sincere, a true friend, possessed of rich learning, a clear and sparkling style, a great wit, and the most powerful Freethinker of his age.

A. C.

CONDORCET

In the history of the French Revolution, we read of a multitude of sections, each ruled by a man, and each man representing a philosophy. Not that each man was the contriver of a system, but the effervescence of one. As true as Robespierre was the advocate of Rousseau, as Marat was the Wilkes of Paris, as Danton was the Paine, and Mirabeau the expediency-politician of reflex England, so true is it that Condorcet was the type of the philosophic Girondists, the offspring of Voltaire.

The two great schools of metaphysics fought out the battle on the theatre of the Constituent Assembly, in a spirit as bitterly uncompromising as when under different phraseological terms, they met in the arguments of the School-men, or further in the womb of history, on the forum of Athens. It is a fact no less true than singular, that after each mental excitement amongst the *savons*, whether in ancient or in modern times, after the literary shock has passed away, the people are innoculated with the strife, and, destitute of the moderation of their leaders, fight for that doctrine which they conceive oppresses their rights. The French Revolution was one of those struggles. It gave rise to epoch-men. Not men who originated a doctrine, but those who attempted to carry it out. Condorcet was one of those men. He was the successor of Voltaire in the Encyclopædic warfare. The philosopher amongst the orators. Destitute of the amazing versatility of the sage of Ferney, he imbibed the prophet's antipathy to superstition, and after a brilliant career, fell in the wild onslaught of passion. The Revolution was the arena on which was fought the battle involving the question whether Europe was to be ruled for a century by Christianity or Infidelity. The irresolution of Robespierre lost to us the victory of the first passage of arms, equally as decisive as Lafayette in 1830, and Lamartine in 1848, being Liberals, lost in each case the social Republic by their vacillating policy. The true Freethinkers of that age were the Girondists. With their heroic death, the last barrier to despotism disappeared; the Consulate became the only logical path for gilded chains and empire. With the ostracism of the Republicans by Napoleon the Little, a Parallel is completed between the two eras of French history.

The family name of Condorcet was Caritat. His father was a scion of an aristocratic family, and an officer in the army. The son who gave honor to the family, was born in the year 1743, at Ribemont, in Picardy. His father dying early, left his son to be educated with his wife, under the guardianship of his brother, the Bishop of Lisieux, a celebrated Jesuit. The mother of Condorcet was extremely superstitious, and in one of her fanatic ecstasies, offered up her son at the shrine of the Virgin Mary. How this act was performed we cannot relate; but it is a notorious fact that until his twelfth year, the embryo philosopher was clothed in female attire, and had young ladies for companions, which, M. Arago says, "accounts for many peculiarities in the *physique* and the *morale* of his manhood." The abstinence from all rude, boyish sports, checked the proper muscular development of his limbs; the head and trunk were on a large scale, but the legs were so meagre that they seemed unfit to carry what was above them; and, in fact, he never could partake in any strong exercises, or undergo the bodily fatigues to which healthy men willingly expose themselves. On the other hand, he had imbibed the tenderness of a delicate damsel, retaining to the last a deep horror for affliction pain on the inferior animals.

In 1775, he entered the Jesuit Academy at Rheiras. Three years afterwards, he was transferred to the College of Navarre, in Paris, and soon made himself the most distinguished scholar there. His friends wished him to enter the priesthood, not knowing that even in his seventeenth year he had embraced the Deism of the age.

At the age of nineteen he left college, and immediate-ly published a series of mathematical works, which established his fame. Shortly after this, the Academy of Sciences chose Condorcet for their assistant secretary. In the year 1770 he accompanied D'Alembert in a tour through Italy, making a call for some weeks at Ferney, where he was delighted with the company of Voltaire, and was duly recognised as one of the Encylopædists; and, on his return to Paris, became the literary agent of his great leader.

A Quarterly Reviewer, writing on Voltaire and Condercet, says of the former, "When he himself, in these latter days, was resolved to issue anything that he knew and felt to be pregnant with combustion, he never dreamt of Paris—he had agents enough in other quarters: and the anonymous or pseudonymous mischief was printed at London, Amsterdam, or Hamburgh, from a fifth or sixth copy in the handwriting of some Dutch or English clerk—thence, by cautious steps, smuggled into France—and then, disavowed and denounced by himself, and, for him, by his numberless agents, with an intrepid assurance which, down to the last, confounded and baffled all official inquisitors, until, in each separate case, the scent had got cold. Therefore, he sympathized not at all with any of these, his subalterns, when they, in their own proper matters, allowed themselves a less guarded style of movement."

On one occasion, Condorcet's imprudence extorts a whole series of passionate remonstrants from him and his probable complaints—but the burden is always the same—"Tolerate the whispers of age! How often shall I have to tell you all that no one but a fool will publish such things unless he has 200,000 bayonets at his back? Each Encyclopædist was apt to forget that, though he corresponded familiarly with Frederick, he was not a King of Prussia; and, by-and-by, not one of them more frequently made this mistake than Condorcet—for that gentleman's saintlike tranquillity of demeanor, though it might indicate a naturally languid pulse, covered copious elements of vital passion. The slow wheel could not resist the long attrition of controversy; and when it once blazed, the flame was all the fiercer for its unseen nursing. 'You mistake Condorcet,' said D'Alembert, 'he is a volcano covered with snow.'"

When Turgot became Minister of Marine, he gave Condorcet a post as Inspector of Canals; from this he was subsequently promoted to the Inspector of the Mint. When Turgot was replaced by Necker, Condorcet resigned his office.

In 1782 he was elected one of the forty of the Academy of Sciences, beating the Astronomer, Bailly, by *one* vote. In the next year, D'Alembert, his faithful friend, died, leaving him the whole of his wealth; his uncle, the bishop, likewise died in the same year, from whom he would receive a fresh accession of property. Shortly after this, time, Condorcet married Madame de Grouchy—also celebrated as a lady of great beauty, good fortune, and an educated Atheist. The marriage was a happy one. The only offspring was a girl, who married General Arthur O'Connor, uncle to the late Feargus O'Connor, an Irish refugee who was connected with Emmett's rebellion.

During the excitement of the American War of Independence, Condorcet took an active part in urging the French Government to bestow assistance in arms and money, upon the United States; after the war was concluded, he corresponded with Thomas Paine, who gradually converted him to the extreme Republican views the "illustrious needleman" himself possessed, which, in this case, rapidly led to the *denouement* of 1791, when he was elected a member of the Legislative Assembly by the department of Paris. In the next year he was raised to the rank of President by a majority of near one hundred votes. While in the Assembly, he brought forward and supported the economical doctrines of Adam Smith, proposed the abolition of indirect taxation, and levying a national revenue upon derivable wealth in amount according to the individual, passing over all who gained a livelihood by manual labor. He made a motion for the public burning of all documents relating to nobility—himself being a Marquis. He took a conspicuous place in the trial of the king; he voted him guilty, but refused to vote for his death, as the punishment of death was against his principles. The speech he made on this occasion is fully equal to that of Paine's on the same occasion.

When the divergence took place between the Jacobins and Girondists, Condorcet strove to unite them; but every day brought fresh troubles, and the position of the Seneca of the Revolution was too prominent to escape the opposition of the more violent taction.

Robespierre triumphed; and in his success could be traced the doom of his enemies. An intercepted letter was the means of Condorcet's impeachment. Deprived of the support of Isnard, Brissot, and Vergniaud, the Jacobins proscribed without difficulty the hero whose writings had mainly assisted in producing the Revolution. His friends provided means for his escape. They applied to a lodging-house keeper, a Madame Vernet, if she would conceal him for a time; she asked was he a virtuous man— yes, replied his friend, he is the— — stay, you say he is a good man, I do not wish to pry into his secrets or his name. Once safe in this asylum, he was unvisited by either wife or friends; morover, such was the hurry of his flight, that he was without money, and nearly without books.

While in this forced confinement, he wrote the "*Esquisse d'un Tableau Historique des Progrès de l'Esprit Humain,*" and several other fragmentary essays. In this work he lays down a scheme of society similar to the "New Moral World," of Robert Owen. Opposing the idea of a God, he shows the dominion of science in education, political economy, chemistry, and applies mathematical principles to a series of moral problems. Along with the progress of man he combined the progress of arts—estimating the sanatory arrangements of our time, he prophecied on the gradual extension of longevity, amongst the human race; and with it, enjoyments increased by better discipline in gustatorial duties. He has similar views on the softer sex to M. Proudhomme (his immediate disciple,) and, in the close of the work, Condorcet announced the possibility of an universal language, which is daily becoming more assimilated to modern ideas.

The guillotine had not been idle during the few weeks of Condorcet's retreat. Fancying that (if discovered) he might be the means of injuring his benefactress, he resolved to escape from the house of Madame Vernet. Previous to doing this, he made his will. M. Arago, describing this epoch in his closing days, says:—

"When he at last paused, and the feverish excitement of authorship was at an end, our colleague rested all his thoughts anew on the danger incurred by his hostess. He resolved then (I employ his own words) to quit the retreat which the boundless devotion of his tutelar angel had transformed into a paradise. He so little deceived himself as to the probable consequences of the step he meditated—the chances of safety after his evasion appeared so feeble—that before he put his plan into execution he made his last dispositions. In the pages then written, I behold everywhere the lively reflection of an elevated mind, a feeling heart, and a beautiful soul. I will venture to say, that there exists in no language anything better thought, more tender, more touching, more sweetly expressed, than the 'Avis d'un Proscrit a sa Fill.' Those lines, so limpid, so full of unaffected delicacy, were written on that very day when he was about to encounter voluntarily an immense danger. The presentiment of a violent end almost inevitably did not disturb him—his hand traced those terrible words, *Ma mort, ma mort prochaîne!* with a firmness which the Stoics of antiquity might have envied. Sensibility, on the contrary, obtained the mastery when the illustrious proscribed was drawn into the anticipation that Madame de Condorcet also might be involved in the bloody catastrophe that threatened him. *Should my daughter be destined to lose all*—this is the most explicit allusion that the husband can insert in his last writing."

"The Testament is short. It was written on the fly-leaf of a 'History of Spain.' In it Condorcet directs that his daughter, in case of his wife's death, shall be brought up by Madame Vernet, whom she is to call her second mother, and who is to see her so educated as to have means of independent support either from painting or engraving. 'Should it be necessary for my child to quit France, she may count on protection in England from my Lord Stanhope and my Lord Daer. In America, reliance may be placed on Jefferson and Bache, the grandson of Franklin. She is, therefore, to make the English language her first study.'"

Such was the last epistle ever written by Condorcet. Notwithstanding the precautions taken by his friends, he escaped into the streets—from thence having appealed in vain to friends for assistance, he visited some quarries. Here he remained from the 5th to the evening of the 7th of April, 1794. Hunger drove him to the village of Clamait, when he applied at an hostelry for refreshment. He described himself as a carpenter out of employment, and ordered an omelet. This was an age of suspicion, and the landlord of the house soon discovered that the wanderer's hands were white and undisfigured with labor, while his conversation bore no resemblance to that of a common artificer. The good dame of the house inquired how many eggs he would have in his dish. Twelve, was the answer. Twelve eggs for a joiner's supper! This was heresy against the equality of man. They demanded his passport—he had not got one—the only appearance of anything of the sort was a scrap of paper, scrawled over with Latin epigrams. This was conclusive evidence to the village Dogberries that he was a traitor and an aristocrat. The authorities signed the warrant for his removal to Paris. Ironed to two officers they started on the march. The first evening they arrived at Bourg-la-Reine, where they deposited their prisoner in the gaol of that town. In the morning the gaoler found him a corpse. He had taken a poison of great force, which he habitually carried in a ring. Thus ended the life of the great Encyclopædist—a man great by his many virtues—who reflected honor on France by his science, his literary triumphs, and his moral heroism. He had not the towering energy of Marat, nor the gushing eloquence of Danton, neither had he the superstitious devotion to abstract ideas which characterized the whole course of Robespierre's life. The oratory of Danton, like that of Marat, only excited the people to dissatisfaction; they struck down effete institutions, but they were not the men to inaugurate a new society. It is seldom we find the pioneers of civilization the best mechanics. They strike down the forest—they turn the undergrowth—they throw a log over the stream, but they seldom rear factories, or invent tubular bridges.

Amongst the whole of the heroes of the French Revolution, we must admire the Girondists, as being the most daring, and, at the same time, the most constructive of all who met either in the Constituent Assembly or the Convention. The Jacobin faction dealt simply with politics through the abstract notions of Rousseau: but of what use are "human rights" if we have to begin *de novo* to put into operation?—rather let us unite the conservative educationalism of Socialism with the wild democracy of ignorance. Politics never can be successful unless married to Socialism.

It was not long after Condorcet's death, before the Committee of Public Instruction undertook the charge of publishing the whole of his works. For this they have been censured on many grounds. We consider that it was one of the few good things accomplished by that Committee. There is nothing in the works of this writer which have a distinctive peculiarity to us; few great writers who direct opinion at the time they write, appear to posterity in the same light as they did to a public inflamed by passion, and trembling under reiterated wrongs. When we look at the works of D'Holbach, we find a standard treatise, which is a land-mark to the present day; but at the time the "System of Nature" was written, it had not one tithe the popularity which it now enjoys; it did not produce an effect superior to a new sarcasm of Voltaire, or an epigram of Diderot. Condorcet was rather the co-laborer and *literateur* of the party, than the prophet of the new school. Voltaire was the Christ, and Condorcet the St. Paul of the new faith. In political economy, the doctrines of the English and Scotch schools were elaborated to their fullest extent. Retrenchment in pensions and salaries, diminution of armies, equal taxation, the resumption by the State of all the Church lands, the development of the agricultural and mechanical resources, the abolition of the monopolies, total free trade, local government, and national education; such-were the doctrines for which Turgot fought, and Condorcet popularized. If they had been taken in time, France would have escaped a revolution, and Europe would have been ruled by peace and freedom. It may be asked, who brought about the advocacy of those doctrines, for they were not known before the middle of the eighteenth century? They were introduced as a novelty, and defended as a paradox. France had been exhausted by wars, annoyed by *ennui*, brilliant above all by her genius, she was struck with lassitude for her licentious crimes. There was an occasion for a new school. Without it, France, like Carthage, would have bled to death on the hecatomb of her own lust. Her leading men cast their eyes to England; it was then the most progressive nation in existence. The leading men of that country were intimate with the rulers of the French; the books of each land were read with avidity by their neighbors; a difference was observable between the two: but how that difference was to be reconciled was past the skill of the wisest to unravel. England had liberal institutions, and a people with part of the substance, and many of the forms of Liberalism, along with a degree of education which kept them in comparative ignorance, yet did not offer any obstacles to raising themselves in the social sphere. Before France could compete with England, she had to rid herself of the feudal system, and obtain a Magna Charta. She was above four centuries behind-hand here. She had to win her spurs through revolutions, like those of Cromwell's and that of 1688, and the still greater ones of Parliament. The Freethinkers of England prepared the Whig revolution of William, by advocating the only scheme which was at the time practicable, for of the two—the Protestant and the Catholic religion—the former is far more conducive to the liberties of a people than the latter, and at the time, and we may also say, nearer the present, the people were not prepared for any organic change. This being the case, it is not to be wondered at that the French Revolution was a failure as a constructive effort; it was a success as a grand outbreak of power; showing politicians where (in the future) to rely for success. The men who undertook to bring about this Revolution are not to be censured for its non-success. They wished to copy English institutions, and adapt them to those of the French; for this purpose, the Continental League was formed, each member of which pledged himself to uproot, as far as lay in his power, the Catholic Church in France. A secret name was given to it—L'Infame—and an organized attack was speedily commenced. The men at the head of the movement, besides Voltaire and Frederick, were D'Alembert, Diderot, Grim, St. Lambert, Condillac, Helvetius, Jordan, Lalande, Montesquieu, and a host of others of less note. Con-dorcet, being secretary of the Academy, corresponded with, and directed the movements of all, in the absence of his chief. Every new book was criticised — refutations were published to the leading theological works of the age; but by far the roost effective progress was made by the means of poems, essays, romances, epigrams, and scientific papers. The songs of France at this era were written by the philosophers; and this spirit was diffused among the people. In a country so volatile and excitable as the French, it is difficult to estimate too highly the power of a ballad warfare. The morality of Abbots and Nuns were sung in strains as rhapsodical, and couplets as voluptuous as the vagaries of the Songs of Solomon.

Much discretion was required, that no separate species of warfare should be overdone, lest a nausea of sentiment should revert upon the authors, and thus lead to a reaction more sanguinary than the force of the philosophers could control. In all those cases Condorcet was the prime mover and the agent concerned. He communicated with Voltaire on every new theory, and advised him when and how to strike, and when to *rest*. In all those matters Condorcet was obeyed. There was a smaller section of the more serious philosophers who sympathized with, yet did not labor simultaneously for the common cause — those men, the extreme Atheists — clever but cautious — men who risked nothing — Mirabeau and D'Holbach were the types of this class. It is well known that both Frederick, Voltaire, and Condorcet opposed those sections, as likely to be aiming at too much for the time.

When it was considered prudent to take a more decided step, the Encyclopædia was formed. Condorcet had a principal part in this work, which shook priestcraft on its throne; it spread consternation where-ever it appeared, and was one of the main causes of the great outbreak. No one can sufficiently praise a work of such magnitude; nor can any one predicate when its effects will cease.

In the "Life of Condorcet," by Arago, there is a curious extract copied from a collection of anecdotes, said to be compiled from his note-books, and dignified with the title of "Mémoires de Condorcet." It relates to a conversation between the Abbe Galiana and Diderot, in which it is said Condorcet acquiesced. The subject is the fair sex: —

Diderot. — How do you define woman?

Galiana. — An animal naturally feeble and sick.

Diderot. — Feeble? Has she not as much courage as man?

Galiana.—Do you know what courage is? It is the effect of terror. You let your leg be cut off, because you are afraid of dying. Wise people are never courageous—they are prudent—that is to say, poltroons.

Diderot.—Why call you woman naturally sick!

Galiana.—Like all animals, she is sick until she attains her perfect growth. Then she has a peculiar symptom which takes up the fifth part of her time. Then come breeding and nursing, two long and troublesome complaints. In short, they have only intervals of health, until they turn a certain corner, and then *elles ne sont plus de malades peut-être—elles ne sont que des reilles.*

Diderot.—Observe her at a ball, no vigor, then, M. l'Abbe?

Galiana.—Stop the fiddles! put out the lights! she will scarcely crawl to her coach.

Diderot.—See her in love.

Galiana.—It is painful to see anybody in a fever.

Diderot.—M. l'Abbe, have you no faith in education?

Galiana.—Not so much as in instinct. A woman is habitually ill. She is affectionate, engaging, irritable, capricious, easily offended, easily appeased, a trifle amuses her. The imagination is always in play. Fear, hope, joy, despair, and disgust, follow each other more rapidly, are manifested more strongly, effaced more quickly, than with us. They like a plentiful repose, at intervals company; anything for excitement. Ask the doctor if it is not the same with his patients. But ask yourself, do we not all treat them as we do sick people, lavish attention, soothe, flatter, caress, and get tired of them?

Condorcet, in a letter, remarking on the above conversation, says:—"I do not insist upon it as probable that woman will ever be Euler or Voltaire; but I am satisfied that she may one day be Pascal or Rousseau." This very qualification, we consider, is sufficient to absolve Condorcet from, the charge of being a "woman hater." His opponents, when driven from every other source, have fallen back on this, and alleged that he viewed the sexes as unequal, and that the stronger had a right to lord it over the weaker. But which is the weaker? Euler and Voltaire were masculine men. A woman to be masculine, in the true sense of the word, is an anomaly, to be witnessed with pain. She is not in a normal condition. She is a monster. Women should live in society fully educated and developed in their physical frame, and then they would be more feminine in proportion as they approach the character of Mary Wollstonecraft. They have no right to domineer as tyrants, and then fall into the most abject of slaves. In each of the characters of Pascal and Rousseau, was an excess of sensibility, which overbalanced their other qualities, and rendered their otherwise great talents wayward, and, to a certain extent, fruitless. The peculiarity of man is physical power, and intellectual force; that of woman is an acute sensibility. Condorcet, then, was justified in expressing the opinions he avowed upon the subject.

In a paper, in the year 1766, read before the "Academy," on "Ought Popular Errors to be Eradicated!" Condorcet says, "If the people are often tempted to commit crimes in order that they may obtain the necessaries of life, it is the fault of the laws; and, as bad laws are the product of errors, it would be more simple to abolish those errors than to add others for the correction of their natural effects. Error, no doubt, may do some good; it may prevent some crimes, but it will occasion mischiefs greater than these. By putting nonsense into the heads of the people, you make them stupid; and from stupidity to ferocity there is but a step. Consider—if the motives you suggest for being just make but a slight impression on the mind, that will not direct the conduct—if the impressions be lively, they will produce enthusiasm, and enthusiasm for error. Now, the ignorant enthusiast is no longer a man; he is the most terrible of wild beasts. In fact, the number of criminals among the men with prejudices (Christians) is in greater proportion to the total number of our population, than the number of criminals in the class above prejudices (Freethinkers) is to the total of that class. I am not ignorant that, in the actual state of Europe, the people are not, perhaps, at all prepared for a true doctrine of morals; but this degraded obtuseness is the work of social institutions and of superstitions. Men are not born blockheads; they become such. By speaking reason to the people, even in the little time they give to the cultivation of their intellect, we might easily teach them the little that it is necessary for them to know. Even the idea of the respect that they should have for the property of the rich, is only difficult to be insinuated among them—first, because they look on riches as a sort of usurpation, of theft perpetrated upon them, and unhappily this opinion is in great part true—secondly, because their excessive poverty makes them always consider themselves in the case of absolute necessity—a case in which even very severe moralists have been of their mind—thirdly, because they are as much despised and maltreated for being poor, as they would be after they had lowered themselves by larcenies. It is merely, therefore, because institutions are bad, that the people are so commonly a little thievish upon principle."

We should have much liked to have given some extended quotations from the works of Condorcet; but, owing to their general character, we cannot extract any philosophic formula which would be generally interesting. His "Lettres d'un Théologien" are well deserving of a reprint; they created an astounding sensation when they appeared, being taken for the work of Voltaire—the light, easy, graceful style, with deeply concealed irony, the crushing retort and the fiery sarcasm. They made even priests laugh by their Attic wit and incongruous similes. But it was in the "Academy" where Condorcet's influence was supreme. He immortalized the heroes as they fell, and pushed the cause on by his professional duties. He was always awake to the call of duty, and nobly did he work his battery. He is now in the last grand sleep of man—the flowers of poesy are woven in amarynth wreaths over his tomb.

A.C.

SPINOZA

Baruch Spinoza, or Espinoza, better known under the name of Benedict Spinoza (as rendered by himself in the Latin language,) was born at Amsterdam, in Holland, on the 24th of November, 1632. There is some uncertainty as to this date, as there are several dates fixed by different authors, both for his birth and death, but we have adopted the biography given by Dr. C. H. Bruder, in the preface to his edition of Spinoza's works. His parents were Jews of the middle, or, perhaps, somewhat humbler class. His father was originally a Spanish merchant, who, to escape persecution, had emigrated to Holland. Although the life of our great philosopher is one full of interesting incidents, and deserves to be treated fully, we have but room to give a very brief sketch, referring our readers, who may wish to learn more of Spinoza's life, to Lewes's "Biographical History of Philosophy," *Westminster Review*, No. 77, and "Encyclopædia Brittannica." p. 144. His doctrines we will let speak for themselves in his own words, trusting thereby to give the reader an opportunity of knowing who and what Spinoza really was. One man shrinks with horror from him as an Atheist. Voltaire says, that he was an Atheist, and taught Atheism. Another calls him "a God-intoxicated man." We present him a mighty thinker, a master mind, a noble, fearless utterer of free and noble thoughts, a hard-working, honest, independent man; as one who, two centuries ago, gave forth to the world a series of thinkings which have crushed, with resistless force, the theological shell in the centre of which the priests hide the kernel "truth."

Spinoza appears in his boyhood to have been an apt scholar, and to have rapidly mastered the tasks set him by his teachers. Full of rabbinical lore he won the admiration of the Rabbi Moses Mortira, but the pupil rose higher than his master, and attempted to solve problems which the learned rabbis were content to reverence as mysteries not capable of solution. First they remonstrated, then threatened; still Spinoza persevered in his studies, and in making known the result to those around him. He was threatened with excommunication, and withdrew himself from the synagogue. One more effort was made by the rabbis, who offered Spinoza a pension of about £100 a-year if he would attend the synagogue more frequently, and consent to be silent with regard to his philosophical thinkings. This offer he indignantly refused. Reason failing, threats proving futile, and gold being treated with scorn, one was found sufficiently fanatic to try a further experiment, which resulted in an attempt on Spinoza's life; the knife, however, luckily missed its aim, and our hero escaped. At last, in the year 1660, Spinoza, being then twenty-eight years of age, was solemnly excommunicated from the synagogue. His friends and relations shut their doors against him. An outcast from the home of his youth, he gained a humble livelihood by polishing glasses for microscopes, telescopes, etc., at which he was very expert. While thus acquiring, by his own handiwork, the means of subsistence, he was studying hard, devoting every possible hour to philosophical research. Spinoza became master of the Dutch, Hebrew, German, Spanish, Portuguese, and Latin languages, the latter of which he acquired in the house of one Francis Van den Ende, from whom it is more than probable he received as much instruction in Atheism as in Latin. Spinoza only appears to have once fallen in love, and this was with Van den Ende's daughter, who was herself a good linguist, and who gave Spinoza instruction in Latin. She, however, although willing to be his instructress and companion in a philogical path, declined to accept his love, and thus Spinoza was left to philosophy alone. After his excommunication he retired to Rhynsburg, near the City of Leyden, in Holland, and there studied the works of Descartes. Three years afterwards he published an abridgment of the "Meditations" of the great father of philosophy, which created a profound sensation. In an appendix to this abridgment were contained the germs of those thinkings in which the pupil outdid the master, and the student progressed beyond the philosopher. In the month of June, 1664, Spinoza removed to Woorburg, a small village near the Hague, where he was visited by persons from different parts, attracted by his fame as a philosopher; and at last, after many solicitations he came to the Hague, and resided there altogether. In 1670 he published his "Tractatus Theologico-Politicus." This raised him a host of opponents; many writers rushed eager for the fray, to tilt with the poor Dutch Jew. His book was officially condemned and forbidden, and a host of refutations (?) were circulated against it. In spite of the condemnation it has outlived the refutations.

Spinoza died on the 21st or 22nd of February, 1677, in his forty-fifth year, and was buried on the 25th of February at the Hague. He was frugal in his habits, subsisting independently on the earnings of his own hands. Honorable in all things, he refused to accept the chair of Professor of Philosophy, offered to him by the Elector, and this because he did not wish to be circumscribed in his thinking, or in the freedom of utterance of his thoughts. He also refused a pension offered to him by Louis XIV, saying that he had no intention of dedicating anything to that monarch. The following is a list of Spinoza's works:—"Principiorum Philosophise Renati

Descartes;" "Tractatus Theologico-Politicus;" "Ethica;" "Tractatus Politicus;" "De Emandatione Intellectus;" "Epistolæ;" "Grammaticus Hebracæ," etc. There are also several spurious works ascribed to Spinoza. The "Tractatus Politicus" has been translated into English by William Maccall, who seems fully to appreciate the greatness of the philosopher, although he will not admit the usefulness of Spinoza's logic. Maccall does not see the utility of that very logic which compelled him to admit Spinoza's truth. We are not aware of any other translation of Spinoza's works except that of a small portion of his "Ethica," by Lewes. This work, which was originally published in 1677, commenced with eight definitions, which, together with the following axioms and propositions, were reprinted from the *Westminster Review* in the *Library of Reason*:—

DEFINITIONS.

I. By cause of itself I understand that, the essence of which involves existence: or that, the nature of which can only be considered as existent.

II. A thing finite is that which can be limited (terminari potest) by another thing of the same nature—*ergo*, body is said to be finite because it can always be conceived as larger. So thought is limited by other thoughts. But body does not limit thought, nor thought limit body.

III. By substance I understand that which is in itself, and is conceived *per se*—that is, the conception of which does not require the conception of anything else as antecedent to it.

IV. By attribute I understand that which the mind perceives as constituting the very essence of substance.

V. By modes I understand the accidents (affectiones) of substance; or that which is in something else, through which also it is conceived.

VI. By God I understand the being absolutely infinite; that is, the substance consisting of infinite attributes, each of which expresses an infinite and eternal essence.

Explication, I say absolutely infinite, but not in *suo genere*; for to whatever is infinite, but not in *suo genere*, we can deny infinite attributes; but that which is absolutely infinite, to its essence pertains everything which implies essence, and involves no negation.

VII. That thing is said to be free which exists by the sole necessity of its nature, and by itself alone is determined to action. But that is necessary, or rather constrained, which owes its existence to another, and acts according to certain and determinate causes.

VIII. By eternity I understand existence itself, in as far as it is conceived necessarily to follow from the sole definition of an eternal thing.

AXIOMS.

I. Everything which is, is in itself, or in some other thing.

II. That which cannot be conceived through another, *per aliud* must be conceived, *per se.*

III. From a given determinate cause the effect necessarily follows, and *vice versa*. If no determinate cause be given, no effect can follow.

IV. The knowledge of an effect depends on the knowledge of the cause, and includes it.

V. Things that have nothing in common with each other cannot be understood by means of each other—that is, the conception of one, does not involve the conception of the other.

VI. A true idea must agree with its original in nature.

VII. Whatever can be clearly conceived as non-existent does not, in its essence, involve existence.

PROPOSITIONS.

I. Substance is prior in nature to its accidents. Demonstration. Per definitions three and five.

II. Two substances, having different attributes, have nothing in common with each other. Dem. This follows from def. three; for each substance must be conceived in itself and through itself; in other words, the conception of one does not involve the conception of the other.

III. Of things which have nothing in common, one cannot be the cause of the other. Dem. If they have nothing in common, then (per axiom five) they cannot be conceived by means of each other; *ergo* (per axiom four,) one cannot be the cause of the other.—Q. E. D.

IV. Two or more distinct things are distinguished among themselves, either through the diversity of their attributes, or through that of their modes. Dem. Everything which is, in itself, or in some other thing (per ax. one)—that is (per def. three and five,) there is nothing out of ourselves (*extra intellectum,* outside the intellect) but substance and its modes. There is nothing out of ourselves whereby things can be distinguished amongst one another, except substances, or (which is the same thing, per def. lour) their attributes and modes.

V. It is impossible that there should be two or more substances of the same nature, or of the same attributes. Dem. If there are many different substances they must be distinguished by the diversity of their attributes or of their modes (per prop. 4.) If only by the diversity of their attributes, it is thereby conceded that there is, nevertheless, only one substance of the same attribute; but if their diversity of modes, then, substance being prior in order of time to its modes, it must be considered independent of them—that is (per def. three and six,) cannot be conceived as distinguished from another—that is (per prop, four,) there cannot be many substances, but only one substance.—Q. E. D.

VI. One substance cannot be created by another substance. Dem. There cannot be two substances with the same attributes (per prop, five)—that is (per prop. two,) that hare anything in common with each other; and, therefore (per prop, three,) one cannot be the cause of the other.

Corollary 1. Hence it follows that substance cannot be created by anything else. For there is nothing in nature except substance and its modes (per axiom one, and def. three and five.) Now, this substance, not being produced by another, is self-caused.

Corollary 2. This proposition is more easily to be demonstrated by the absurdity of its contradiction; for if substance can be produced by anything else, the conception of it would depend on the conception of the cause (per axiom four,) and hence (per def. three,) it would not be substance.

VII. It pertains to the nature of substance to exist. Dem. Substance cannot be produced by anything else (per coroli. prop, six,) and is therefore the cause of itself—that is (per def. one,) its essence necessarily involves existence; or it pertains to the nature of substance to exist.—Q. E. D.

VIII. All substance is necessarily infinite. Dem. There exists but one substance of the same attribute; and it must either exist as infinite or finite. But not finite, for (per def. two) as finite it must be limited by another substance of the same nature, and in that case there would be two substances of the same attributes, which (per prop, five) is absurd. Substance therefore is infinite.—Q. E. D.

"Scholium I.—I do not doubt but that to all who judge confusedly of things, and are not wont to inquire into first causes, it will be difficult to admit the demonstration of prop. 7, because they do not sufficiently distinguish between the modifications of substances, and substances themselves, and are ignorant of the manner in which things are produced. Hence it follows, that the commencement which they see natural things have, they attribute to substances; for he who knows not the true cause of things, confounds all things, and feigns that trees talk like men; that men are formed from stones as well as from seeds, and that all forms can be changed into all other forms. So, also, those who confound the divine nature with the human, naturally attribute human affections to God, especially as they are ignorant of how these affections are produced in the mind. If men attended to the nature of substance, they would not, in the least, doubt proposition seven; nay, this proposition would be an axiom to all, and would be numbered among common notions. For by substance they would understand that which exists in itself, and is concerned through itself—*i.e.,* the knowledge of which does not require the knowledge of anything as antecedent to it. But by modification they would understand that which is in another thing, the conception of which is formed by the conception of the thing in which it is, or to which it belongs. We can have, therefore, correct ideas of non-existent modifications, because, although out of the understanding they have no reality, yet their essence is so comprehended in that of another, that they can be conceived through this other. The truth of substance (out of the understanding) lies nowhere but in itself, because it is conceived *per se.* If therefore any one says he has a clear idea of substance, and yet doubt whether such substance exist, this would be as much as to say that he has a true idea, and nevertheless doubts whether it be not false (as a little attention sufficiently manifests;) or if any man affirms substance to be created, he at the same time affirms that a true idea has become false, than which nothing can be more absurd. Hence it is necessarily confessed that the existence of substance, as well as its essence, is an eternal truth. And hence we must conclude that there is only one substance possessing the same attribute, which requires here a fuller development. I note therefore—1. That the correct definition of a thing includes and expresses nothing but the nature of the thing defined. From which follows—2. That no definition includes or expresses a distinct number of individuals, because it expresses nothing but the nature of the thing defined; *ergo,* the definition of a triangle expresses no more than the nature of a triangle, and not any fixed number of triangles. 3. There must necessarily be a distinct cause for the existence of every existing thing. 4. This cause, by reason of which anything exists, must either be contained in the nature and definition of the existing thing (viz., that it pertains to its nature to exist,) or else must be beyond it—must be something different from it.

"As therefore it pertains to the nature of substance to exist, so must its definition include a necessary existence, and consequently from its sole definition we must conclude its existence. But as from its definition, as already shown in notes two and three, it is not possible to conclude the existence of many substances—*ergo,* it necessarily follows that only one substance of the same nature can exist."

It will be necessary for the reader to remember that Spinoza commenced his philosophical studies at the same point with Descartes. Both recognized existence as the primal fact, self-evident and indisputable.

But while Descartes had, in some manner, fashioned a quality—God and God-created substance—Spinoza only found one, substance, the definition of which included existence. By his fourth proposition ("of things which have nothing in common, one cannot be the cause of the other, ") he destroyed the creation theory, because by that theory God is assumed to be a spirit having nothing in common with matter, yet acting on matter; and Lewes speaks of the fourth proposition in the following terms:—"This fallacy has been one of the most influential corrupters of philosophical speculation. For many years it was undisputed, and most metaphysicians still adhere to it. The assertion is that only like can act upon like; but although it is true that *like* produces (causes) *like*, it is also true that like produces *unlike*; thus fire produces pain when applied to our bodies; *explosion* when applied to gunpowder; *charcoal* when applied to wood; all these effects are unlike the cause." We cannot help thinking that in this instance, the usually thoughtful Lewes has either confused substance with its modes, or, for the sake of producing a temporary effect, has descended to mere sophism. Spinoza's proposition is, that *substances* having nothing in common, cannot act on one another. Lewes deals with several modes of the same substance as though they were different substances. Way, more, to make his argument the more plausible, he entirely ignores in it that *noumenon* of which he speaks as underlying all phenomena, and uses each phenomenon as a separate existence. In each of the instances mentioned, however varied may be the modification, the essence is the same. They are merely examples of one portion of the whole acting upon another portion, and there is that in each mode which is common to the whole, and by means of which the action takes place.

Much has been said of Spinoza's "God" and "Divine Substance," and we must refer the reader to Definition Six, in which God is defined as being "infinite substance." Now, although we should be content to strike the word "God" out of our own tablet of philosophical nomenclature, as being a much misused, misrepresented, and entirely useless word, yet we must be very careful, when we find another man using the word, to get his precise definition, and not to use any-other ourselves while in his company.

Spinoza, when asked "What name do you attach to infinite substance?" says, "God."—If he had said any other word we could not have quarrelled with him so long as he defined the word, and adhered strictly to the terms of his definition, although we might regret that he had not either coined a word for himself, or used one less maltreated by the mass. Spinoza said, "I can only take cognizance of one substance (of which I am part) having infinite attributes of extension and thought. I take cognizance of substance by its modes, and in my consciousness of existence. Every thing is a mode of the attribute of extension, every thought, wish, or feeling, a mode of the attribute of thought. I call this, substance, with infinite attributes, God." Spinoza, like all other thinkers, found himself overpowered by the illimitable vastness of the infinite when attempting to grasp it by his mental powers, but unlike other men he did not endeavor to relieve himself by separating himself from that infinite; but, knowing he was a part of the whole, not divisible from the remainder, he was content to aim at perfecting his knowledge of existence rather than at dogmatising upon an indefinable word, which, if it represented anything, professed to represent an incomprehensible existence far beyond his reach.

We ought not to wonder that in many parts of Spinoza's writings we find the word "God" treated in a less coherent manner than would be possible under the definition given in his "Ethics," and for these reasons:— Spinoza, from his cradle upwards, had been surrounded with books and traditions sanctified by the past, and impressed on his willing mind by his family, his tutors, and the heads of his church; a mind like his gathered all that was given, even more quickly than it was offered, still craving for more—"more light"—"more light"—and at last light came bursting on the young thinker like a lightning flash at dark midnight, revealing his mind in chains, which had been cast round him in his nursery, his school, his college, his synagogue. By a mighty effort he burst these chains, and walked forth a free man, despite the entreaties of his family, the reasonings of the rabbis, the knife of the fanatic, the curse of his church, and the edict of the state. But should it be a matter of surprise to us that some of the links of those broken chains should still hang on the young philosopher, and, seeming to be a part of himself, almost imperceptibly incline to old ways of thinking, and to old modes of utterance of those thoughts! Wonder not that a few links bang about him, but rather that he ever succeeded in breaking those chains at all. Spinoza, after his secession from his synagogue, became logically an Atheist; education and early impressions enlarged this into a less clearly-defined Pantheism; but the logic comes to us naked, disrobed of all by which it might have been surrounded in Spinoza's mind. If that logic be correct, then all the theologies of the world are false. We have presented it to the reader to judge of for himself. Many men have written against it; of these some have misunderstood, some have misrepresented, some have failed, and few have left us a proof that they had endeavored to deal with Spinoza on his own ground. Maccall says, "In the glorious throng of heroic names, there are few nobler than Spinoza's. Apart altogether from the estimate we may form of his philosophy, there is something unspeakably interesting in the life and the character of the man. In his metaphysical system there are two things exceedingly distinct. There is, first, the immense and prodigious, but terrible mathematical skeleton, which his subtle intellect binds up and throws as calmly into space as we drop a pebble into the water, and whose bones, striking against the wreck of all that is sacred in belief, or bold in speculation, rattle a wild response to our wildest phantasies, and drive us almost to think in despair that thinking is madness; and there is, secondly, the divinest vision of the infinite, and the divinest incense which the intuition of the infinite ever yet poured forth at the altar of creation."

The "Treatise on Politics" is not Spinoza's greatest work; it is, in all respects, inferior to the "Ethics," and to the "Theologico-Political Treatise." But there are in politics certain eternal principles, and it is for setting forth and elucidating these that the Treatise of Spinoza is so valuable.

In the second chapter of that Treatise, after defining what he means by nature, etc., he, on the sixth section, proceeds as follows:—"But many believe that the ignorant disturb more than follow the order of nature, and conceive of men in nature as a state within the state. For they assert that the human mind has not been produced by any natural causes, but created immediately by God, and thereby rendered so independent of other things as to have absolute power of determining itself, and of using reason aright. But experience teaches us more than enough, that it is no more in our power to have a sound mind than a sound body. Since, moreover, everything, as far as it is able, strives to conserve its being, we cannot doubt that if it were equally in our power to live according to the prescripts of reason, as to be led by blind desire, all would seek the guidance of reason and live wisely, which is not the case. For every one is the slave of the particular pleasure to which he is most attached. Nor do theologians remove the difficulty when they assert that this inability is a vice, or a sin of human nature, which derives its origin from the fall of the first parent. For if it was in the power of the first man to stand rather than to fall, and if he was sound in faculty, and had perfect control over his own mind, how did it happen that he, the wise and prudent, fell? But they say he was deceived and tempted by the devil. But who was it that led astray and tempted the devil himself? Who, I ask, rendered this the most excellent of intelligent creatures so mad, that he wished to be greater than God? Could he render himself thus mad—he who had a sane mind, and strove as much as in him lay to conserve his being? How, moreover, could it happen that the first man in possession of his entire mental faculties, and master of his will, should be both open to temptation, and suffer himself to be robbed of his mind? For if he had the power of using his reason aright, he could not be deceived; for as far as in him lay, he necessarily sought to conserve his own being, and the sanity of his mind. But it is supposed he had this in his power, therefore he necessarily conserved his sane mind, neither could he be deceived. Which is evidently false from his history; and, consequently, it must be granted that it was not in the power of the first person to use reason aright, but that he, like us, was subject to passions."

Spinoza is scarcely likely to become a great favorite with the "Woman's Rights Convention." In his ninth chapter of the same Treatise, he says, "If by nature women were equal to men, and excelled as much as they in strength of mind and in talent, truly amongst nations, so many and so different, some would be found where both sexes ruled equally, and others where the men were ruled by the women, and so educated as to be inferior to them in talent; but as this has never happened, we are justified in assuming that women, by nature, have not an equal right with men, but that they are necessarily obedient to men, and thus it can never happen that both sexes can equally rule, and still less that men be ruled by women."

Lewes, in his seventh chapter on Modern Philosophy, thus sums up Spinoza's teachings and their result. He says:—

"The doctrine of Spinoza was of great importance, if for nothing more than having brought about the first crisis in modern philosophy. His doctrine was so clearly stated, and so rigorously deduced from admitted premises, that he brought philosophy into this dilemma:—

"'Either my premises are correct; and we must admit that every clear and distinct idea is absolutely true; true not only subjectively, but objectively.

"'If so, my objection is true;

"'Or my premises are false; the voice of consciousness is not the voice of truth;

"'And if so, then is my system false, but all philosophy is impossible; since the only ground of certitude—our consciousness—is pronounced unstable, our only means of knowing the truth is pronounced fallacious.'"

"Spinozism or scepticism, choose between them, for you have no other choice.

"Mankind refused, however, to make a choice. If the principles which Descartes had established could have no other result than Spinozism, it was worth while inquiring whether those principles might not themselves be modified.

"The ground of discussion was shifted, psychology took the place of ontology. It was Descartes's theory of knowledge which led to Spinozism; that theory must therefore he examined; that theory becomes the great subject of discussion. Before deciding upon the merits of any system which embraced the great questions of creation, the Deity, immortality, etc., men saw that it was necessary to decide upon the competency of the human mind to solve such problems. All knowledge must be obtained either through experience or independent of experience. Knowledge dependent on experience must necessarily be merely knowledge of *phenomena*. All are agreed that experience can only be experience of ourselves as modified by objects. All are agreed that to know things *per se*—*noumena*—we must know them through some other channel then experience. Have we or have we not that other channel? This is the problem."

"Thus, before we can dogmatize upon on to logical subjects, we must settle this question—Can we transcend the sphere of our consciousness, and know things *per se?*"

"I."

ANTHONY COLLINS

Freethought, as developed in the Deistic straggles of the seventeenth century, had to battle for existence against the Puritanic reaction which took its second rise from the worn-out licentious age of the last of the Stuarts, and that of the no less dangerous (though concealed) libertinism of the Dutch king. A religious rancor also arose which, but for the influence of a new power, would have re-enacted the tragedy of religious persecution. But this rancor became somewhat modified, from the fact that the various parties now were unlike the old schismatics, who were each balanced at the opposite ends of the same pole—extreme Papacy on the one hand, and Fifth-monarchists on the other—when each oscillation from the Protestant centre deranged the balance of enthusiasm, and drove it to the farthest verge of fanaticism, until all religious parties were hurled into one chaos of disunion. Such were the frequent changes of the seventeenth century—but at its close the power of Deism had evolved a platform on which was to be fought the hostilities of creeds. Here, then, could not exist that commingling of sects, which were deducible in all their varied extravagance from the Bible. Theology had no longer to fight with itself, but with philosophy. Metaphysics became the Jehu of opinion, and sought to drive its chariot through the fables of the saints. The old doctrines had to be re-stated to meet new foes. For the Papists, Nonconformists, and Brownists, were excluded to make way for the British Illuminati, who spread as much consternation through England as did the French Encyclopædists across Europe. The new field of action was only planned, for when Catholicism first opposed Protestantism, its leaders little thought what a Pandoric box it was opening—nor did the Divines of the latter sect ever doubt the finality of their own doctrines. They wished to replace one infallibility by another. And the same charge can be substantiated against Deism. When in this Augustan age the Free-thinking leaders, fresh from the trammels of Christism, first took the name of Moral Philosophers, they little knew they were paving the way for an Atheism they so much dreaded—a democracy more unbridled than their most constitutional wishes—a political economy to be tried for half a century, and then to be discarded—a revolutionary fervor which should plough up Europe, and then give place to a Communism, which the first founders of this national agitation would have gazed upon with amazement, and shrunk from with despair. Such is the progress of change. The rise of the Deistic movement may be defined in a sentence. It was the old struggle of speculative opinion shifting its battle-ground from theology to philosophy, prior to the one being discarded, and the other developed into positive science.

Amongst the most distinguished of these reformers, stands the name of Anthony Collins.

Who and what he was, we have little opportunity of knowing, save from the scattered notices of contemporaries; but sufficient is left on record to prove him one of the best of men, and the very Corypheus of Deism. The twin questions of Necessity and Prophecy have been examined by him perhaps more ably than by any other liberal author. There are slight discrepancies in relation to the great events of his life. The Abbe Lodivicat says he was born June 21st, 1676, of a rich and noble family, at Heston, in Middlesex, and was appointed treasurer of the county; but another account says "Hounslow," which we think was the more likely place. He was educated at Eton and Cambridge. He studied for the bar for sometime, but (being wealthy) ultimately renounced jurisprudence, while his youthful studies admirably fitted him for his subsequent magisterial duties. He was clever, honest, learned, and esteemed by all who knew his character. The elder D'Israeli says, "that he was a great lover of literature, and a man of fine genius, while his morals were immaculate, and his personal character independent."

The friendship of Locke alone is sufficient to stamp the character of Collins with honor, and he was one of the most valued friends of this great man. In a volume published by P. Des Maizeaux (a writer we shall have occasion to notice) in the year 1720, containing a collection of the posthumous works of Locke, there are several letters addressed to Collins which fully substantiate our opinion. Locke was then an old man, residing in the country, and Collins was a young man in London, who took a pleasure in executing the commissions of his illustrious friend. In one of them, dated October 29th, 1703, he says—"If I were now setting out in the world, I should think it my greatest happiness to have such a companion as you, who had a true relish of truth, would in earnest seek it with me, from whom I might receive it undisguised, and to whom I might communicate what I thought true, freely. Believe it my good friend, to love truth for truth's sake, is the principal part of human perfection in this world, and the seed-plot of all other virtue; and, if I mistake not, you have as much of it as ever I met with in anybody. What, then, is there wanting to make you equal to the best—a friend for any one to be proud of?"

During the following year the correspondence of Locke appears in a most interesting light—the affectionate inquiries, the kind advice, and the most grateful acknowledgments are made to Collins. On Sept. 11th, Locke writes:—"He that has anything to do with you, must own that friendship is the natural product of your constitution, and your soul, a noble soil, is enriched with the two most valuable qualities of human nature—truth and friendship. What a treasure have I then in such a friend with whom I can converse, and be enlightened about the highest speculations!" On the 1st of October he wrote Collins on his rapid decay, "But this, I believe, he will assure you, that my infirmities prevail so fast on me, that unless you make haste hither, I may lose the satisfaction of ever seeing again a man that I value in the first rank of those I leave behind me." This was written twenty-seven days before his death. Four days before his decease, he wrote a letter to be given to Collins after his death. This document is one of the most important in relation to the life of the great Freethinker—it irrefragably proves the falsity of everything that may be alleged against the character of Collins:—

"Oates, August 23, 1704. For Anthony Collins, Esq.

"Dear Sir—By my will, you will see that I had some kindness for * * * And I knew no better way to take care of him, than to put him, and what I designed for him, into your hands and management. The knowledge I have of your virtues of all kinds, secures the trust, which, by your permission, I have placed in you; and the peculiar esteem and love I have observed in the young man for you, will dispose him to be ruled and influenced by you, so of that I need say nothing. May you live long and happy, in the enjoyment of health, freedom, content, and all those blessings which Providence has bestowed on, you, and your virtues entitle you to. I know you loved me living, and will preserve my memory now I am dead. * * * I leave my best wishes with you.

"John Locke."

Such is the honorable connection which existed between Locke and Collins. Collins's first publication was a tract, "Several of the London Cases Considered," in the year 1700. In 1707, he published an "Essay Concerning the Use of Reason on Propositions, the evidence whereof depends upon Human Testimony;" "in which," says Dr. Leland, "there are some good observations, mixed with others of a suspicious nature and tendency." It principally turned on the Trinitarian controversy then raging, and is of little interest now. In this year Collins united with Dodwell in the controversy carried on by Dr. Samuel Clarke. One of Clarke's biographers alludes to it thus: "Dr. Clarke's arguments in favor of the immateriality, and consequent immortality of the soul, called out, however, a far more formidable antagonist than Dodwell, in the person of Anthony Collins, an English gentleman of singular intellectual acuteness, but, unhappily, of Infidel principles. The controversy was continued through several short treatises. On the whole, though Clarke, in some instances, laid himself open to the keen and searching dialectics of his gifted antagonist, the victory certainly remained with the Divine." Of course it is only to be expected that such will be the opinion of an opponent—but it is further proof of Collins's ability and character. In 1703 appeared his celebrated "Discourses of Freethinking," which perhaps created the greatest sensation in the religious world (with the exception of the "Age of Reason") of any book published against Christianity. This book is as able a defence of the freedom of the expression of thought without penalty, as was ever published. It is divided into four sections. In the 1st, Freethinking is defined—in five arguments. In the 2nd, That it is our duty to think freely on those points of which men are denied the right to think freely: such as of the nature and attributes of God, the truth and authority of Scriptures, and of the meaning of Scriptures, in seven arguments and eleven instances. The third section is the consideration of six objections to Freethinking—from the whole of which he concludes (1) That Freethinkers must have more understanding, and that they must necessarily be the most virtuous people. (2) That they have, in fact, been the most understanding and virtuous people in all ages. Here follows the names of a great number of men whom Collins classified as Freethinkers, and of whom we have no reason to be ashamed.

This book was answered by many divines, but none of them emerged from the contest with such Christian honors as the famous Dr. Bentley—considered England's greatest classical scholar. In the same year, the Dr. published his reply under the signature of "Phileleutheros Lipsiensis." The fame of Bentley was considered equal to Collins's; and it has always been represented that this reply completely crushed the Freethinker—nothing could be farther from the truth. Bentley principally attacked the Greek quotations and denounced Collins for his ignorance in not putting his (Bentley's) construction on every disputed word. For this reply, Bentley received the thanks of the University of Cambridge. In condition with this work, Collins is also charged with wilful deception—which has been reproduced in our own lives by devines who perhaps never read a line of Collins. A French edition of the "Discourse" was translated under the personal inspection of Collins: and it is said that he altered the construction of several sentences to evade the charges brought against him by Bentley Dr. Leland is particularly eloquent upon this; and the Rev. Mr. Lorimer, of Glasgow, triumphantly plagiarises the complaint of the men whose defects he can only imitate. There is another charge connected with Bentley and his friends, which it is desirous should be exposed. The elder D'Israeli says:—"Anthony Collins wrote several well-known works, without prefixing his name; but having pushed too far his curious and polemical points, he incurred the odium of a Freethinker—a term which then began to be in vogue, and which the French adopted by translating it, in their way—'a strong thinker,' or *esprit fort*. Whatever tendency to 'liberalise' the mind from the dogmas and creeds prevails in these works, the talents and learning of Collins were of the first class. His morals were immaculate, and his personal character independent; but the *odium theologicum* of those days combined every means to stab in the dark, till the taste became hereditary with some. I may mention a fact of this cruel bigotry which occurred within my own observation, on one of the most polished men of the age. The late Mr. Cumberland, in the romance entitled his 'Life' gave this extraordinary fact. He said that Dr. Bentley, who so ably replied to Collins's 'Discourse,' when many years after he discovered him fallen into great distress, conceiving that by having ruined Collins's character as a writer for ever, he had been the occasion of his personal misery, he liberally contributed to his maintenance. In vain I mentioned to that elegant writer, who was not curious about facts, that this person could never have been Anthony Collins, who had always a plentiful fortune; and when it was suggested to him that this 'A. Collins' as he printed it, must have been Arthur Collins, the historic compiler, who was often in pecuniary difficulties, still he persisted in sending the lie down to posterity, without alteration, in his second edition, observing to a friend of mine, that 'the story, while it told well, might serve as a striking instance of his great relative's generosity; and that it should stand because it could do no harm to any but to Anthony Collins, whom he considered as little short of an Atheist.'" Such is a specimen of Christian honor and justice.

In 1715, appeared his "Philosophical inquiry into Human Liberty." Dr. Clarke was again his opponent. The publication of this work marked an epoch in metaphysics. Dugald Stewart, in criticising the discussion on Moral Liberty between Clarke and Leibnitz, says, "But soon after this controversy was brought to a conclusion by the death of his antagonist, he (Clarke) had to renew the same argument, in reply to his countryman, Anthony Collins, who, following the footsteps of Hobbes, with logical talents not inferior to his master (and with a weight of personal character in his favor to which his master had no pretensions,) gave to the cause which he so warmly espoused, a degree of credit amongst sober and inquiring politicians, which it had never before possessed in England." The following are the principal arguments of Collins in reference to Liberty and Necessity:—

First. Though I deny Liberty in a certain meaning of that word, yet I contend for Liberty, as it signifies *a power in man to do as he wills or pleases.*

Secondly. When I affirm *Necessity* I contend only for *moral necessity;* meaning thereby that man, who is an intelligent and sensible being, is determined by his reason and senses; and I deny any man to be subject to such necessity as is in clocks, watches, and such other beings, which, for want of intelligence and sensation, are subject to an absolute, physical or mechanical necessity.

Thirdly, I have undertaken to show, that the notions I advance are so far from being inconsistent with, that they are the sole foundation of morality and laws, and of rewards and punishments in society, and that the notions I explode are subversive of them.

From the above premises, Collins sought to show that man is a necessary agent. (1) From our experience (through consciousness.) (2) From the impossibility of liberty. (3) From the consideration of the divine prescience. (4) From the nature and use of rewards and punishments. (5) From the nature of morality. Such were the principles on which the great question of Necessity has ever been advocated—from Hobbes to Collins, Jonathan Ed wards to Mackintosh and Spencer. In the year 1704 Toland dedicated to him a new translation of Æsop's Fables. There are many anecdotes respecting Collins inserted in religious magazines, most of which are false, and all without proof. One of them, related in a most circumstantial manner, appears to be the favorite. It depicts Collins walking out in the country on a Sunday morning, when he meets a countryman returning from Church.

"Well, Hodge," says Collins, "so you have been enjoying the fresh breezes of nature, this fine morning."

The clown replied that "he had been worshipping nature's God," and proved it by repeating the substance of the Athanasian creed. Upon which Collins questions him as to the residence of his God: and for a reply is told that his God is so large, that he fills the universe; and so small that he dwells in his breast. This sublime fact, we are told, had more effect upon Collins's mind than all the books written against him by the clergy. When will sensible men reject such charlatanism?

The next great work of Collins was his "Discourse on the Grounds and Reasons of the Christian Religion," in two parts. The first containing some considerations on the quotations made from the Old in the New Testament, and particularly on the prophecies cited from the former, and said to be fulfilled in the latter. The second containing an examination of the scheme advanced by Mr. Whiston, in his essay towards restoring the true text of the Old Testament, and for vindicating the citations thence made in the New Testament, to which is prefixed an apology for free debate and liberty of writing. This book took the religious world by storm; it is even thought it struck more dismay amongst divines than his former essay on Freethinking. The book proceeds to show that Christianity is not proved by prophecy. That the Apostles relied on the predictions in the Old Testament, and their fulfilment in Jesus as the only sure proof of the truth of their religion; if therefore, the prophecies are not thoroughly literal, and fulfilled distinctly, there can be no proof in Christianity. He then examines the principal prophecies, and dismisses them, as allegorical fables too vague to be of any credit. In less than two years no less than thirty-five books were published in reply to this work, written by the ablest and most influential theologians in England. In 1727 Collins published another large work, "The Scheme of Literal Prophecy Considered," in which he still further defends his view principally against the sophistical reasoning of Whiston, and finally vanquished the whole of his opponents.

Perhaps no Freethinker, with the single exception of Hobbes, was so attacked during his life as Collins. Toland and Woolston were persecuted and driven into prison and poverty; but Collins, with his profusion of wealth, could oppose Christianity with applause—mingle in the gaiety of the Court—occupy a seat on the magisterial bench—be the welcome guest of the most liberal of the aristocracy, contemporary with others who even languished in prison for the propagation of similar sentiments. Since his day the clergy have grown wiser; then the most trivial pamphlet on the Deistic side created a consternation amongst the saints, and they strove who should be the first to answer it—indeed, it was considered a test of honor amongst the clergy to be eager in the exposure of Deism: but this style of warfare was discontinued after the lapse of a few years. The most discerning observers discovered that in proportion to the answers published against liberal works, the influence of the most powerful side decreased. Force, then, gradually interfered, and acts of Parliament were considered the only logical refutation of a philosophical heresy. The anomaly of our laws interfered again. Collins was rich, and so must escape the fangs of the law. Thomas Woolston was poor, so his vitals were pierced by laws which Collins escaped—yet both committed the same offence. In later times Gibbon traced the rise of Christianity, and about the same time Paine accomplished another portion of the same risk—and the Government which prosecuted the plebeian, flattered the patrician. But Collins's time was rapidly drawing nigh. On the 13th of December, 1729, he expired, aged fifty-three years; and to show the esteem in which his character was held, the following notice was inserted in the newspapers of the day—all hostile to his views, yet striving to make it appear that he was, after all, not so great an Infidel as his reputation honored him with:—"On Saturday last, died at his house in Harley Square, Anthony Collins, Esq. He was a remarkably active, up right, and impartial magistrate, the tender husband the kind parent, the good master, and the true friend He was a great promoter of literature in all its branch es; and an immoveable asserter of universal liberty in all civil and religious matters. Whatever his sentiments were on certain points, this is what he declared at the time of his death—viz., that he had always endeavored, to the best of his ability, to serve God, his king, and his country, so he was persuaded he was going to that place which God hath prepared for them that serve him, and presently afterwards he said, the Catholic religion is to serve God and roan. He was an eminent example of temperance and sobriety, and one that had the true art of living. His worst enemies could never charge him with any vice or immorality." With this character the Freethinkers have no right to be dissatisfied. The Abbe Lodivicat says, "His library was curious and valuable; always open to the learned, even to his opponents, whom he furnished with pleasure, both with books and arguments, which were employed in confuting him." Mr. D'Israeli says he has seen a catalogue of Collins's library, elaborately drawn up in his own handwriting, and it must have contained a splendid selection of books. This is proved by the correspondence with Locke, and the extensive number of quotations spread throughout his published works.

By the death of Collins, and the defalcation of one who abused the name of a Deist, the cause of Free-thought was impeded at the time when it most needed assistance. Collins had written a great number of tracts and larger works, intending them to be published after his death: one collection of eight octavo volumes of manuscript containing the attacks upon Christianity, by which he intended his name to be transmitted to posterity, were all arranged ready for publication as his posthumous works. To ensure their credit-able appearance, and to reward a man whom he had thought worthy of confidence, and one who professed to be a disciple of Collins, he bequeathed them to Des Maizeaux, then a popular author and editor. He had edited the correspondence of Locke and Collins, written the lite of Bayle, and subsequently edited Toland. The idea of Collins was to give his work to Des Maizeaux for a recompense for the trouble of publishing them, while he would derive the whole profits of their sale, which no doubt would be very large. It appears that the widow of Collins was much younger than himself—in league with the Church of England; and was in rather a suspicious friendship with more than one clerical antagonist of her late husband. Des Maizeaux being worked upon conjointly by Mrs. Collins and a person named Tomlinson, was induced to accept a present of fifty guineas, and relinquished the possession of the manuscripts. It was not long, however, before his conscience accused him of the great wrong done to the memory of his benefactor, and to the Free-thinking cause. His regret was turned into the most profound compunction for his crime; and in this state of mind he wrote a long letter to one who had been a mutual friend to Collins and himself, acknowledging that he had done "a most wicked thing," saying—"I am convinced that I have acted contrary to the will and intention of my dear deceased friend; showed a disregard to the particular mark of esteem he gave me on that occasion; in short, that I have forfeited what is dearer to me than my own life—honor and reputation.... I send you the fifty guineas I received, which I do now look upon as the wages of iniquity, and I desire you to return them to Mrs. Collins, who, as I hope it of her justice, equity, and regard to Mr. Collinses intentions, will be pleased to cancel my paper."

This appeal (which proved that Des Maizeaux, if he was weak-minded, was not absolutely dishonest) had no effect on Mrs. Collins. The manuscripts were never returned. What their contents were, no one now can inform us. We are justified, however, in supposing that as those eight volumes were the crowning efforts of a mind which in its youth was brilliant in no common degree, must have been even superior to those books which roused England from its dreamy lethargy, and brought about a revolution in controversy. Whether they touched upon miracles, or the external evidences, or the morals of Christism, is unknown. The curtain was drawn over the scene of demolition. Seven years after this time the controversy was reopened by Mrs. Collins, in the year 1737, on account of a report being current that Mrs. C. had permitted transcripts of those manuscripts to get abroad. The widow wrote some very sharp letters to Des Maizeaux, and he replied in a tone which speaks faithfully of the affection he still bore to Collins's memory. He concludes thus:—"Mr. Collins loved me and esteemed me for my integrity and sincerity, of which he had several proofs. How I have been drawn in to injure him, to forfeit the good opinion he had of me, and which, were he now alive, would deservedly expose me to his utmost contempt, is a grief which I shall carry to the grave. It would be a sort of comfort to me if those who have consented I should be drawn in, were in some measure sensible of the guilt towards so good, kind, generous a man."

Such is an epitome of the secret history of the MSS. of Anthony Collins. If we look at the fate of the MSS. of other Deists, we shall have good reasons for believing that some of the ablest writings, meant to give a posthumous reputation to their authors, have disappeared into the hands of either ignorant or designing persons. Five volumes, at least, of Toland's works, meant for publication, were, by his death, irretrievably lost. Blount's MSS. never appeared. Two volumes of Tindall's were seized by the Bishop of London, and destroyed. Woolston's MSS. met with no better fate. Chubb carefully prepared his works, and published them in his lifetime. Bolingbroke made Mallet his confidant, as Collins did by Des Maizeaux. The name of St. John produced £10,000 to Mallet; but those works were left with the tacit acknowledge ment that the Scotch poet should write a suitable life of the peer. The letter of Mallet to Lord Cornbury can only be compared to an invitation for a bid for the suppression of the "Philosophical Works" of St. John; and if this was not sufficient, we need only instance the apparent solicitation with which he stopped a well-known influential dignitary of the church on the day when the works were to appear, by pulling out his watch, and saying, "My Lord, Christianity will tremble at a quarter to twelve." We may be thankful to the pecuniary poverty of our opponents even for the possession of the first philosophy. Some of Hume's and Gibbon's works have not yet appeared. The MSS. of most of the minor Freethinkers disappeared with their authors. There is no doubt but what Robert Taylor left some valuable writings which cannot be recovered. Such is the feeble chance of great men's writings being published when they are no longer alive.

With regard to the literary claims of Collins. His works are logically composed and explicitly worded. He invariably commences by stating the groundwork of his opponent's theories, and from them deduces a great number of facts and axioms of a contrary character, and upon those builds his whole chain of argument. He is seldom witty—never uses the flowers of rhetoric, combining a most rigid analysis with a synthetic scheme, admitting but of one unswerving end. He was characteristically great in purpose. He avoided carrying forward his arguments beyond the basis of his facts. Whether in treating the tangled intricacies of necessity, or the theological quagmires of prophecy, he invariably explained without confusing, and refuted without involving other subjects than those legitimately belonging to the controversy. His style of writing was serious, plain, and without an undue levity, yet withal perfectly readable. Men studied Collins who shrunk from contact with the lion-hearted Woolston, whose brusque pen too often shocked those it failed to convince. There was a timidity in many of the letters of Blount, and a craving wish to rely more on the witticisms of Brown, than was to be found in the free and manly spirit of our hero. To the general public, the abstruse speculations of the persecuted Toland were a barrier which his many classical allusions only heightened; and the musical syllables of Shaftesbury, with his style, at once so elevated, so pompous, and so quaint; or the political economic doctrines of Mandeville, all tended to exalt the name of Collins above those of his contemporaries and immediate successors; and posterity cannot fail to place his bust in that historic niche betwixt Hobbes—his master on one hand—and Bolingbroke, his successor on the other. From the great St. John has descended in the true apostolical descent the mantle of Free-thought upon Hume, Gibbon, Paine, Godwin, Carlile, Taylor, and Owen. And amongst this brilliant galaxy of genius, no name is more deserving of respect than that of Anthony Collins.

A. C.

DES CARTES

Rene des Cartes Duperron, better known as Des Cartes, the father of modern philosophy, was born at La Haye, in Touraine, of Breton parents, near the close of the sixteenth century, at a time when Bacon was like the morning sun, rising to shed new rays of bright light over the then dark world of philosophy. The mother of Des Cartes died while he was but a few days old, and himself a sickly child, he began to take part in the battle of life with but little appearance of ever possessing the capability for action on the minds of his fellows, which he afterwards so fully exercised. Debarred, however, by his physical weakness from many boyish pursuits, he devoted himself to study in his earliest years, and during his youth gained the title of the young philosopher, from his eagerness to learn, and from his earnest endeavors by inquiry and experiment to solve every problem presented to his notice. He was educated in the Jesuits' College of La Flèche; and the monument erected to him at Stockholm informs us, "That having mastered all the learning of the schools, which proved short of his expectations, he betook himself to the army in Germany and Hungary, and there spent his vacant winter hours in comparing the mysteries and phenomena of nature with the laws of mathematics, daring to hope that the one might serve as a key to the other. Quitting, therefore, all other pursuits, he retired to a little village near Egmont, in Holland, where spending twenty-five years in continual reading and meditation, he effected his design."

In his celebrated "Discourse on Method," he says, — "As soon as my age permitted me to leave my preceptors, I entirely gave up the study of letters; and, resolving to seek no other science than that which I could find in myself, or else in the great book of the world, I employed the remainder of my youth in travel — in seeing courts and camps — in frequenting people of diverse humors and conditions — in collecting various experiences; and, above all, in endeavoring to draw some profitable reflection from what I saw. For it seemed to me that I should meet with more truth in the reasonings which each man makes in his own affairs, and which, if wrong, would be speedily punished by failure, than in those reasonings which the philosopher makes in his study upon speculations which produce no effect, and which are of no consequence to him, except perhaps that he will be the more vain of them, the more remote they are from common sense, because he would then have been forced to employ more ingenuity and subtlety to render them plausible."

At the age of thirty-three Des Cartes retired from the world for a period of eight years, and his seclusion was so effectual during that time, that his place of residence was unknown to his friends. He there prepared the "Meditations," and "Discourse on Method," which have since caused so much pen-and-ink warfare amongst those who have aspired to be ranked as philosophical thinkers. He became European in fame; and, invited by Christina of Sweden, he visited her kingdom, but the rudeness of the climate proved too much for his delicate frame, and he died at Stockholm in the year 1650, from inflammation of the lungs, being fifty-four years of age at the time of his death.

Des Cartes was perhaps the most original thinker that France had up to that date produced; and, contemporary with Bacon, he exercised a powerful influence or the progress of thought in Europe; but although a great thinker, he was not a brave man, and the fear of giving offence to the church and government, has certainly prevented him from making public some of his writings, and perhaps has toned down some of these thoughts which, when first uttered, took a higher flight, and struck full home to the truth itself.

The father and founder of the deductive method, Des Cartes still proudly reigns to the present day, although some of his conclusions have been over-turned, and others of his thinkings have been carried to conclusions which he never dared to dream of. He gave a strong aid to the tendency of advancing civilization, to separate philosophy from theology, thereby striking a blow, slow in its effect, and effectual in its destructive operation, on all priestcraft. In his dedication ol the "Meditations," he says,—"I have always thought that the two questions of the existence of God and the nature of the soul, were the chief of those which ought to be demonstrated rather by philosophy than by theology; for although it is sufficient for us, the faithful, to believe in God, and that the soul does not perish with the body, it does not seem possible ever to persuade the Infidels to any religion, unless we first prove to them these two things by natural reason."

Having relinquished faith, he found that he must choose an entirely new faith in which to march with reason; the old ways were so cumbered with priests and Bibles, that progression would have been impossible. This gave us his method. He wanted a starting point from which to reason, some indisputable fact upon which to found future thinkings.

"He has given us the detailed history of his doubts. He has told us how he found that he could, plausibly enough, doubt of everything except his own existence. He pushed his scepticism to the verge of self-annihilation. There he stopped: there in self, there in his consciousness, he found at last an irresistible fact, an irreversible certainty. Firm ground was discovered. He could doubt the existence of the external world, and treat it as a phantasm. He could doubt the existence of God, and treat the belief as a superstition. But of the existence of his own thinking, doubting mind, no sort of doubt was possible. He, the doubter, existed if nothing else existed. The existence that was revealed to him in his own consciousness, was the primary fact, the first indubitable certainty. Hence his famous *Cogito ergo Sum*: I think, therefore I am." (*Lewes's Bio. Hist. Phil.*)

Proceeding from the certainty of his existence, Des Cartes endeavors to rind other equally certain tacts, and for that purpose presents the following doctrine and rules for our guidance:—The basis of all certitude is consciousness, consciousness is the sole foundation of absolute certainty, whatever it distinctly proclaims must be true. The process is, therefore, rendered clear and simple: examine your consciousness—each distinct reply will be a fact.

He tells us further that all clear ideas are true—that whatever is clearly and distinctly conceived is true—and in these lie the vitality of his system, the cause of the truth or error of his thinkings.

The following are the rules he gave us for the detection and separation of true ideas from false, (*i.e.*, imperfect or complex):—

"1. Never to accept anything as true but what is evidently so; to admit nothing but what so clearly and distinctly presents itself as true, that there can be no reason to doubt it.

"2. To divide every question into as many separate parts as possible, that each part being more easily conceived, the whole may be more intelligible.

"3. To conduct the examination with order, beginning by that of objects the most simple, and therefore the easiest to be known, and ascending little by little up to knowledge of the most complex.

"4. To make such exact calculations, and such circumspections as to be confident that nothing essential has been omitted. Consciousness being the basis of all certitude, everything of which you are clearly and distinctly conscious must be true: everything which you clearly and distinctly conceive, exists, if the idea of it involve existence."

In these four rules we have the essential part of one half of Des Cartes's system, the other, which is equally important, is the attempt to solve metaphysical problems by mathematical aid. To mathematics he had devoted much of his time. He it was who, at the age of twenty three, made the grand discovery of the applicability of algebra to geometry. While deeply engaged in mathematical studies and investigations, he came to the conclusion that mathematics were capable of a still further simplification, and of much more extended application. Impressed with the certainty of the conclusions arrived at by the aid of mathematical reasoning, he began to apply mathematics to metaphysics.

His ambition was to found a system which should be solid and convincing. Having searched for certitude, he had found *its basis* in consciousness; he next wanted a *method*, and hoped he had found it in mathematics.

He tells us that "those long chains of reasoning, all simple and easy, by which geometers used to arrive at their most difficult demonstrations, suggested to him that all things which came within human knowledge, must follow each other in a similar chain; and that provided we abstain from admitting anything as true which is not so, and that we always preserve in them the order necessary to deduce one from the other, there can be none so remote to which we cannot finally attain, nor so obscure but that we may discover them."

Acting out this, he dealt with metaphysics as we should with a problem from Euclid, and expected by rigorous reasoning to discover the truth. He, like Archimedes, had wished for a standing place from which to use the lever, that should overturn the world; but, having a sure standing place in the indubitable fact of his own existence, he did not possess sufficient courage to put forth the mighty power—it was left for one who came after him to fairly attempt the over-throw of the world of error so long existent.

Cartesianism was sufficiently obnoxious to the divines to provoke their wrath; and yet, from some of its peculiarities, it has found many opponents amongst the philosophical party. The Cartesian philosophy is founded on two great principles, the one metaphysical, the other physical. The metaphysical is Des Cartes's foundation-stone—the "I think, therefore I am." This has been warmly attacked as not being logical. Des Cartes said his existence was a fact—a fact above and beyond all logic; logic could neither prove nor disprove it. The *Cogito ergo Sum* was not new itself, but it was the first stone of a new building—the first step in a new road: from this fact Des Cartes tried to reach another, and from that others.

The physical principle is that nothing exists but substance, which he makes of two kinds—the one a substance that thinks, the other a substance extended. Actual thought and actual extension are the essence of substance, so that the thinking substance cannot be without some actual thought, nor can anything be retrenched from the extension of a thing, without taking away so much of its actual substance.

In his physical speculations, Des Cartes has allowed his imagination to run very wild. His famous theory of vortices is an example of this. Assuming extension to be the essence of substance, he denied the possibility of a vacuum by that assumption; for if extension be the essence of substance, wherever extension is, there substance must be. This substance he assumes to have originally been divided into equal angular particles, each endowed with an equal degree of motion; several systems or collections of these particles he holds to have a motion about certain equidistant points, or centres, and that the particles moving round these composed so many vortices. These angular particles, by their intestine motions, he supposes to become, as it were, ground into a spherical form; the parts rubbed off are called matter of the first element, while the spherical globules he calls matter of the second element; and since there would be a large quantity of this element, he supposes it to be driven towards the centre of each vortex by the circular motion of the globules, and that there it forms a large spherical body such as the suu. This sun being thus formed, and moving about its own axis with the common matter of the vortex, would necessarily throw out some parts of its matter, through the vacuities of the globules of the second element constituting the vortex; and this especially at such places as are farthest from its poles: receiving, at the same time in, by these poles, as much as it loses in its equatorial parts. And, by these means, it would be able to carry round with it those globules that are nearest, with the greater velocity; and the remoter, with less. And, further: those globules which are nearest the centre of the sun, must be smallest; because, were they greater, or equal, they would, by reason of their velocity, have a greater centrifugal force, and recede from the centre. If it should happen that any of these sun-like bodies, in the centres of the several vortices, should be so in-crusted and weakened, as to be carried about in the vortex of the true sun: if it were of less solidity, or had less motion than the globules towards the extremity of the solar vortex, it would descend towards the sun, till it met with globules of the same solidity, and susceptible of the same degree of motion with itself* and thus, being fixed there, it would be for ever after carried about by the motion of the vortex, without either approaching any nearer to, or receding from the sun, and so become a planet. Supposing, then, all this, we are next to imagine that our system was at first divided into several vortices, in the centre of each of which was a lucid spherical body; and that some of these being gradually incrustated, were swallowed up by others which were larger, and more powerful, till at last they were all destroyed and swallowed up by the biggest solar vortex, except some few which were thrown off in right lines from one vortex to another, and so became comets. It should also be added, that in addition to the two elements mentioned above, those particles which may yet exist, and be only in the course of reduction to their globular form an it still retain their angular proportions, form a third element.

This theory has found many opponents; but in this state of our work we conceive our duty to be that of giving a simple narrative of the philosopher's ideas, rather than a history of the various criticisms upon those ideas, the more especially as our pages scarcely afford room for such a mode of treatment.

Having formed his method, Des Cartes proceeded to apply it. The basis of certitude being consciousness, he interrogated his consciousness, and found that he had an idea of a substance infinite, eternal, immutable, independent, omniscient, omnipotent. This he called an idea of God: he said, "I exist as a miserably imperfect finite being, subject to change—ignorant, incapable of creating anything—I find by my finitude that I am not the infinite; by my liability to change that I am not the immutable; by my ignorance that I am not the omniscient: in short, by my imperfection, that I am not the perfect. Yet an infinite, immutable, omniscient, and perfect being must exist, because infinity, immutability, omniscience, and perfection are applied as correlatives in my ideas of finitude, change, etc. God therefore exists: his existence is clearly proclaimed in my consciousness, and therefore ceases to be a matter of doubt any more than the fact of my own existence. The conception of an infinite being proved his real existence, for if there is not really such a being I must have made the conception; but if I could make it I can also unmake it, which evidently is not true; therefore there must be externally to myself, an archetype from which the conception was derived.".... "All that we clearly and distinctly conceive as contained in anything is true of that thing."

"Now, we conceive clearly and distinctly that the existence of God is contained in the idea we have of him: ergo—God exists." —(*Lewes's Bio. Hist. Phil.*)

Des Cartes was of opinion that his demonstrations of the existence of God "equal or even surpass in certitude the demonstrations of geometry." In this opinion we must confess we cannot share. He has already told us that the basis of all certitude is consciousness—that whatever is clearly and distinctly conceived, must be true—that imperfect and complex conceptions are false ones. The first proposition, all must admit, is applicable to themselves. I conceive a fact clearly and distinctly, and, despite all resistance, am compelled to accept that fact; and if that fact be accepted beyond doubt, no higher degree of certainty can be attained, That two and two are four—that I exist—are facts which I never doubt. The *Cogito ergo Sum* is irresistible, because indubitable; but *Cogito ergo Deus est* is a sentence requiring much consideration, and upon the face of it is no syllogism, but, on the contrary, is illogical. If Des Cartes meant "I" am conscious that I am not the whole of existence, he would be indisputable; but if he meant that "I" can be conscious of an existence entirely distinct, apart from, and external to, that very consciousness, then his whole reasoning from that point appears fallacious.

We use the word "I" as given by Des Cartes. Mill, in his "System of Logic," says, "The ambiguity in this case is in the pronoun I, by which in one place is to be understood *my will*: in another *the laws of my nature*. If the conception, existing as it does in my mind, had no original without, the conclusion would unquestionably follow that '1' had made it—that is, that the laws of my nature had spontaneously evolved it; but that my *will* made it would not follow. Now, when Des Cartes afterwards adds that I cannot unmake the conception, he means that I cannot get rid of it by an act of my will, which is true; but is not the proposition required. That what some of the laws of my nature have produced, other laws, or those same laws in other circumstances, might not subsequently efface, he would have found it difficult to establish."

Treating the existence of God as demonstrated from the *a priori* idea of perfection and infinity, and by the clearness of his idea of God's existence, Des Cartes then proceeds to deal with the distinction between body and soul. To prove this distinction was to him an easy matter. The fundamental and essential attribute of substance must be extension, because we can denude substance of every quality but that of extension; this we cannot touch without at the same time affecting the substance.. The fundamental attribute of mind is thought; it is in the act of thinking that the consciousness of existence is revealed; to be without thought would be to be without consciousness.

Des Cartes has given us, among others, the axiom "That two substances are really distinct when their ideas are complete, and no way imply each other. The idea of extension is complete and distinct from the idea of thought, which latter is also clear and distinct by itself. It follows, therefore, that substance and mind are distinct in essence."

Des Cartes has, from the vagueness of some of his statements, subjected himself to the charge of asserting the existence of innate ideas, and the following quotations will speak for themselves on the subject:—"When I said that the idea of God is innate in us, I never meant more than this, that Nature has endowed us with a faculty by which we may know God; but I have never either said or thought that such ideas had an actual existence, or even that they were a species distinct from the faculty of thinking.... Although the idea of God is so imprinted on our minds, that every person has within him the faculty of knowing him, it does not follow that there may not have been various individuals who have passed through life without ever making this idea a distinct object of apprehension; and, in truth, they who think they have an idea of a plurality of Gods, have no idea of God whatever." This seems explicit as negativing the charge of holding the doctrine of innate ideas; but in the *Edinburgh Review* several passages are given, amongst which is the following:—"By the word idea I understand all that can be in our thoughts; and I distinguish three sorts of ideas—adventitious, like the common idea of the sun, framed by the mind, such as that which astronomical reasoning gives of the sun; and innate, as the idea of God, mind, body, a triangle, and generally all those which represent true, immutable, and eternal essences." With regard to these rather opposite statements, Lewes says, "If Des Cartes, when pressed by objections, gave different explanations, we must only set it down to a want of a steady conception of the vital importance of innate ideas to his system. The fact remains that innate ideas form the necessary groundwork of the Cartesian doctrine.... The radical error of all ontological speculation lies in the assumption that we have ideas independent of experience; because experience can only tell us of ourselves or of phenomena; of noumena it can tell us nothing.... The fundamental question, then, of modern philosophy is this—Have we any ideas independent of experience?"

Des Cartes's disciples are of two classes, the "mathematical cultivators of physic," and the "deductive cultivators of philosophy." The first class of disciples are far in advance of their chief, and can only be considered as having received an impulse in a true direction. The second class unhesitatingly accepted his principles, and continued his thinking, although they developed his system in a different manner, and arrived at stronger conclusions than Des Cartes's courage would have supported. Some of the physical speculations of Des Cartes have been much ridiculed by subsequent writers; but many reasons may be urged, not only against that ridicule, but also against the more moderate censure which several able critics have dealt out against the intellectual character of Des Cartes. It should be remembered that the theories of all his predecessors were mere conjectural speculations respecting the places and paths of celestial bodies, etc. Innumerable hypotheses had been formed and found useless; and we ought rather to look to what Des Cartes did accomplish under the many difficulties of his position, in respect to the then, state of scientific knowledge, than to judge harshly of those speculations, which, though attended with no beneficial result to humanity at large, were doubtless well intended by their author. He was the first man who brought optical science under the command of mathematics, by the discovery of the law of refraction of the ordinary ray through diaphanous bodies; and probably there is scarcely a name on record, the bearer of which has given a greater impulse to mathematical and philosophical inquiry than Des Cartes. Although, as a mathematician, he published but little, yet in every subject which he has treated he has opened, not only a new field lor investigation, but also a new road for the investigators to proceed by. His discovery of the simple application of the notation of indices to algebraical powers, has totally remodelled the whole science of algebra. His conception of expressing the fundamental property of curve lines and curve surfaces by equations between the co-ordinates has led to an almost total supersedence of the geometry of the ancients. Contemporary with Galileo, and with a knowledge of the persecution to which that father of physics was being subjected by the Church, we are tempted to express our surprise that Des Cartes did not extend the right hand of fellowship, help, and sympathy to his brother philosopher; but it is, nevertheless, the fact, that either jealous of the fame of Galileo (as some have alleged.) or from a fear of being involved in the same persecutions, Des Cartes abstained from visiting the astronomer, although travelling for some time near his place of abode in Italy. Lewes, in his "Life of Des Cartes," says, "Des Cartes was a great thinker; but having said this we have almost exhausted the praise we can bestow on him as a man. In disposition he was timid to servility. While promulgating the proofs of the existence of the Deity, he was in evident alarm lest the Church should see something objectionable in them. He had also written an astronomical treatise; but hearing of the fate of Galileo he refrained from publishing, and always used some chicanery in speaking of the world's movement. He was not a brave man; he was also not an affectionate one. There was in him a deficiency of all finer feelings. But he was even-tempered, and studious of not giving offence."

We are tempted, after a careful perusal of the life and writings of Des Cartes and his contemporaries, to be of opinion that he was a man who wished to be considered the chief thinker of his day, and who shunned and rejected the offers of friendship from other philosophers, lest they, by being associated with him, should jointly wear laurels which he was cultivating solely to form a crown for himself. Despite all, his brow still bears a crown, and his fame has a freshness that we might all be justly proud of, if appertaining to ourselves.

We trust that in these few pages we have succeeded in presenting Des Cartes, to such of our readers who were unacquainted with his writings, sufficiently well to enable them to appreciate him, and to induce them to search further; and at the same time we hope that those better acquainted with him will not blame as for the omission of much which they may consider more important than the matter which appears in this little tract. We have endeavored to picture Des Cartes as the founder of the deductive method, as having the foundation-stone of all his reasoning in his consciousness.

"I"

M. DE VOLTAIRE

François Marie Arouet, better known by the name of Voltaire, was born at Chatenay, on the 20th of February, 1694. By assuming the name of Voltaire, young Arouet followed the custom, at that time generally practiced by the rich citizens and younger sons, who, leaving the family name to the heir, assumed that of a fief, or perhaps of a country house. The father of M. de Voltaire was treasurer to the Chamber of Accounts, and his mother, Margaret d'Aumart, was of a noble family of Poitou. The fortune which the father enjoyed, enabled him to bestow a first-class education upon the young Arouet, who was sent to the Jesuits' College, where the sons of the nobility received their education. While at school, Voltaire began to write poetry, and gave signs of a remarkable genius. His tutors, Fathers Poree and Jay, from the boldness and independence of his mind predicted that he would become the apostle of Deism in France. This prediction he fulfilled. "Voltaire was," says Lord Brougham, "through his whole life, a sincere believer in the existence and attributes of the Deity. He was a firm and decided, and an openly declared unbeliever in Christianity; but he was, without any hesitation or any intermission, a Theist." His open declaration of disbelief in the inspiration of the Bible, and his total rejection of the dogmas of Christianity, laid him open to the malignant attacks and misrepresentations of the priesthood and the bigots of Europe; and so strong were they, that his life was continually in danger. Lord Brougham, in his "Men of Letters of the Time of George III.." says:—"Voltaire's name is so intimately connected in the minds of all men with Infidelity, in the minds of most men with irreligion, and, in the minds of all who are not well-informed, with these qualities alone, that whoever undertakes to write his life and examine his claims to the vast reputation which all the hostile feelings excited by him against himself have never been able to destroy, or even materially to impair, has to labor under a great load of prejudice, and can hardly expect, by any detail of particulars, to obtain for his subject even common justice at the hands of the general reader."

Voltaire was born in a corrupt age, and in a capital where it was fashionable to be immoral. When he left College, he was introduced by his own godfather, the Abbe de Chateauneuf, to the notorious Ninon de l'Enclos, who, at her death, left him by will two thousand livres to purchase books. In estimating the character of Voltaire, a due consideration must be had for the period in which he lived, and of the nature of the society amidst which he was reared. He lived twenty, years under the reign of Louis XIV., and during the whole of the reign of the infamous Louis XV., when kings, courtiers, and priests set the example of the grossest immorality. It was then, as Voltaire said, "that to make the smallest fortune, it was better to say four words to the mistress of a king, than to write a hundred volumes."

Voltaire's life, from his youth upwards, was a stormy one. After he left College, his father, finding him persist in writing poetry, and living at large, forbade him his house. He insisted upon his son binding himself to an attorney. But his restless disposition quite unfitted him for regular employment, and he soon quitted the profession. He early made the acquaintance of the most celebrated men of his time, but his genius, his wit, and his sarcasm, soon raised up numerous enemies. At the age of twenty-two, he was accused of having written a satire upon Louis XIV., who was just dead, and was thrown into the Bastile. But he was not cast down. It was here that he sketched his poem of the "League," corrected his tragedy of "Oedipus," and wrote some merry verses on the misfortune, of being a prisoner. The Regent, Duke of Orleans, being informed of his innocence, restored him to freedom, and granted him a recompense. "I thank your royal highness," said Voltaire, "for having provided me with food; but I hope you will not hereafter trouble yourself concerning my lodging."

Voltaire, with his activity of mind, and living to so great an age, must necessarily produce many works. They are voluminous, consisting of history, poetry, and philosophy. His dramatic pieces are numerous, many of which are considered second only to Shakespeare's. "Oedipus," "Zadig," "Ingénu," "Zaire," "Henri-ade," "Irene," "Tancred," "Mahomet," "Merope," "Saul," "Alzire," "Le Fanatisme," "Mariamne," "Gaston de Foix," "Enfant Prodigue," "Pucelle d'Orléans," an essay on "Fire," the "Elements," "History of Charles XII.," "Lectures on Man," "Letters on England," "Memoirs," "Voyage of Sacramentado," "Micromegas," "Maid of Orleans," "Brutus," "Adelaide," "Death of Cæsar," "Temple of Taste," "Essay on the Manners and Spirit of Nations," "An Examination of the Holy Scriptures," and the "Philosophical Dictionary," are works that emanated from the active brain of this wit, poet, satirist, and philosopher.

In 1722, while at Brussels, Voltaire met Jean Baptiste Rousseau, whose misfortunes he deplored, and whose poetic talents he esteemed. Voltaire read some of his poems to Rousseau, and he in return read to Voltaire his "Ode addressed to Posterity," which Voltaire, it is asserted, told him would never arrive at the place to which it was addressed. The two poets parted irreconcileable foes.

In 1725, Voltaire was again shut up in the Bastile, through attempting to revenge an insult inflicted upon him by a courtier. At the end of six months he was released, but ordered to quit Paris. He sought refuge in England, in 1726. He was the guest in that country of a Mr. Falconer, of Wandsworth, whose hospitality he remembered with affection so long as life lasted. Voltaire was known to most of the wits and Freethinkers of that day in England. At this early age he was at war with Christianity. "His visit to England," says Lamartine, "gave assurance and gravity to his incredulity; for in France he had only known libertines—in England he knew philosophers." He went to visit Congreve, who had the affectation to tell him that he (Congreve) valued himself, not on his authorship, but as a man of the world. To which Voltaire administered a just rebuke by saying, "I should never have come so far to see a gentleman!"

Voltaire soon acquired an ample fortune, much of which was expended in aiding men of letters, and in encouraging such youth as he thought discovered the seeds of genius. The use he made of riches might prevail on envy itself to pardon him their acquirement. His pen and his purse were ever at the service of the oppressed. Calas, an infirm old man, living at Toulouse, was accused of having hung his son, to prevent his becoming a Catholic. The Catholic population became inflamed, and the young man was declared to be a martyr. The father was condemned to the torture and the wheel, and died protesting his innocence. The family of Calas was ruined and disgraced. Voltaire, assuring himself of the innocence of the old man, determined to obtain justice for the family. To this end he labored incessantly for three years. In all this time, he said, a smile did not escape him for which he did not reproach himself as for a crime. His efforts were successful. Nor was this the only cause in which he was engaged on the side of the weak and the wronged against the powerful and the persecuting. His whole life, though maligned as an Infidel and a-scoffer, was one long act of benevolence. On learning that a young niece of Corneille languished in a condition unworthy of his name, Voltaire, in the most delicate manner, invited her to his house, and she there received an education suitable to the rank that her birth had marked lor her in society. "It is the duty of a soldier," he said, "to succor the niece of his general."

Voltaire lived for a time at the Court of Frederick the Great of Prussia, and for many years carried on a correspondence with that monarch. He quarrelled with the king, and left the court in a passion. An emissary was despatched to him to request an apology, who said he was to carry back to the king his answer *verbatim*. Voltaire told him that "the king might go to the devil!" On being asked if that was the message he meant to be delivered! "Yes," he answered, "and add to it that I told you that you might go there with him." In his "Memoirs," he has drawn a most amusing picture of his Prussian Majesty. He, also says, "Priests never entered the palace; and, in a word, Frederick lived without religion, without a council, and without a court."

Wearied with his rambling and unsettled mode of living, Voltaire bought an estate at Ferney, in the Pays des Gex, where he spent the last twenty years of his life. He rebuilt the house, laid out gardens, kept a good table, and had crowds of visitors from all parts, of Europe. Removed from whatever could excite momentary or personal passion, he yielded to his zeal for the destruction of prejudice, which was the most powerful and active of all the sensations he felt. This peaceful life, seldom disturbed except by the threats of persecution rather than persecution itself, was adorned by those acts of enlightened and bold benevolence, which, while they relieve the sufferings of certain individuals, are of any service to the whole human race. He was known to Europe as the "Sage of Ferney." After an absence of more than twenty-seven years, he re-visited Paris in the beginning of 1778. He had just finished his play of "Irene," and was anxious to see it performed. His visit was an ovation. He had outlived all his enemies. After having been the object of unrelenting persecution by the priests and corrupt courtiers of France for a period of more than fifty years, he yet lived to see the day when "all that was most eminent in station or most distinguished in talents—all that most shone in society, or most ruled in court, seemed to bend before him." At this period he, for the first time, saw Benjamin Franklin. They embraced each other in the midst of public acclamations, and it was said to be Solon who embraced Sophocles.

Voltaire did not survive his triumph long. His unwearied activity induced him, at his great age, to commence a "Dictionary" upon a novel plan, which he prevailed upon the French Academy to take up. These labors brought on spitting of blood, followed by sleeplessness, to obviate which he took opium in considerable quantities. Condorcet says that the servant mistook one of the doses, which threw him into a state of lethargy, from which he never rallied. He lingered for some time, but at length expired on the 30th of May, 1778, in his eighty-fifth year.

It was the custom in those days, and prevails to a considerable extent even in our own time, for the religious world to fabricate "horrible death-beds" of all Freethinkers. Voltaire's last moments were distorted by his enemies after the approved fashion; and notwithstanding the most unqualified denial on the part of Dr. Burard and others, who were present at his death, there are many who believe these falsehoods at this moment. Voltaire died in peace, with the exception of the petty annoyances to which he was subjected by the priests. The philosophers, too, who wished that no public stigma should be cast upon him by the refusal of Christian burial, persuaded him to undergo confession and absolution. This, to oblige his friends, he submitted to; but when the cure one day drew him from his lethargy by shouting into his ear, "Do you believe the divinity of Jesus Christ?" Voltaire exclaimed, "In the name of God, Sir, speak to me no more of that man, but let me die in peace!" This put to flight all doubts of the pious, and the certificate of burial was refused. But the prohibition of the Bishop of Troyes came too late. Voltaire was buried at the monastery of Scellieres, in Champagne, of which his nephew was abbot. Afterwards, during the first French Revolution, the body, at the request of the citizens, was removed to Paris, and buried in the Pantheon. Lamartine, in his "History of the Girondists," p. 149, speaking of the ceremony, says:—

"On the 11th of July, the departmental and municipal authorities went in state to the barrier of Charenton, to receive the mortal remains of Voltaire, which were placed on the ancient site of the Bastile, like a conqueror on his trophies; his coffin was exposed to public gaze, and a pedestal was formed for it of stones torn from the foundations of this ancient stronghold of tyranny; and thus Voltaire when dead triumphed over those stones which had triumphed over and confined him when living. On one of the blocks was the inscription, '*Receive on this spot, where despotism once fettered thee, the Honors decreed to thee by thy country*'.... The coffin of Voltaire was deposited between those of Descartes and Mirabeau—the spot predestined for this intermediary genius between philosophy and policy, between the design and the execution."

The aim of Voltaire's life was the destruction of prejudice and the establishment of Reason. "Deists," said W. J. Fox in 1819, "have done much for toleration and religious liberty. It may be doubted if there be a country in Europe, where that cause has not been advanced by the writings of Voltaire." In the Preface and Conclusion to the "Examination of the Scriptures," Voltaire says:—

"The ambition of domineering over the mind, is one of the strongest passions. A theologian, a missionary, or a partisan of any description, is always for conquering like a prince, and there are many more sects than there are sovereigns in the world. To whose guidance shall I submit my mind? Must I be a Christian, be-cause I happened to be born in London, or in Madrid? Must I be a Mussulman, because I was born in Turkey? As it is myself alone that I ought to consult, the choice of a religion is my greatest interest. One man adores God by Mahomet, another by the Grand Lama, and another by the Pope. Weak and foolish men! adore God by your own reason.... I have learnt that a French Vicar, of the name of John Meslier, who died a short time since, prayed on his death-bed that God would forgive him for having taught Christianity. I have seen a Vicar in Dorsetshire relinquish a living of £200 a year, and confess to his parishioners that his conscience would not permit him to preach the shocking absurdities of the Christians. But neither the will nor the testament of John Meslier, nor the declaration of this worthy Vicar, are what I consider decisive proofs. Uriel Acosta, a Jew, publicly renounced the Old Testament in Amsterdam; however, I pay no more attention to the Jew Acosta than to Parson Meslier. I will read the arguments on both sides of the trial, with careful attention, not suffering the lawyers to tamper with me; but will weigh, before God, the reasons of both parties, and decide according to my conscience. I commence by being my-own instructor.... I conclude, that every sensible man, every honest man, ought to hold Christianity in abhorrence. 'The great name of Theist, which we can never sufficiently revere,' is the only name we ought to adopt. The only gospel we should read is the grand book of nature, written with God's own hand, and stamped with his own seal. The only religion we ought to profess is, 'to adore God, and act like honest men.' It would be as impossible for this simple and eternal religion to produce evil, as it would be impossible for Christian fanaticism not to produce it.... But what shall we substitute in its place? say you. What? A ferocious animal has sucked the blood of my relatives. I tell you to rid yourselves of this beast, and you ask me what you shall put in its place! Is it you that put this question to me? Then you are a hundred times more odious than the Pagan Pontiffs, who permitted themselves to enjoy tranquillity among their ceremonies and sacrifices, who did not attempt to enslave the mind by dogmas, who never disputed the powers of the magistrates, and who introduced no discord among mankind. You have the face to ask what you must substitute in the place of your fables!"

As will be seen by his exclamation on his death-bed, Voltaire was no believer in the *divinity* of Christ. He disbelieved the Bible *in toto*. The accounts of the doings of the Jewish kings, as represented in the Old Testament, he has unsparingly ridiculed in the drama of "Saul." The quiet irony of the following will be easily appreciated:—

Divinity of Jesus.—The Socinians, who are regarded as blasphemers, do not recognize the divinity of Jesus Christ. They dare to pretend, with the philosophers of antiquity, with the Jews, the Mahometans, and most other nations, that the idea of a god-man is monstrous; that the distance from God to man is infinite; and that it is impossible for a perishable body to be infinite, immense, or eternal. They have the confidence to quote Eusebius, Bishop of Cæsarea, in their favor, who, in his "Ecclesiastical History," book i., chap.

9, declares that it is absurd to imagine the uncreated and unchangeable nature of Almighty God taking the form of a man. They cite the fathers of the church, Justin and Tertullian, who have said the same thing: Justin in his "Dialogue with Triphonius;" and Tertullian, in his "Discourse against Praxeas." They quote St. Paul, who never calls Jesus Christ, God, and who calls him man very often. They carry their audacity so far as to affirm, that the Christians passed three entire ages in forming by degrees the apotheosis of Jesus; and that they only raised this astonishing edifice by the example of the Pagans, who had deified mortals. At first, according to them, Jesus was only regarded as a man inspired by God, and then as a creature more perfect than others. They gave him some time after, a place above the angels, as St. Paul tells us. Every day added to his greatness. He in time became an emanation, proceeding from God. This was not enough; he was even born before time. At last he was God consubstantial with God. Crellius, Voquelsius, Natalis, Alexander, and Hornbeck, have supported all these blasphemies by arguments, which astonish the wise and mislead the weak. Above all, Faustus Socinus spread the seeds of this doctrine in Europe; and at the end of the sixteenth century, a new species of Christianity was established. There were already more than three hundred. — [Philosophical Dictionary, vol. i. p. 405.]

Though a firm and consistent believer in the being of a God, Voltaire was no bigot. The calm reasoning of the following passage does honor to its author: —

Faith. — Divine faith, about which so much has been written, is evidently nothing more than incredulity brought under subjection; for we certainly have no other faculty than the understanding by which we can believe; and the objects of faith are not those of the understanding. We can believe only what appears to be true; and nothing can appear true but in one of the three following ways—by intuition or feeling, as I exist, I see the sun; or by an accumulation of probability amounting to certainty, as there is a city called Constantinople; or by positive demonstration, as triangles of the same base and height are equal. Faith, therefore, being nothing at all of this description, can no more be a belief, a persuasion, than it can be yellow or red. It can be nothing but the annihilation of reason, a silence of adoration at the contemplation of things absolutely incomprehensible. Thus, speaking philosophically, no person believes the Trinity; no person believes that the same body can be in a thousand places at once; and he who says, I believe these mysteries, will see, beyond the possibility of a doubt, if he reflects for a moment on what passes in his mind, that these words mean no more than, I respect thee, mysteries; I submit myself to those who announce them. For they agree with me, that my real reason, their own reason, believe them not; but it is clear if my *reason* is not persuaded, I am not persuaded, and my reason cannot possibly be two different beings. It is an absolute contradiction that I should receive that as true which my understanding rejects as false. Faith, therefore, is nothing but submissive or deferential incredulity. But why should this submission be exercised when my understanding invincibly recoils? The reason, we well know, is, that my understanding has been persuaded that the mysteries of my faith are laid down by God himself. All, then, that I can do, as a reasonable being, is to be silent and adore. That is what divines call external faith; and this faith neither is, nor can be, anything more than respect for things incomprehensible, in consequence of the reliance I place on those who teach them; If God himself were to say to me, "Thought is of an olive colour;" "the square of a certain number is bitter;" I should certainly understand nothing at all from these words. I could not adopt them either as true or false. But I will repeat them, if he commands me to do it; and I will make others repeat them at the risk of my life. This is faith; it is nothing more than obedience. In order to obtain a foundation then for this obedience, it is merely necessary to examine the books which require it. Our understanding, therefore, should investigate the books of the Old and New Testament, just as it would Plutarch or Livy; and if it finds in them incontestable and decisive evidences—evidences obvious to all minds, and such as would be admitted by men of all nations— that God himself is their author, then it is our incumbent duty to subject our understanding to the yoke of faith.

Prayer.—We know of no religion without prayers; even the Jews had them, although there was no public form of prayer among them before the time when they sang their canticles in their synagogues, which did not take place until a late period. The people of all nations, whether actuated by desires or fears, have summoned the assistance of the Divinity. Philosophers, however, more respectful to the Supreme Being, and rising more above human weakness, have been habituated to substitute, for prayer, resignation. This, in fact, is all that appears proper and suitable between creature and Creator. But philosophy is not adapted to the great mass of mankind; it soars too highly above the vulgar; it speaks a language they are unable to comprehend. To propose philosophy to them, would be just as weak as to propose the study of conic sections to peasants or fish-women. Among philosophers themselves, I know of no one besides Maximus Tyrius who has treated of this subject. The following is the substance of his ideas upon it:—The designs of God exist from all eternity. If the object prayed for be conformable to his immutable will, it must be perfectly useless to request of him the very thing which he has determined to do. If he is prayed to for the reverse of what he has determined to do, he is prayed to be weak, fickle, and inconstant; such a prayer implies that this is thought to be his character, and is nothing better than ridicule or mockery of him. You either request of him what is just and right, in which case he ought to do it, and it will be actually done without any solicitation, which in fact, shows distrust of his rectitude; or what you request is unjust, and then you insult him. You are either worthy or unworthy of the favour you implore; if worthy, he knows it better than you do yourself; if unworthy, you commit an additional crime in requesting that which you do not merit. In a word, we offer up prayers to God only because we have made him after our own image. We treat him like a pacha, or a sultan, who is capable of being exasperated and appeased. In short, all nations pray to God; the sage is resigned, and obeys him. Let us pray with the people, and let us be resigned to him with the sage. We have already spoken of the public prayer of many nations, and of those of the Jews. — That people have had one from time immemorial, which deserves all our attention, from its resemblance to the prayer taught us by Jesus Christ himself. This Jewish prayer is called the Kadish, and begins with these words: — "Oh! God! let thy name be magnified and sanctified; make thy kingdom to prevail; let redemption flourish, and the Messiah come quickly!" As this Radish is recited in Chaldee, it has induced the belief, that it is as ancient as the captivity, and that it was at that period that the Jews began to hope for a Messiah, a Liberator, or Redeemer, whom they have since prayed for in ihe seasons of their calamities. — [Ibid, vol. ii., p. 350.]

Voltaire's contempt for the Bible led him to use the language of "holy writ" in the coarsest jokes; though, perhaps, with such material, the jokes could not well be otherwise than *coarse*. The following letter he addressed to M. Bâillon, Intendant of Lyons, on account of a poor Jew taken up for uttering contraband goods. This kind of writing obtained for Voltaire the title of "scoffer:" —

"Blessings on the Old Testament, which gives me this opportunity of telling you, that amongst all those who adore the New, there is not one more devoted to your service than myself, a certain descendant of Jacob, a pedlar, as all these gentlemen are, whilst he is waiting for the Messiah, waits also for your protection, which at present he has the most need of. Some honest men of the first trade of St. Matthew, who gather together the Jews and Christians at the gates of your city, have seized something in the breeches pocket of an Israelitish page, belonging to the poor circumcised, who has the honour to tender you this billet, with all proper submission and humility. I beg leave to join my Amen to his at a venture. I but just saw you at Paris as Moses saw the Deity, and should be very happy in seeing you face to face. If the word face can any ways be applied to me, preserve some remembrance of your old eternal humble servant, who loves you with that chaste and tender affection, which the religious Solomon had for his three hundred Shuhamites."

Voltaire's prodigious wit and sarcasm were so exuberant, that he expended them upon all people and all subjects—even *himself*, when occasion admitted of it, In one of his letters,-addressed to the Elector Palatine, Sept. 9, 1761, he gives this excuse for not attending at the court:—

"I should really make an excellent figure amidst the rejoicings of your electoral highness. It was only, I think, in the Egypt of antiquity that *skeletons* were admitted to a place in their festivals. To say the truth, my lord, it is all over with me. I laugh indeed sometimes; but am forced to acknowledge that pain is an evil. It is a comfort to me that your highness is well; but I am fitter for an extreme unction than a baptism. May the peace serve for an era to mark the prince's birth; and may his august father preserve his regard for, and accept the profound respects of his little Swiss, Voltaire."

In politics, Voltaire was not very far advanced. He seems to have had no idea of a nation without a *king*. A monarch who should not commit any very flagrant acts of tyranny, was as much as he appeared to desire. He evidently did not foresee the great revolution that was so soon to burst forth in France, but that he mainly contributed by his writings to bring it about, there can be no doubt. His influence upon the men of his time, both in France and Europe, is ably depicted by such writers as Lamartine, Quinet, and Brougham. Voltaire's was the one great mind of his day, whose thoughts engrossed the attention of all men. He was great by his learning, his genius, and his benevolence—and this man was the champion of Reason, the enemy of superstition, and an "Infidel." Quinet, in his lectures on the Romish Church, says:—"I watch, for forty years, the reign of one man who is in himself the spiritual director, not of his country, but of his age. From the corner of his chamber, he governs the kingdom of spirits; intellects are every day regulated by his; one word written by his hand traverses Europe. Princes love, and kings fear him; they think they are not sure of their kingdom if he be not with them. Whole nations, on their side, adopt without discussion, and emulously repeat, every syllable that falls from his pen. Who exercises this incredible power, which had been nowhere seen since the middle ages? Is he another Gregory II.? Is he a Pope? No—Voltaire."

We conclude our sketch with the eloquent words of Lamartine, who describes, in a few sentences, the inestimable services rendered to Freethought and intellectual progression by the Sage of Ferney:—

"If we judge of men by what they have *done*, then Voltaire is incontestably the greatest writer of modern Europe. No one has caused, through the powerful influence of his genius alone, and the perseverance of his will, so great a commotion in the minds of men; his pen aroused a world, and has shaken a far mightier empire than that of Charlemagne, the European empire of a theocracy. His genius was not *force* but *light*. Heaven had destined him not to destroy but to illuminate, and wherever he trod, light followed him, for Reason (which is *light*) had destined him to be first her poet, then her apostle, and lastly her idol."

J. W.

JOHN TOLAND

In the Augustan age of Freethought, no British writer achieved more renown, or performed greater services to Biblical criticism, than John Toland. His life would fill a volume, while his works would stock a library. True to his convictions, he spoke like a man, and died as a hero. His books are strewn with classical illustrations, and deal so with abstract (and to us) uninteresting arguments, that we shall simply give a brief sketch of the life of this extraordinary man. He gave his thoughts to the scholars at the same time that Woolston addressed the people; conjointly they revolutionized opinion in our favor.

Toland was born on November 30, 1670, at Londonderry, in Ireland. It is said his registered name was "James Junius," another account says "Julius Cæsar;" but we have been unable to find any authentic date for either supposition, and whatever his name was registered, we have indisputable evidence that he was always called John Toland. We have less proof as to his parentage; some writers allege that he was the natural son of a Catholic priest; while others contend that he was born of a family once affluent, but at the time of his birth in very reduced circumstances. Whether this was the case or the reverse, young Toland received a liberal education. He was early taught the classics, studied in the Glasgow College; and on leaving Glasgow he was presented with letters of credit from the city magistrates, highly flattering to him as a man and a scholar. He received the diploma of A.M. at Edinburgh, the day previous to the Battle of the Boyne. He finished his studies at the University of Leyden.

The first work of importance which Toland published, was a "Life of John Milton, containing besides the History of his Works, several extraordinary Characters of Men and Books, Sects, Parties, and Opinions." This work being violently opposed, was speedily followed by "Amyntor," or a defence of Milton's life, containing—1. A general apology for all writings of that kind. 2. A catalogue of books, attributed in the primitive times to Jesus Christ, his apostles, and other eminent persons, with several important remarks relating to the canon of Scripture. 3. A complete history of the Book, entitled "Icon Basilike, proving Dr. Gauden, and not King Charles I., to be the author of it," etc. Those works established the fame of Toland, as well as formed the groundwork for persecution, which hunted him even on his death-bed. In the year 1699 Toland collected, edited, and published, from the original MSS., the whole of the works of James Harrington, prefixed by a memoir of this extraordinary theorist. In his preface he says that he composed this work "in his beloved retirement at Cannon, near Bansted, in Surrey." From this, along with other excerpts scattered through his works, we cannot but infer that at the outset of his career he possessed a moderate competence of worldly wealth and social position. He says his idea was "to transmit to posterity the worthy memory of James Harrington, a bright ornament to useful learning, a hearty lover of his native country, and a generous benefactor to the whole world; a person who obscured the false lustre of our modern politicians, and equalled (if not exceeded) all the ancient legislators." This to us is an interesting fact, for it shows the early unanimity which existed between the earlier reformers in politics and those of theology. The supervision of the "Oceana" by Toland, bears the same inferential analogy, as if Mr. Holyoake were the biographer and publisher of the "New Moral World" and its author. In 1700, he published "Anglia Libera; or, the Limitation and Succession of the Crown of England, explained and Asserted," etc. This book is concluded by the following apothegm, assuring the people "that no king can ever be so good as one of their own making, as there is no title equal to their approbation, which is the only divine right of all magistracy, for the voice of the people is the voice of God." In 1702, Toland spent some time in Germany, publishing a series of Letters to a friend in Holland, entitled "Some Remarks on the King of Prussia's Country, on his Government, his Court, and his numerous Palaces." About this time appeared "The Art of Governing by Parties;" this was always a favorite subject of the old Freethinkers, and is still further elucidated by Bolingbroke.

In 1707 he published a large treatise in English and Latin, as "A Philippic Oration, to incite the English against the French," a work I have never seen. We now return to an earlier date, and shall trace the use of his theological works. The first of note (1696) was "Christianity not Mysterious" — showing that there is nothing in the gospel contrary to reason, nor above it; and that no Christian doctrine can be properly called a mystery. As soon as this book was issued from the press, it was attacked with unmanly virulence. One man (Peter Brown) who was more disgustingly opposed to Toland than the rest, was made a bishop; and by far the greatest majority amongst the Anglican clergy, who attacked him, were all rewarded by honors and preferment. The author was accused of making himself a new Heresiarch; that there was a tradition amongst the Irish that he was to be a second Cromwell, and that Toland himself boasted that before he was forty years old, he would be governor over a greater country than Cromwell; and that he would be the head over a new religion before he was thirty. One of his opponents publicly stigmatises him as saying that he (Toland) himself designed to be as great an impostor as Mahomet, and more powerful than the Pope; while the Puritans denounced him as a disguised Jesuit, and the Papists as a rancorous Nonconformist. To complete the comedy, the Irish Parliament condemned his book to be publicly burnt, some ecclesiastics loudly murmuring that, the author should be burned with it; others, more moderate, were anxious that Toland should burn it himself, while at last they came to an unanimous resolution to burn it in front of the threshold of his door, so that when the author appeared, he would be obliged to step oyer the ashes of his own book, which was accordingly done amid the brutal cheers of an ignorant and infuriated populace.

As a proof of the high esteem in which Toland was held by the *few* able and liberal men of the day, we extract the following account from the correspondence of John Locke and Mr. Molyneux. * The latter gentleman, writing to the former, says:—"I am told the author of 'Christianity not Mysterious' is of this country, and that his name is Toland, but he is a stranger in these parts, I believe. If he belongs to this kingdom, he has been a good while out of it, or I have not heard of any such *remarkable* man amongst us." In another letter, the same writer says:—"In my last to you, there was a passage, relating to the author of 'Christianity not Mysterious.' I did not then think he was so near me as within the bounds of this city; but I find since that he has come over hither, and have had the favor of a visit from him. I now understand that he was born in this country, but that he has been a great while abroad, and his education was for some time under the great Le Clerc. But that for which I can never honor him too much, is his acquaintance and friendship to you, and the respect which upon all occasions he expresses for you. I propose a great deal of satisfaction in his conversation. I take him to be a candid Freethinker, and a good scholar. But there is a violent sort of spirit which reigns here, which begins already to show itself against him, and I believe will increase daily, for I find the clergy alarmed to a mighty degree against him. And last Sunday he had his welcome to this city, by hearing himself harangued against out of the pulpit, by a prelate of this country."

* Locke's posthumous works. Edited by Die Maizeaus.

Mr. Locke, in return, says:—"For the man I wish very well, and could give you, if it needed, proofs that I do so. And therefore I desire you to be kind to him: but I must leave it to your prudence in what way and how far. For it will be his fault alone, if he proves not a very valuable man, and have not you for his friend." To this, Mr. Molyneux writes to Mr. Locke—"I look upon Mr. Toland as a very ingenuous man, and I should be very glad of any opportunity of doing him service, to which I think myself indispensably bound by your recommendation." Soon after this, Mr. Molyneux describes the treatment Toland underwent in Ireland. In another letter to Locke—"He has had his opposers here, as you will find by a book which I have sent to you. The author (Peter Brown) is my acquaintance, but two things I shall never forgive in his book: the one is the foul language and opprobrious names he gives Mr. Toland; the other is upon several occasions, calling in the aid of the civil magistrate, and delivering up Mr. Toland to secular punishment. This, indeed, is a killing argument, but some will be apt to say, that where, the strength of his reason failed him, then he flies to the strength of his sword; and this reminds me of a business that was very surprising to many, the presentment of some pernicious books and their authors by the grand jury of Middlesex. This is looked upon as a matter of dangerous consequence, to make our civil courts judges of religious doctrines; and no one knows upon a change of affairs whose turn it may be next to be condemned. But the example has been followed in this country, and Mr. Toland and his book have been presented here by a grand jury, not one of whom I am persuaded ever read one leaf in 'Christianity not Mysterious.'

"Let the Sorbonne forever now be silent; a learned grand jury, directed by as learned a judge, does the business much better. The Dissenters here were the chief promoters of this matter, but, when I asked one of them 'What if a violent Church of England jury should present Mr. Baxter's books as pernicious, and condemn them to the flames by the common executioner,' he was sensible of the error, and said he wished it had never been done." Mr. Locke, in his reply, coincides with his friend, and says, "The Dissenters had best *consider*; but they are a sort of men which will always be the same." A remark which 150 years has not failed in its truthfulness. Mr. Molyneux concludes his remarks in reference to Toland, as follows:—"Mr. Toland is at length driven out of our kingdom; the poor gentleman at last wanted a meal's meat, and the universal outcry of the clergy ran so strong against him, that none durst admit him to their tables. The little stock of money which he had was soon exhausted, he fell to borrowing, and to complete his hardships, the Parliament fell on his book, voted it to be burnt by the common hangman, and ordered the author to be taken into custody by the Serjeant-at-Arms, and to be prosecuted by the Attorney General. Hereupon he is fled out of this kingdom, and none here knows where he has directed his course." From this correspondence we glean the following facts:—

1. That John Locke and Mr. Molyneux were favorable to Freethought.

2. That (on Locke's authority) Toland possessed abilities of no common order.

3. That Toland was unjustly persecuted, and he met with the sympathy of the Liberals.

Toland, having received a foretaste of his country's vengeance, retired for two years to Germany, where he was welcomed by the first scholars of the age. Hearing that the House of Convocation, in London, was about to denounce two of his works as heretical ("Christianity not Mysterious," and "Amyntor,") he hastened to England, and published two letters to the Prolucutor, which were never laid before Convocation. He insisted that he should be heard in his own defence before sentence was passed on his works; but as usual this wish was denied him. A legal difficulty prevented the bishops from prosecuting the works, and Toland gave the world a full account in his "Vindicius Liberius."

The "Letters to Serena," written in a bold, honest, unflinching manner, were the next performances of Toland. The first letter is on "The Origin and Force of Prejudices." It is founded on a reflection of Cicero, that all prejudices spring from moral, and not physical sources, and while all admit the power of the senses to be infallible, all strive to corrupt the judgment, by false metaphor and unjust premises. Toland traces the progress of superstition from the hands of a midwife to those of a priest, and shows how the nurse, parent, schoolmaster, professor, philosopher, and politician, all combine to warp the mind of man by fallacies from his progress in childhood, at school, at college, and in the world. How the child is blinded with an idea, and the man with a word. The second letter is "A History of the Soul's Immortality Among the Heathens." A lady had been reading Platers "Phædo," and remarked as to how Cato could derive any consolation from the slippery and vague suppositions of that verbiant dialogue. Toland, therefore, for her edification, drew up a list of the specifications of the ancients on the subject, analysing (in its progress) the varying phases of the fables of the Elysian fields, the Charons, the Styx, etc., deriving them all from the ancient Egyptians. Toland thought the idea had arisen among the people, like our witches, ghosts, and fairy stories, and subsequently defended by the philosophers, who sought to rule their passions by finding arguments for their superstitions, and thus the rise of their exoteric and esoteric doctrines were the first foundations of the belief in the immortality of the soul. The third letter is on "The Origin of Idolatry," or, as it might rather be called, a history of the follies of mankind. He traces the causes, the origin, and the science of superstition—its phenomena and its devotees, proving that all the sacrifices, prayers, and customs of idolatry are the same in all ages, they only differ in language and adaptability of climate, and that with the fall of judicial astrology, idolatry received its greatest blow, for while men thought that priests could control destiny, they feared them—but this idea destroyed, it removed the terror which so long had existed as an immediate object betwixt the man and this sacerdotal tyrant.

In letter fourth, addressed "To a Gentleman in Holland, showing Spinoza's System of Philosophy to be without any principle or foundation," and in the concluding article, Toland argues that "motion is essential to matter, in answer to some remarks by a noble friend on the above." In the fifteenth section of this argument, Toland thus rebuts the allegation that were motion indissolubly connected with matter, there must be extension without surface for motion or matter to exert their respective powers upon. It is often used as an argument, that if a vase was filled with any commodity to the utmost extent, where would be the space for motion? We know that in a kettle of water, if there is no outlet for the steam (which is the motion of the water,) the kettle will burst. Toland says, "'You own most bodies are in actual motion, which can be no argument that they have been always so, or that there are not others in actual repose.' I grant that such a consequence does not necessarily follow, though the thing may itself be true. But, however, it may not be amiss to consider how far this actual motion reaches, and is allowed, before we come to treat of rest. Though the matter of the universe be everywhere the same, yet according to its various modifications it is conceived to be divided into numberless particular systems, vortices or whirlpools of matter; and these again are subdivided into other systems greater or less, which depend oh one another, as every one on the whole, in their centres, textures, frame, and coherence. Our sun is the centre of one of the larger systems, which contains a great many small ones within the sphere of its activity, as all the planets which move about it; and these are subdivided into lesser systems that depend on them, as his satelites wait upon Jupiter, and the moon on the earth; the earth again is divided into the atmosphere, ground, water, and other principal parts; these again into the vegetable, animal, and mineral kingdoms. Now, as all these depend in a link on one another, so their matter is mutually resolved into each other, for earth, air, fire, and water are not only closely blended and united, but likewise interchangeable, transformed in a perpetual revolution: earth becoming water, water air, air ether, and so back again in mixtures without end or number. The animals we destroy contribute to preserve us, till we are destroyed to preserve other things, and become parts of grass, or plants, or water, or air, or something else that helps to make other animals, and they one another, or other men, and these again into stone, or wood, or metals, or minerals, or animals again, or become parts of all these and of a great many other things, animals, or vegetables, daily consuming and devouring each other—so true it is that everything lives by the destruction of another. All the parts of the universe are in this constant motion of destroying and begetting, of begetting and destroying, and the greater systems are acknowledged to have their ceaseless movements as well as the smallest particles, the very central globes of the vortices revolving on their own axis, and every particle in the vortex gravitating towards the centre. Our bodies, however we may flatter ourselves, do not differ from those of other creatures, but like them receive increase or diminution by nutrition or evacuation, by accretion, transpiration, and other ways, giving some parts of ours to other bodies, and receiving again of theirs, not altogether the same yesterday as to-day, nor to continue the same to-morrow, being alive in a perpetual flux like a river, and in the total dissolution of our system at death to become parts of a thousand other things at once, our bodies partly mixing with the dust and the water of the earth, partly exhaled and evaporated into the air, flying to so many different places, mixing and incorporating with numerous things.

"No parts of matter are bound to any one figure or form, losing and changing their figures and forms continually, that is being in perpetual motion, dipt, or worn, or ground to pieces, or dissolved by other parts, acquiring their figures, and these theirs, and so on incessantly: earth, air, fire, and water, iron, wood, and marble, plants and animals, being rarefied, condensed, liquified, congealed, dissolved, coagulated, or any other way resolved into one another. The whole face of the earth exhibits those mutations every moment to our eyes, nothing continuing one hour numerically the same; and these changes being but several kinds of motion, are therefore the incontestable effects of universal action. But the changes in the parts make no change in the universe; for it is manifest that the continual alterations, successions, revolutions, and transmutations of matter, cause no accession or diminution therein, no more than any letter is added or lost in the alphabet by the endless combinations and transpositions thereof into so many different words and languages, for a thing no sooner quits one form than it puts on another, leaving as it were the theatre in a certain dress, and appearing again in a new one, which produces a perpetual youthfulness and vigor, without any decay or decrepitness of the world, as some have falsely imagined, contrary to reason and experience; the world, with all the parts and kinds thereof, continuing at all times in the same condition."

"But the species still continue by propagation, notwithstanding the decay of the individuals, and the death of our bodies is but matter going to be dressed in some new form; the impressions may vary, but the wax continues still the same, and indeed death is in effect the very same thins with our birth; for as to die is only to cease to be what we formerly were, so to be born is to begin to be something which we were not before. Considering the numberless successive generations that have inhabited this globe, returning at death into the common mass of the same, mixing with all the other parts thereof, and to this, the incessant river-like flowing and transpiration of matter every moment from the bodies of men while they live, as well as their daily nourishment, inspiration of air, and other additions of matter to their bulk; it seems probable that there is no particle of matter on the whole earth which has not been a part of man. Nor is this reasoning confined to our own species, but remains as true of every order of animals or plants, or any other beings, since they have been all resolved into one another by ceaseless revolutions, so that nothing is more certain than that every material Thing is all Things, and that all Things are but manifestations of one."

In his reply to Wotton, who attacks those "Letters to Serena," Toland says they were addressed "to a lady, the most accomplished then in the world." The name of the lady will probably, remain forever a mystery.

In 1718, he published the celebrated work "Nazarenus, or Jewish, Gentile, and Mahometan Christianity," which caused an immense sensation at the time it appeared, and led to his "Mangonentes" (1720,) a work singularly profound and effective. In the same year he gave the world "Tetradymus," containing "Hodegus, or the Pillar of Cloud and Fire," that guided the Israelites in the Wilderness, *not miraculous*, but a thing equally practiced by other nations; and "Clidophorus, or of the Exoteric and Esoteric Philosophy;" and "Hypatia." There is a long preface to those books, "from under an elm in Bensbury (or Chebem's camp,) on the 'warren at the south end of Wimbledon Common (1720.") About this time "Pantheisticon" appeared, written as a caricature on Church Liturgies, which Archdeacon Hare denounced as "downright Atheism."

Along with the above, Toland wrote a multitude of small pamphlets; he translated the fables of Æsop, and published a poem, entitled "Clito," which caused much excitement at the time; and, as it represented Toland's ideal character, we reprinted it in the London Investigator. His earlier political works were esteemed so valuable in the defence of the Protestant succession, and advancing the interests of the Elector, subsequently King of England, that in one of his visits paid to that Court, he was presented by the Electress with miniature portraits of herself and family.

The following is a catalogue of the works of Toland, which have never yet been published, and the works in which they are mentioned:—

1. The History of Socrates (in the Life of Harrington.)

2. Systems of Divinity Exploded. An Epistolary Dissertation. (Christianity not Mysterious.)

3. The History of the Canon of the New Testament. (Nazarenus.)

4. Repubiica Mosaica. (Nazarenus.)

5. A Treatise Concerning Tradition. (Tetradymus.)

There were several other works, part of them written, which passed into the hands of Lord Molesworth (we believe,) part of which were published (the "History of the Druid" and also "Giordano Bruno;") but whether they exist at the present time or not, we are unable to say.

There is also great difficulty in deciding as to the manner of Toland's life; of this, however, we are certain, that he caused great opposition in his own day, and he was patronised by able man. He edited an edition of Lord Shaftesbury's Letters, and published a work of that noble Lord's surreptitiously; he mingled amongst the German Courts, and appeared on terms of equality with the *elite* of the philosophers and the aristocracy. The brief memoir prefaced to one of his works is an epistolary document addressed to a noble Lord. His acquaintance with Locke, Shaftesbury, Collins, Molesworth, and Molyneux, must have proceed-. ed from other causes than his genius, or why was Toland exalted when Mandeville, Chubb, and the brave Woolston are never so much as alluded to? We consider that there is a strong probability that he was wealthy—or at least possessed of a moderate competence. His abilities were of a curious order. He seemed to be one of a school which rose about his time to advocate Freethought, but shackled by a dogma. His collegiate education gave him an early liking for the dead languages, and he carried out the notion of the ancients, that the exoteric or esoteric methods were still in force. From a careful perusal of the works of the "Fathers," and the contemporary books of the heathens, he fancied that all the superstitions in the world differed but in degree— that religion was but the organic cause of superstition, the arguments made for it by the philosophers to propitiate the vulgar. This idea (in the main) was agreed to by Woolston, although his violent "Discourses," which were addressed to the unlearned, contained within them the germ of their intrinsic popularity. Yet even Woolston's works, notwithstanding their bluff exterior, had something more within them than what the people could appreciate, or even the present race of Freethinkers can always understand; for underneath that unrivalled vein of sarcasm, there was in every instance an esoteric view, which comprehended the meaning by which the earlier Christians understood the gospels, and rendered them on the same scale as the works of the ancients. The renowned William Whiston was another who interpreted Scripture in a similar manner. All those writers would have been Swedenborgians if there had been no Freethought, while Whiston would have been an Atheist had there been no representative of that school. We do not consider Toland, then, as an absolute Deist. At that time the age was not so far progressed as to admit a Biblical scholar into the extreme advanced list; and when a man has spent the whole of his childhood in a sectarian family, and his youth and early manhood in a University, it is an impossibility to throw off at one struggle the whole of his past ideas; he may be unfettered in thought, and valiant in speech, still there is the encyclopædia of years hanging upon him as a drag to that extreme development which he wishes, but cannot bring his passions to follow. Not that we would by any means observe that Toland was comparatively behind his age, but that even in his more daring works he still had a vague idea of Scripture being partly inspired, although overlaid with a mass of ecclesiastical verbiage.

It also seems a mystery how the works of Woolston could be condemned, his person seized, while in the case of Toland we hear of nothing but his works being burnt. Why was Convocation so idle? Why make idle threats, and let their victim ramble at large! Was it because the one had powerful friends and the other had none? or was it that in the earlier portion of the career of Toland, the invisible hand of Bolingbroke stayed the grasp of persecution? Or was Shaftesbury's memory so esteemed, that hid friend was untouched! Those particulars we cannot learn, but they will take rank with other parallel cases, as when the same government prosecuted Paine, and gave Gibbon a sinecure, or nearer our own times when a series of men were imprisoned for Atheism, and Sir William Moles worth published similar sentiments without hindrance.

In the "History of the Soul's Immortality," Toland thus gives the explanation respecting the exoteric and esoteric doctrines of Pythagoras:— "Pythagoras himself did not believe the transmigration which has made his name so famous to posterity; for in the internal or secret doctrine he meant no more than the eternal revolution of forms in matter, those ceaseless vicissitudes and alterations which turn everything into all things, and all things into anything; as vegetables and animals become part of us, we become part of them, and both become parts of a thousand other things in the universe, each turning into water, water into air, etc., and so back again in mixtures without end or number. But in the external or popular doctrine he imposed on the mob by an equivocal expression that they should become various kinds of beasts after death, thereby to deter them the more effectually from wickedness.... Though the poets embellished their pieces with the opinion of the soul's immortality, yet a great number of them utterly rejected it for Seneca was not single in saying:—

'Naught's after death, and death itself is naught,
Of a quick race, only the utmost goal;
Then may the saints lose all their hope of heaven,
And sinners quit their racky fears of hell.'"

We now dismiss John Toland from our view. He was one of the most honest, brave, truthful, and scholastic of the old Deists. His memory will be borne on the wings of centuries, and if ever a true millennium does arise, the name of this sterling Freethinker will occupy one of the brightest niches in its Pantheon of Worthies.

A. C.

COMPTE DE VOLNEY

Constantine Francis Chasshboeuf, de Volney, was born on February 3rd, 1757, at Craon, in Anjou. His father, a distinguished advocate, not wishing his son to bear the name of *Chasseboeuf*, resolved that he should assume that of *Boisgirais*. With this name Constantine Francis was first known in the world, studying at the College of Ancenis and Angers. He afterwards commenced his Oriental travels, changing his name to Volney.

At the age of seventeen, finding himself his own master, and possessed of £50 a-year, inherited from his mother, he went to Paris, in order to study the sciences, preferring the study of medicine and physiology, although giving great attention to history and the ancient languages. On inheriting a legacy of £240, he visited Egypt and Syria, starting on foot, a knapsack on his back, a gun on his shoulder, and his £240, in gold, concealed in a belt. When he arrived in Egypt, he shut himself up for eight months in a Coptic monastery, in order to learn Arabic; after which he commenced his travels through Egypt and Syria, returning to France after an absence of four years, and publishing his "Voyage en Egypte et en Syrie," which was acknowledged by the French army, on their conquering Egypt, to be the only book "that had never deceived them." The French Government named him Director of Commerce and Agriculture in Corsica, but being elected a deputy of the tiers-etat of the Senechausse of Anjou, he resigned the government appointment, holding the maxim, that a national deputy ought not in any way to be a pensioner. He opposed all secret deliberations, and wished to admit the constituents and the citizens. He was made secretary on the 23rd of November, 1790, and in the debates, which arose upon the power of the king to determine peace and war, Volney proposed and carried the resolution that "The French nation renounces from this moment the undertaking any war tending to increase their territory." In 1792, he accompanied Pozzo di Borgo to Corsica, in compliance with invitations from many influential inhabitants, who sought his information. In Corsica he became acquainted with Napoleon Buonaparte, who was then an artillery officer; and some years after, hearing that Buonaparte had obtained the command of the army of Italy, Volney exclaimed, "If circumstances favor him, we shall see the head of a Cæesar upon the shoulders of an Alexander." When Volney returned to Paris, he published an "Account of the State of

Corsica." He was afterwards appointed Professor of History, attracting large audiences; but the Normal School being suppressed, he embarked for the United States of America, in 1795. He was received by Washington, who bestowed publicly on him marks of honor and friendship. In 1798, Volney returned to France, and gave up to his mother-in-law the property which he was entitled to from the death of his father, which had just occurred. During his absence, he had been chosen a member of the Institute. Buonaparte also, on Volney's return, tried to win his esteem and assistance, soliciting him as colleague in the consulship. But he refused the co-operation, as also the office of Minister of the Interior.

Seldom do men find so many inducements to "accept office" as was offered to Volney; and seldom do men appear who are disinterested enough to reject the inducements then held out to him. Although he refused to work *with* the ruling powers of that day, he ever ceased to work *for* the *people!* He occupied himself till the last year of his life in giving to the world that literature which will never be forgotten.

It would be impossible to notice all the works written by such an indefatigable thinker as the *"heretic"* of our sketch. We ought to mention, however, that subsequently to his being made Peer of France, by Louis XVIII.; and when there existed an intention of crowning Louis, Volney published "The History of Samuel, the inventor of Royal Coronations." This book represents Samuel as an impostor, Saul as the blind instrument of sacerdotal cunning, and David as an ambitious youth. In September, 1791, Volney presented to the Assembly "The Ruins, or Meditations on the Revolutions of Empires," a book which will immortalize him in the memory of Freethinkers. The originality of style, and the eloquence of expression, cannot fail to interest all who read it. We give the following extracts, from the above work, but as it contains so much that ought to be read, we must return to the subject in another number:—

"Legislators, friends of evidence and of truth!

"That the subject of which we treat should be involved in so many clouds, is by no means astonishing, since, beside the difficulties that are peculiar to it, thought itself has, till this moment, ever had shackles imposed upon it, and free inquiry, by the intolerance of every religious system, been interdicted. But now that thought is unrestrained, and may develope all its powers, we will expose in the face of day, and submit to the common judgment of assembled nations, such rational truths as unprejudiced minds have by long and laborious study discovered: and this, not with the design of imposing them as a creed, but from a desire of provoking new lights, and obtaining better information.

"Chiefs and instructors of the people! you are not ignorant of the profound obscurity in which the nature, origin, and history of the dogmas you teach are enveloped. Imposed by force and authority, inculcated by education, maintained by the influence of example, they were perpetuated from age to age, and habit and inattention strengthened their empire. But if man, enlightened by experience and reflection, summon to the bar of mature examination the prejudices of his infancy, he presently discovers a multitude of incongruities and contradictions, which awaken his sagacity, and call forth the exertion of his reasoning powers.

"At first, remarking the various and opposite creeds into which nations are divided, we are led boldly to reject the infallibility claimed by each; and arming ourselves alternately with their reciprocal pretensions, to conceive that the senses and the understanding, emanating directly from God, are a law not less sacred, and a guide not less sure, than the indirect and contradictory codes of the prophets.

"If we proceed to examine the texture of the codes themselves, we shall observe that their pretended divine laws, that is to say, laws immutable and eternal, have risen from the complexion of times, of places, and of persons; that these codes issue one from another in a kind of genealogical order, mutually borrowing a common and similar fund of ideas, which *every* institutor modifies agreeably to his fancy.

"If we ascend to the source of those ideas, we shall find that it is lost in the night of time, in the infancy of nations, in the very origin of the world, to which they claim alliance: and there, immersed in the obscurity of chaos, and the fabulous empire of tradition, they are attended with so many prodigies as to be seemingly inaccessible to the human understanding. But this prodigious state of things gives birth to a ray of reasoning, that resolves the difficulty; for if the miracles held out in systems of religion have actually existed; if, for instance, metamorphoses, apparitions and the conversations of one or more Gods, recorded in the sacred books of the Hindoos, the Hebrews, and the Parses, are indeed events in real history, it follows that nature in those times was perfectly unlike the nature that we are acquainted with now; that men of the present age are totally different from the men that formerly existed; but, consequently, that we ought not to trouble our heads about them.

"On the contrary, if those miraculous facts have had no real existence in the physical order of things, they must be regarded solely as productions of the human intellect: and the nature of man, at this day, capable of making the most fantastic combinations, explains the phenomenon of those monsters in history. The only difficulty is to ascertain how and for what purpose the imagination invented them. If we examine with attention the subjects that are exhibited by them, if we analyze the ideas which they combine and associate, and weigh with accuracy all their concomitant circumstances, we shall find a solution perfectly conformable to the laws of nature. Those fabulous stories have a figurative sense different from their apparent one; they are founded on simple and physical facts; but these facts being ill-conceived and erroneously represented, have been disfigured and changed from their original nature by accidental causes dependent on the human mind, by the confusion of signs made use of in the representation of objects, by the equivocation of words, the defect of language, and the imperfection of writing. These Gods, for example, who act such singular parts in every system, are no other than the physical powers of nature, the elements, the winds, the meteors, the stars, all which have been personified by the necessary mechanism of language, and the manner in which objects are conceived by the understanding. Their life, their manners, their actions, are only the operation of the same powers, and the whole of their pretended history no more than a description of their various phenomena, traced by the first naturalist that observed them, but taken in a contrary sense by the vulgar, who did not understand it, or by succeeding generations, who forgot it. In a word, all the theological dogmas respecting the origin of the world, the nature of God, the revelation of his laws, the manifestation of his person, are but recitals of astronomical facts, figurative and emblematical narratives of the motion and influence of the heavenly bodies. The very idea itself of the divinity, which is at present so obscure, abstracted, and metaphysical, was in its origin merely a composite of the powers of the material universe, considered sometimes analytically, as they appear in their agents and their phenomena, and sometimes synthetically, as forming one whole, and exhibiting an harmonious revelation in all its parts. Thus the name of God has been bestowed sometimes upon the wind, upon fire, water, and the elements; sometimes upon the sun, the stars, the planets, and their influences; sometimes upon the universe at large, and the matter of which the world is composed; sometimes upon abstract and metaphysical properties, such as space, duration, motion, and intelligence; but in every instance, the idea of a Deity has not flowed from the miraculous revelation of an invisible world, but has been the natural result of human reflection, has followed the progress and undergone the changes of the successive improvement of intellect, and has had for its subject the visible universe and its different agents.

"It is then in vain that nations refer the origin of their religion to heavenly inspiration; it is in vain that they pretend to describe a supernatural state of things as first in order of events; the original barbarous state of mankind, attested by their own monuments, belies all their assertions. These assertions are still more victoriously refuted by considering this great principle, *that man receives no ideas but through the medium of his senses*: for from hence it appears that every system which ascribes human wisdom to any other source than experience and sensation, includes in it a ysteron vroteron, and represents the last results of understanding as earliest in the order of time. If we examine the different religious systems which have been formed respecting the actions of the Gods, and the origin of the world, we shall discover at every turn an anticipation in the order of narrating things, which could only be suggested by subsequent reflection. Reason, then, emboldened by these contradictions, hesitates not to reject whatever does not accord with the nature of things, and accepts nothing for historical truth that is not capable of being established by argument and ratiocination. Its ideas and suggestions are as follows:—

"Before any nation received from a neighbor nation dogmas already invented; before one generation inherited the ideas of another, none of these complicated systems had existence. The first men, the children of nature, whose consciousness was anterior to experience, and who brought no preconceived knowledge into the world with them, were born without any idea of those articles of faith which are the result of learned contention; of those religious rites which had relation to arts and practices not yet in existence; of those precepts which suppose the passions already developed; of those laws which have reference to a language and a social order hereafter to be produced; of that God, whose attributes are abstractions of the knowledge of nature, and the idea of whose conduct is suggested by the experience of a despotic government; in fine, of that soul and those spiritual existences which are said not to be the object of the senses, but which, however, we must forever have remained unacquainted with, if our senses had not introduced them to us. Previously to arriving at these notions, an immense catalogue of existing facts must have been observed. Man, originally savage, must have learned from repeated trials the use of his organs. Successive generations must have invented and refined upon the means of subsistence; and the understanding, at liberty to disengage itself from the wants of nature, must have risen to the complicated art of comparing ideas, digesting reasonings, and seizing upon abstract similitudes.

"It was not till after having surmounted those obstacles, and run a long career in the night of history, that man, reflecting on his state, began to perceive his subjection to forces superior to his own and independent of his will. The sun gave him light and warmth; fire burned, thunder terrified, the winds buffeted, water overwhelmed him; all the various natural existences acted upon him in a manner not to be resisted. For a long time an automaton, he remained passive, without inquiring into the cause of this action; but the very moment he was desirous of accounting to himself for it, astonishment seized his mind; and passing from the surprise of a first thought to the reverie of curiosity, he formed a chain of reasoning.

"At first, considering only the action of the elements upon him, he inferred relatively to himself, an idea of weakness, of subjection, and relatively to them, an idea of power, of domination; and this idea was the primitive and fundamental type of all his conceptions of the divinity.

"The action of the natural existences, in the second place, excited in him sensations of pleasure or pain, of good or evil; by virtue of his organization, he conceived love or aversion for them, he desired or dreaded their presence: and fear or hope was the principle of every idea of religion.

"Afterwards, judging everything by comparison, and remarking in those beings a motion spontaneous like his own, he supposed there to be a will, an intelligence inherent in that motion, of a nature similar to what existed in himself; and hence, by way of inference, he started a fresh argument. Having experienced that certain modes of behavior towards his fellow-creatures wrought a change in their affections and governed their conduct, he applied those practices to the powerful beings of the universe. 'When my fellow-creature of superior strength,' said he to himself, 'is disposed to injure me, I humble myself before him, and my prayer has the art of appeasing him. I will pray to the powerful beings that strike me. I will supplicate the faculties of the planets, the waters, and they will hear me. I will conjure them to avert the calamities, and to grant me the blessings which are at their disposal. My tears will move, my offerings propitiate them, and I shall enjoy complete felicity.'

"And, simple in the infancy of his reason, man spoke to the sun and the moon; he animated with his understanding and his passions the great agents of nature; he thought by vain sounds and useless practices to change their inflexible laws. Fatal error! He desired that the water should ascend, the mountains be removed, the stone mount in the air; and substituting a fantastic to a real world, he constituted for himself beings of opinion, to the terror of his mind and the torment of his race.

"Thus the ideas of God and religion sprung, like all others, from physical objects, and were in the understanding of man, the products of his sensations, his wants, the circumstances of his life, and the progressive state of his knowledge.

"As these ideas had natural beings for their first models, it resulted from hence that the divinity was originally as various and manifold as the forms under which he seemed to act: each being was a power, a genius, and the first men found the universe crowded with innumerable Gods.

"In like manner the ideas of the divinity having had for motors the affections of the human heart, they underwent an order of division calculated from the sensations of pain: and pleasure, of love and hatred: the powers of nature, the Gods, the genii, were classed into benign and maleficent, into good and evil ones: and this constitutes the universality of these two ideas in every system of religion.

"These ideas, analogous to the condition of their inventors, were for a long time confused and cross. Wandering in woods, beset with wants, destitute of resources, men in their savage state had no leisure to make comparisons and draw conclusions. Suffering more ills than they tasted enjoyments, their most habitual sentiment was fear, their theology terror, their worship was confined to certain modes of salutation, of offerings which they presented to beings whom they supposed to be ferocious and greedy like themselves. In their state of equality and independence, no one took upon him the office of mediator with Gods as insubordinate and poor as himself. No one having any superfluity to dispose of, there existed no parasite under the name of priest, nor tribute under the name of victim, nor empire under the name of altar; their dogmas and morality, jumbled together, were only self-preservation; and their religion, an arbitrary idea without influence on the mutual relations existing between men, was but a vain homage paid to the visible powers of nature.

"Such was the first and necessary origin of every idea of the divinity...."

"In reality, when the vulgar heard others talk of a new heaven and another world, they gave a body to these fictions; they erected on it a solid stage and real scenes; and their notions of geography and astronomy served to strengthen, if they did not give rise to the delusion.

"On the one hand, the Phoenician navigators, those who passed the pillars of Hercules to fetch the pewter of Thule and the amber of the Baltic, related that at the extremity of the world, the boundaries of the ocean (the Mediterranean,) where the sun sets to the countries of Asia, there were Fortunate Islands, the abode of an everlasting spring; and at a farther distance, hyperborean regions, placed under the earth (relatively to the tropics,) where reigned an eternal night. From those stories, badly understood, and no doubt confusedly related, the imagination of the people composed the Elysian Fields, delightful spots in a world below, having their heaven, their sun, and their stars; and Tartarus, a place of darkness, humidity, mire, and chilling frost. Now, inasmuch as mankind, inquisitive about all that of which they are ignorant, and desirous of a protracted existence, had already exerted their faculties respecting what was to become of them after death; inasmuch, as they had early reasoned upon that principle of life which animates the body, and which quits it without changing the form of the body, and had conceived to themselves airy substances, phantoms and shades, they loved to believe that they should resume in the subterranean world that life which it was so painful to lose; and this abode appeared commodious for the reception of those beloved objects which they could not prevail on themselves to renounce.

"On the other hand, the astrological and philosophical priests told such stories of their heavens as perfectly quadrated with these fictions. Having, in their metaphorical language, denominated the equinoxes and solstices the gates of heaven, or the entrance of the seasons, they explained the terrestrial phenomena by saying, that through the gate of horn (first the bull, afterwards the ram,) vivifying fires descended, which, in spring, gave life to vegetation, and aquatic spirits, which caused, at the solstice, the overflowing of the Nile: that through the gate of ivory (originally the bowman, or Sagittarius, then the balance,) and through that of Capricorn, or the urn, the emanations or influences of the heavens returned to their source and re-ascended to their origin; and the Milky Way which passed through the doors of the solstices, seemed to them to have been placed there on purpose to be their road and vehicle. The celestial scene farther presented, according to their Atlas, a river (the Nile, designated by the windings of the Hydra;) together with a barge (the vessel Argo,) and the dog Sirius, both bearing relation to that river, of which they foreboded the overflowing. These circumstances, added to the preceding ones, increased the probability of the fiction; and thus to arrive at Tartarus or Elysium, souls were obliged to cross the rivers Styx and Acheron, in the boat of Charon the ferryman, and to pass through the doors of horn and ivory, which were guarded by the mastiff Cerberus. At length a civil usage was joined to all these inventions, and gave them consistency.

"The inhabitants of Egypt having remarked that the putrefaction of dead bodies became in their burning climate the source of pestilence and diseases, the custom was introduced in a great number of States, of burying the dead at a distance from the inhabited districts, in the desert which lies at the West. To arrive there it was necessary to cross the canals of the river in a boat, and to pay a toll to the ferryman, otherwise the body remaining unburied, would have been left a prey to wild beasts. This custom suggested to her civil and religious legislators, a powerful means of affecting the manners of her inhabitants, and addressing savage and uncultivated men with the motives of filial piety and reverence for the dead; they introduced, as a necessary condition, the undergoing that previous trial which should decide whether the deceased deserved to be admitted upon the footing of his family honors into the *black city*. Such an idea too well accorded with the rest of the business not to be incorporated with it; it accordingly entered for an article into religious creeds, and hell had its Minos and its Radamanthus, with the wand, the chair, the guards, and the urn, after the exact model of this civil transaction. The divinity then, for the first time, became a subject of moral and political consideration, a legislator, by so much the more formidable as, while his judgment was final and his decrees without appeal, he was unapproachable to his subjects. This mythological and fabulous creation, composed as it was of scattered and discordant parts, then became a source of future punishments and rewards, in which divine justice was supposed to correct the vices and errors of this transitory state. A spiritual and mystical system, such as I have mentioned, acquired so much the more credit as it applied itself to the mind by every argument suited to it. The oppressed looked thither for an indemnification, and entertained the consoling hope of vengeance; the oppressor expected by the costliness of his offerings to secure to himself impunity, and at the same time employed this principle to inspire the vulgar with timidity; kings and priests, the heads of the people, saw in it a new source of power, as they reserved to themselves the privilege of awarding the favors or the censure of the great Judge of all, accord-ing to the opinion they, should inculcate of the odiousness of crimes and the meritoriousness of virtue.

"Thus, then, an invisible and imaginary world entered into competition with that which was real. Such, O Persians! was the origin of your renovated earth, your city of resurrection, placed under the equator, and distinguished from all other cities by this singular attribute, that the bodies of its inhabitants cast no shade. Such, O Jews and Christians! disciples of the Persians, was the source of your New Jerusalem, your paradise and your heaven, modelled upon the astrological heaven of Hermes. Meanwhile your hell, O ye Musselmans! a subterraneous pit surmounted by a bridge, your balance of souls and good works, your judgment pronounced by the angels Monkir and Nekir, derives its attributes from the mysterious ceremonies of the cave of Mithra; and your heaven is exactly coincident with that of Osiris, Ormuzd, and Brama."....

"It is evident, that it is not truth for which you contend; that it is not her cause you are jealous of maintaining, but the cause of your own passions and prejudices; that it is not the object as it really exists that you wish to verify, but the object as it appears to you; that it is not the evidence of the thing that you are anxious should prevail, but your personal opinion, your mode of seeing and judging. There is a power that you want to exercise, an interest that you want to maintain, a prerogative that you want to assume:

in short, the whole is a struggle of vanity. And as every individual, when he compares himself with every other, finds himself to be his equal and fellow, he resists by a similar feeling of right; and from this right, which you all deny to each other, and from the inherent consciousness of your equality, spring your disputes, your combats, and your intolerance.

"Now the only way of restoring unanimity is by returning to nature, and taking the order of things which she has established for your director and guide, and this farther truth will then appear from your uniformity of sentiment.

"If we would arrive at uniformity of opinion, we must previously establish certainty, and verify the resemblance which our ideas have to their models. Now, this cannot be obtained, except so far as the objects of our inquiry can be referred to the testimony, and subjected to the examination of our senses. Whatever cannot be brought to this trial is beyond the limits of our understanding: we have neither rule to try it by, nor measure by which to institute a comparison, nor source of demonstration and knowledge concerning it.

"Whence it is obvious that, in order to live in peace and harmony, we must consent not to pronounce upon such objects, nor annex to them importance; we must draw a line of demarcation between such as can be verified and such as cannot, and separate, by an inviolable barrier, the world of fantastic beings from the world of realities: that is to say, all civil effect must be taken away from theological and religious opinions.

"This, O nations! is the end that a great people, freed from their fetters and prejudices, have proposed to themselves; this is the work in which, by their command, and under their immediate auspices, we were engaged, when your kings and your priests came to interrupt our labors.... Kings and priests! you may yet for awhile suspend the solemn publication of the laws of nature; but it is no longer in your power to annihilate or to subvert them."

We conclude with the following:—"Investigate the laws which nature, for our direction, has implanted in our breasts, and form from thence an authentic and immutable code. Nor let this code be calculated for one family, or one nation only, but for the whole with-out exception. Be the legislators of the human race, as ye are the interpreters of their common nature. Show us the line that separates the world of chimeras from that of realities: and teach us, after so many religions of error and delusion, the religion of evidence and truth."

Our space prohibits further quotation in this number; but when we return to the subject, we shall notice chapter xxi., "Problem of Religious Contradictions," and also "The Law of Nature; or Principles of Morality."

Few men wrote more on various topics than Volney; and few have been more respected while living, and esteemed when dead, by those whose respect and esteem it is always an honor to possess. At the age of fifty-three, after much travel and great study, Volney consoled his latter days by marrying his cousin—the hope of his youth—Mdlle. de Chassebouf. A disorder of the bladder, contracted when traversing the Arabian deserts, caused his death at the age of sixty-three. He was buried in the cemetery of Pere Lachaise, when Laya, Director of the French Academy, pronounced a noble panegyric over his grave; and months after his death he was spoken highly of by some of the most illustrious men of France. Thus ended the days of one of the Freethinkers of the past whose works, despite all suppression, will never die.

J. W.

CHARLES BLOUNT

Look with me through the dark vista of 150 years of clouded history. Throw your mind across the bridge of time, for we are about to visit a tragic scene—a scene which might be depicted by a poet—so much of beauty, of truth, and of goodness, all blasted by the perjuries of the priest. Yonder, in the dim library of an ancestral mansion, embowered amid the woods of the south, close by the gurgling waters which beat an echo to the stormy breezes—those breezes which will never more fan his cheek—that water where he has often bathed his limbs will be his rippling monument. The shady moonlight of an August evening is gilding the rich pastures of Hertfordshire; the gorse bushes have not yet lost their beauty, the pheasants are playing in the woods—woods that so lately resounded with laughter—laughter ringing like a bell—the music of a merry heart. Withdraw those curtains which hide the heart-struck and the dead. Above you is the exquisite picture of Eleanora, gazing into the very bed at that form which lay shrouded in nothingness. You see the broad manly brow—even now the brown hair rises in graceful curls over that damp forehead. The lips are locked in an eternal smile, as if to mock the closed eyes and the recumbent form. Is it true that pictures of those we love are endowed with a clairvoyant power of gazing at those who have caressed them in life? If it is, then on that August night the wife of Charles Blount was watching over his bier.

But who is that pale form, with dishevelled hair and weeping eyes, with an alabaster skin stained with the blue spots of grief? The rapid upheaving swells of that fair bosom tell of affection withered, not by remorse, but by superstition? See her how she nervously grasps that dead man's hand, how she imprints kisses on his lips! Her hair, which yesterday was glossy as the raven's, is now as bleached as the driven snow; to-day she utters her plaintive cries, to-morrow she hastens to join her lover in the tomb. This is a sad history. It should be written with the juice of hemlock, as a warning to Genius of impatient love.

While the fair girl watches by the couch of the suicide, while from the painted canvass Eleanora gleams on the living and the dead, while the clouds of night gather silently over that ancestral hall, around the drooping corn on the bold sloping park, and the clear blue river—all so quiet and gentle—let us gather up the events of the past, and learn the cause of a death so tragic, a grief so piercing.

In the year 1672, at the age of nineteen years, a young man (the son of a baronet) led to the altar the lovely daughter of Sir Timothy Tyrrel. Flowers strewed the path of the wedded pair, and for years their life was one scene of bliss. At last, struck down by disease, Charles Blount stood by the side of his dying wife—in his arms *his* Eleanora yielded her last sigh. He buried her by the willow-tree in the old churchyard. The lily blended with the white rose, and the myrtle overshadowed the grave. It was here where the widower rested in the evening—here where he taught his children the virtues of their dead mother. Sometimes he gazed at the azure skies, and strange fancies beguiled the mind of the mourner. When he saw the sun sink to the west, gilding the world with its glorious rays, he mused on the creeds of many lands. He fancied he saw a heaven and a God, and traced in the lines of light the patriarchal worshippers of the world. He looked at the sun and its worshippers—those who sought the origin of purity by worshipping that which is the origin of all good. He looked at the fables of Greece, and found delight in the thought of Sappho uttering her diapason of joy in lyrics which told of love and beauty; at Egypt, where the priests, in their esoteric cunning, searched in vain for that which gives life, and motion, and joy; and then he glanced at the Christian heaven, but here all was dark—dark as the Plutonian caverns of Homer's hell. He wished to meet his Eleanora—not in Pagan dreams—not in Christian parables—but in the world of realities. He looked with eager eyes upon the world around him, in society, at Court, and, in the homes of his country. But wherever he went, there was but one thought—one feeling. He wished a mother for his children—a mother like the sainted dead. There was but one who answered the ideal—like in features, in passion, and in beauty—to the lost Eleanora. Born of the same parents, loved by the same brother, educated by the same teachers, imbued with the same thoughts, she was the model of her dead sister; with a sisterly love for her brother, she was already both mother and aunt to her sister's children.

With deliberate thoughts, with convulsive passion, the love of Charles Blount passed the bounds of that of a brother; longing to make her his wife, he adored her with the passion he had lavished on the dead. It seemed as if the shade of Eleanora was perpetually prompting him to bestow all his affection on the young and beautiful Eliza. She caressed his children with the pride of an aunt, she traced the image of her sister in the laughing eyes of the merry babes—still she was not happy. How could she be happy? She loved him as a man—as a brother. She was a Christian—he an Infidel. She was bound by creeds—he by conduct. She was doing the duty she owed to the dead. He sought to do it by uniting himself to the living. Eliza was anxious to marry, but there existed something which, to her mind, was greater than human duties, and it often outraged them. God and the Church demanded her first attention, and then her lover and his children. The Church, in cruel mockery of human rights, stepped between her judgment and her affections. It denied the power of a woman to occupy the married home of her deceased sister. She was willing to pledge her love to Charles Blount at the altar, but the priest mocked her prayers and denounced her affections. The occasion was too good to be lost. Episcopalism sought revenge on its opponent, and it triumphed. Eliza felt the force of Blount's arguments. She wandered with him through the green fields, but her sorrow was too great to pluck the wild roses. The luscious fruits of summer were passed untasted. A heart sick and in trouble, a mind wandering from her sister's grave to her children, and then at the anathema of the Church, made her a widowed maid. To overcome her scruples, her lover wrote a book (inviting the clergy to refute it,) defending the marriage with a deceased wife's sister. But ever as he spoke there was a film before her eyes. There was a gaunt priest, with canonical robes, stood before the gates of heaven. Before him and through him was the way to an eternal happiness, below him was a fiery hell; and he shouted with hoarse voice, *Incest, incest, incest!* — And ever as he shouted, he pointed with his finger of scorn at this Christian hell, and she conjured up in her mind the old stories of this priest, until she saw the livid flames rising up higher till they encircled her form, and then the priest screamed with fury, *Anathema maranatha, incest, incest!* And in terror she stood, with the big drops of sweat dripping from her brow, with her heart beating, with her mind distracted, but her affections unclouded.

This priest was the Church of England, and those fancies were driven into her imagination by her creed, her litanies, and her sermons. Eliza Tyrrel was miserable; she was placed between her love, her duty, and her religion. If she had been a woman of a strong mind, she would have torn her creed into shreds, she would have dared the anathema of the priest— the ostracism of its dupes—and would have clung to the man she loved so truly, in defiance of that which was, at the best, but a faint possibility.

The arguments in that pamphlet of Blount's were conclusive, but she distrusted reason. The plainest dictates of common logic were referred to the promptings of the Devil. How could it be otherwise? Can the teachings of a lifetime be overthrown by the courtship of a few months? Eliza Tyrrel, true to Blount, loved him; true to her religion, she durst not marry him without the sanction of the Church. So Blount, as a last resolve, laid the matter before the Lord's Vicegerent at Canterbury, and many of the most learned divines of England; and from those ecclesiastical leeches there was a Shylock cry of *incest, incest, incest!* And those terrible words came greeting the ears of Charles Blount, making his home like a charnel-house, and they nearly sent his beautiful Eliza to a maniac's grave. Still she lingered on. Denied the power of a wife, she would not relinquish her duties as a mother to her sister's babes. There was a calm heroism here which few can imitate. The passions of Blount could not brook further insults. The last kick of bigotry against the broken-hearted Freethinker was given. He could no longer rise with the lark, and roam over the hills of his ancestral home. To him the birds, as they warbled, spoke of joys never to return. The broad river told him of the days when the little skiff floated on its waters with Eleanora; and even his friends only too bitterly reminded him of the tournaments of wit where Hobbes, Brown, and Gildon, jousted each other in the presence of his wife. His life was one scene of misery. He saw no chance of amendment. In a fit of despair, he loaded his pistol with due deliberation, placed it to his head, and shot himself. He lingered for sometime, and then died on the breast of Eliza.

This was a strange suicide. Blount's memory bears its weight of obloquy. It is hard to draw the line when and where a man has a right to take away his life. Common sense tells us that so long as our families are dependent upon us, we have no right to end our lives; and if we have no dependents, no friends, then our country has a claim upon us. But, at the same time, the one sole end of existence is to be happy. If a man cannot find happiness in life, if there is a great coalition against him, he is justified in taking up arms against them; but, at the same time, it proves a greater amount of courage "to bear up against the ills of life" than to madly leave it, and thus weaken the force of those who wish to stem its injustice.

Charles Blount died, and with him expired much of the chivalry of Freethought. His friend, Charles Gil-don, writing of him to a lady, says, "You know Astrea (Eliza,) and have an exact friendship with her. You can attest her beauty, wit, honor, virtue, good humor, and discretion. You have been acquainted with the charms of her conversation and conduct, and condemn her, only adhering to a national custom to the loss of so generous a friend, and so faithful a lover. But custom and obedience meeting the more easily, betrayed her virtue into a crime. I know my friend loved her to his last breath; and I know, therefore, that all who love his memory must, for her sake, love and value her, as being a lady of that merit, that engaged the reason of Philander (C. Blount) to so violent a passion for her."

The same writer says, "His father was Sir Henry Blount, the Socrates of the age, for his aversions to the reigning sophisms and hypocrisies, eminent in all capacities: the best husband, father, and master, extremely agreeably in conversation, and just in all his dealings. From such a father our hero derived him self; to such a master owed his generous education, unmixed with the nauseous methods and profane opinions of the schools. Nature gave him parts capable of the noblest sciences, and his industrious studies bore a proportion to his capacities. He was a generous and constant friend, an indulgent parent, and a kind master. His temper was open and free; his conversation pleasant; his reflections just and modest; his repartees close — not scurrilous; he had a great deal of wit, and no malice. His mind was large and noble — above the little designs of most men; an enemy to dissimulation, and never feared to own his thoughts. He was a true Englishman, and lover of the liberties of his country, and declared it in the worst of times. He was an enemy to nothing but error, and none were his enemies that knew him, but those who sacrificed more to mammon than reason."

This was the man who died, because a dominant priesthood insisted on a dogma which interfered with a purely Secular rite, which blasted two hearts in a vain attempt to perpetuate a system, which dashes its rude fingers, and tears out the heart of human felicity to sprinkle the altar of superstition with the gore of offended innocence. Charles Blount was a Deist; as such, he believed in a God; which he described in his account of a Deist's religion. Let us examine his thoughts, and see if they bear the interpretation which Christianity has always placed upon them. Blount gives the Deist's opinion of God. He says, "Whatever is adorable, amiable, and imitable by mankind, is in one Supreme, perfect Being." An Atheist cannot object to this. He speaks in the manner in which God is to be worshipped. He says, not by sacrifice, or by a Mediator, but by a steady adherence to all that is great and good and imitable in nature. This is the brief religious creed of Charles Blount. He never seeks to find out fabled attributes of Deity. He knows what is of value to mankind, and sedulously practices whatever is beneficial to society.

In his "Anima Mundi, or, History of the Opinions of the Heathens on the Immortality of the Soul," (p. 97,) Blount says: —

"The heathen philosophers were much divided concerning the soul's future state; some held it mortal, others immortal. Of those who held the mortality of the soul, the Epicureans were the chief sect, who, notwithstanding their doctrines, led virtuous lives." Cardan had so great a value for their moral actions, that he appeared in justification of them. It appears (says he) "by the writings of Cicero, Diogenes, and Laertius, that the Epicureans did more religiously observe laws, piety, and fidelity among men than either the Stoics or the Platonists; and I suppose the cause thereof was, that a man is either good or evil by custom, but none confideth in those that do not possess sanctity of life. Wherefore they were compelled to use greater fidelity, thereby the better to justify their profession, from which reason it likewise proceeds, that at this day few do equal the fidelity of usurers, notwithstanding they are most base in the rest of their life. Also among the Jews, whilst the Pharisees, that confessed the resurrection and the immortality of the soul, frequently persecuted Christ, the Sadducees, who denied the resurrection, angels, and spirits, meddled not with him above once or twice, and that very gently. Thus, if you compare the lives of Pliny and Seneca (not their writings,) you shall find Pliny, with his mortality of the soul, did as far exceed Seneca in honesty of manners, as Seneca excels him in religious discourse. The Epicureans observed honesty above others, and in their conversation were usually found inoffensive and virtuous, and for that reason were often employed by the Romans when they could persuade them to accept of great employs, for their fault was not any want of ability or honesty, but their general desire of leading a private life of ease, and free from trouble, although inglorious. For when immortality is not owned, there can be no ambition of posthumous glory.

"The Epicureans, instead of those bloody scenes of gallantry (which tyrants applaud,) undertook to manage carefully the inheritance of orphans; bringing up, at their own charge, the children of their deceased friends, and were counted good men, unless it were in front of religious worship; for they constantly affirmed that there were no Gods, or, at least, such as concerned themselves with human affairs, according to the poets. Neither doth the hope of immortality conduce to fortitude, as some vainly suggest, for Brutus was not more valiant than Cassius; and if we will confess the truth, the deeds of Brutus were more cruel than those of Cassius; for he used the Rhodians, who were his enemies, far more kindly than Brutus did those amicable cities which he governed. In a word, though they both, had a hand in Cæsar's murder, yet Brutus was the only parricide. So that the Stoics, which believed a Providence, lived as if there were none; whereas the Epicureans, who denied it, lived as if there were.... The next sect to the Epicureans, in point of incredulity, concerning the soul, I conceive to be the Sceptics, who were by some esteemed, not only the modestest, but the most perspicuous of all sects. They neither affirmed nor denied anything, but doubted of all things. They thought all our knowledge seemed rather like truth, than to be really true, and that for such like reasons as these:—

"1. They denied any knowledge of the Divine Nature, because, they say, to know adequately is to comprehend, and to comprehend is to contain, and the thing contained must be less than that which contains it; to know inadequately is not to know.

"2. From the uncertainty of our senses, as, for instance, our eyes represent things at a distance to be less than they really are. A straight stick in the water appears crooked; the moon to be no bigger than a cheese; the sun greater at rising and setting than at noon. The shore seems to move, and the ship to stand still; square things to be round at a distance; an erect pillar to be less at the top. Neither (say they) do we know whether objects are really as our eyes represent them to us, for the same thing which seems white to us seems yellow to a jaundiced man, and red to a creature afflicted with red eyes; also, if a man rubs his eyes, the figure which he beholds seems long or narrow, and therefore it is not improbable that goats, cats, and other creatures, which have long pupils of the eye, may think those things long which we call round, for as glasses represent the object variously, according to their shape, so it may be with our eyes. And so the sense of hearing deceives. Thus, the echo of a trumpet, sounded in a valley, makes the sound seem before us, when it is behind us. Besides, how can we think that an ear, which has a narrow passage, can receive the same sound with that which has a wide one? Or the ear, whose inside is full of hair, to hear the same with a smooth ear? Experience tells us that if we stop, or half stop, our ears, the sound cometh different as when the ears are open. Nor is the smelling, taste, or touch less subject to mistake; for the same scents please some, and displease others, and so in our tastes. To a rough and dry tongue that very thing seems bitter (as in an ague,) which to the most moist tongue seems otherwise, and so is it in other creatures. The like is true of the touch, for it were absurd to think that those creatures which are covered with shells, scales, or hairs, should have the same sense in touching with those that are smooth. Thus one and the same object is diversely judged of, according to the various qualities of the instruments of sense, which convinceth to the imagination; from all which the Sceptic concluded, that what these things are in their own nature, whether red, white, bitter, or sweet, he cannot tell; for, says he, why should I prefer my own conceit in affirming the nature of things to be thus, or thus, because it seemeth so to me—when other living creatures, perhaps, think it is otherwise? But the greatest fallacy is in the operation of our inward senses; for the fancy is sometimes persuaded that it hears and sees what it does not, and our reasoning is so weak, that in many disciplines scarce one demonstration is found, though this alone produces science. Wherefore it was Democritus's opinion that truth is hid in a well, that she may not be found by men. Now, although this doctrine be very inconsistent with Christianity, yet I could wish Adam had been of this persuasion, for then he would not have mortgaged his posterity for the purchase of a twilight knowledge. Now, from these sinister observations it was that they esteemed all our sciences to be but conjectures, and our knowledge but opinion. Whereupon, doubting the sufficiency of human reason, they would not venture to affirm or deny anything of the soul's future state; but civilly and quietly gave way to the doctrines and ordinances under which they lived, without raising or espousing any new opinions." Speaking of the "origin of the world," Gildon gives the following as a translation from Ocellus Lucanas:—"Again (says he,) as the frame of the world has been always, so it is necessary that its parts should likewise always have existed; by parts, I mean the heaven, earth, and that which lieth betwixt—viz., the sky; for not without these, but with these, and of these, the world consists. Also, if the parts exist, it is necessary that the things which are within them should also coexist; as with the heavens, the sun, moon, fixed stars, and planets; with the earth, animals, plants, minerals, gold, and silver; with the air, exhalations, winds, and alterations of weather, sometimes heat and sometimes cold, for with the world all those things do, and ever have existed, as parts thereof. Nor hath man had any original production from the earth, or elsewhere, as some believe, but have always been, as now he is, coexistent with the world, whereof he is a part. Now, corruptions and violent alterations are made according to the parts of the earth, by winds and waters imprisoned in the bowels thereof; but a universal, corruption of the earth never hath been, nor ever shall be. Yet these alterations have given occasion for the invention of many lies and fables. And thus are we to understand them that derive the original of the Greek history from Inachus, the Argive; not that he really was the original, as some make him, but because a most memorable alteration did then happen, and some were so unskilful as to attribute it to Inachus.... But for the universe, and all the parts whereof it subsists, as it is at present, so it ever was, and ever shall be; one nature perpetually moving, and another perpetually suffering, one always governing, and the other always being governed. The course which nature takes in governing the world, is by one contrary prevailing over another, as thus:—The moisture in the air prevaileth over the dryness of the fire; and the coldness of the wafer over the heat of the air, and the dryness of the earth over the moisture of the water; and so the moisture of the water over the dryness of the earth; and the heat in the air over the coldness of the water; and the dryness in the fire over the moisture of the air. And thus the alterations are made and produced, out of one another.... As nature cannot create by making something out of nothing, so neither can it annihilate, by turning something into nothing; whence it consequently follows, as there is no access, so there is no diminution in the universe, no more than in the alphabet, by the infinite combination and transposition of letters, or in the wax by the alteration of the seal stamped upon it. Now, as for the forms of natural bodies, no sooner doth any one abandon the matter he occupied, but another instantly steps into the place thereof; no sooner hath one acted his part and is retired, but another comes presently forth upon the stage, though it may be in a different shape, and so act a different part; so that no portion of the matter is, or at any time can be, altogether void and empty, but like Proteus, it burns itself into a thousand shapes, and is always supplied with one form or another, there being in nature nothing but circulation."

The following are the principal works of Blount:—"Anima Mundi; or, an Historical Narration of the Opinions of the Ancients concerning Man's Soul after this Life, according to Enlightened Nature;" published in 1679. Upwards of twenty answers were published to this work. In 1680 he published a translation, with notes, of the life of Apolloninis, of Tyana. This work was suppressed. During the same year, he gave the world "Great is Diana of the Ephesians; or, the Original of Idolatry."

By able critics this is considered one of his ablest works in 1683, "Religio Laici" appeared, which is published from a Latin work of Lord Herbert's. In 1688 he wrote "A Vindication of Learning, and of the Liberty of the Press." This tractate sparkles with wit and argument. But by far the most important work he was connected with, was published in the year he died, and mainly written by himself, "The Oracles of Reason" a favorite title with both American and English Freethinkers. It consists of sixteen sections; the most interesting being the first four, containing "A Vindication of Dr. Burnett's Archiologie." The seventh and eighth chapters (translated) of the same, of "Moses's Description of the Original State of Man," and Dr. Burnett's "Appendix of the Brahmin's Religion." We would quote from these sections of the "Oracles," but intend to form separate "Half-Hours," with sketches of Drs. Brown and Burnett; it will be more appropriate to use Blount's translation in describing those quaint, but highly instructive authors. In the general style of Blount's works, he is not seen to advantage; there is too much heaviness, enhanced by the perpetual Greek and Latin quotations; but as his works were intended for scholars, and the time in which they were written was essentially the most pedantic era of our literary history, we cannot expect that vivacity and clearness which other writers in a later age possessed. It was in his character as a man that Blount excelled—he was the leader of the chivalry of the period, as in the next age Woolston was his successor. At the Court he was the gayest of the gay, without the taint of immorality, in a period of the grossest licentiousness; he defended the honor of his friends, frequently at the expense of calumny and danger. In witty repartees he was equal to Rochester; while for abstruse learning he was superior to many of the most learned theologians. Daintily brave and skilfully alive to the requirements of friends and foes, he passed through life in the gilded barge of pleasure, and ended it sailing through a cloud where he foundered. But the darkness which enveloped his history is now charged with that sympathetic power which draws the young to his grave, and compels the gloomiest to shed a tear over his unhappy fate.

At the close of August, in 1693, a few friends met near the grave of Blount, to join in their last respects to their lost friend. Foremost amongst them was Charles Gildon, who so soon repented of the part he had taken in the "Oracles of Reason," but never forgot the kindness he experienced from Blount. He lived long enough for Pope to be revenged on his apostacy, by inserting his name in his great satire. At the time we speak he was mournful and deeply grieved at the loss he had sustained; near him was Harvey Wilwood, whose bold demeanor and sorrowful countenance told of heart-struck grief, for of the few able to appreciate the genius of Blount, he was one of the earliest and most devoted in his friendship. Now we see the noble Lord, whom Blount always addressed as "the most ingenious Strephon;" along with him there is the pretty Anne Rogers, with Savage, and Major Arkwright; we look in vain for Eliza Tyr-rel; they talk slowly over him that is no more; they recount to themselves the intellectual achievements, and the brilliant hours they have spent in the past; and while they speak so kindly, and think so deeply, they kneel on the hallowed spot, but not to pray; some of them pledge their enmity against Christian laws and Christian priests, and they executed it. During this time, the calm radiance of the lunar light shines on the church of Ridge, illumining those ghostly tablets of white marble, where the forefathers of Blount lie entombed. The baronial arms are emblazoned on the wall; heraldic pomp is keeping watch over the mouldering bones of the now-levelled great. Anne Rogers weeps wildly for Eliza and Eleanora. Those metaphysical disquisitions which have exalted woman to so high a nature, that devotion to esthetics which woman should always cultivate, not as a household slave, but as one of equal rights with man, and his leader in everything which concerns taste, elegance, and modesty; such gifts in no ordinary degree had Anne Rogers— and often in dialectic subtlety had she mastered her relative, who stood by her side, and given tokens of her admiration of Blount's philosophy and conduct. "Strephon" was passionately attached to his confidant and friend, and could not give so calm an expression to his loss. He wept wildly, for he had lost one who tempered his rebuke with a kind word, and pointed out that Epicurean path which leads to enjoyment without excess: to pleasure, without a reaction. It was a memorable meeting. While the remembrance of past deeds of love lighted up the eye and made the blood course faster through their veins, Anne Rogers detailed the following episode in his character:—Blount had visited the Court of King James, and had been singled out by that monarch for one of his savage fits of spleen. "I hear, Mr. Blount, you are very tenacious of the opinions of Sir Henry, your father, and you consider his conduct during the Rebellion as worthy of imitation. Is it so?" "Your Majesty," replies Blount, "has been correctly informed; I admire my father's conduct." "What!" says James, "in opposing his king?" Blount quickly answered, "A king, my liege, is the chief magistrate of the

Commonwealth, and is so hereditarily while he obeys the laws of that Commonwealth, whose power he represents; but when he usurps the direction of that power, he is king no longer, and such was the case with your royal father." With a scowl of defiance on his face, King James left the Freethinker, and sought more congenial company; and as Anne Rogers told the story, each eye was dimmed with tears. The moon had risen high in the heavens ere the mourners prepared to depart—the first streaks of dawn broke through the Eastern sky, and revealed the grave watered with tears, where the most chivalrous Freethinker of his age reposed, in that sleep which knows of no awakening.

"A. C."

PERCY BYSSHE SHELLEY

Percy Bysshe Shelley (the son and heir of a wealthy English baronet, Sir Timothy Shelley, of Castle Goring, in the county of Sussex) was born at Field Place, near Horsham, in that county, on the 4th of August, 1792. Ushered into the world in the midst of wealth and fashion, with all the advantages of family distinction, the future of Shelley's life appeared a bright one; but the sunshine of the morning only served to render the darkness which came over his noontide more dark, and to make poor Shelley still more susceptible of the hardships he had to encounter. First educated at Eton, his spirit there manifested itself by an unflinching opposition to the fagging system, and by revolt against the severe discipline of the school; in his "Revolt of Islam" Shelley has thus portrayed his feeling:—

"I do remember well the hour which burst
My spirit's sleep; a fresh May dawn it was
When I walked forth upon the glittering grass
And wept, I knew not why: until there rose
From the near school-room voices that, alas!
Were but one echo from a world of woes,
The harsh and grating strife of tyrants and of foes.
And then I clasped my hands and looked around,
And none was near to mock my streaming eyes,
Which poured their warm drops on the sunny ground;
So, without shame, I spake—' I will be wise,
And just, and free, and mild, if in me lies
Such power, for I grow weary to behold
The selfish, and the strong still tyrannize
Without reproach or check.'"

And from that hour did I, with earnest thought,
Heap knowledge from forbidden mines of lore;

Yet nothing that ray tyrants knew or taught
I cared to learn, but from that secret store
Wrought linked armour for my soul, before
It might walk forth to war among mankind."

From Eton, Shelley went to Oxford, and while there he, scarce at the age of eighteen, published a volume of political rhymes, entitled "Margaret Nicholson's Remains," the said Margaret being a woman who tried to assassinate George III. He also wrote a pamphlet in defence of Atheism. A copy of this pamphlet he caused to be sent to the head of each of the colleges in Oxford, with a challenge to discuss and answer.—The answer to this was the edict which expelled Shelley from Oxford, and at the same time placed a wide chasm between him and his family. This breach was still further widened in the following year by his marriage, at the age of nineteen, with a beautiful girl named Westbrook. Although Miss Westbrook was respectfully connected, Shelley's aristocratic family regarded this as a *mesalliance*, and withdrew his pecuniary allowance; and had it not been for the bride's father, who allowed the young couple £200 a year, they would have been reduced to actual poverty. This was an unfortunate marriage for both. After having two children, disagreements arose, and Shelley was separated from his wife. She (like all beautiful women) was soon attacked by the busy tongue of slander, and, unable to bear the world's taunts, committed suicide by throwing herself into a pond, just four years from the date of their marriage. Shelley, on this account, suffered much misery and misrepresentation, and this misery was much increased by his family, who applied to the Court of Chancery, and obtained a decree, by which Shelley was deprived of the custody of his children, on the ground of his Atheism. The same spirit even now pervades the Shelley family, and scarce a copy of his poems can be found in the neighborhood of his birth-place. Shelley afterwards contracted a second marriage with the daughter of Godwin, the author of "Caleb Williams," and Mary Wollstonecroft (who died in giving birth to Shelley's wife), and for sometime the poet resided at Marlow in Buckinghamshire, where he composed the "Revolt of Islam;" and it is a strong proof of the reality of Shelley's poetical pleadings for the oppressed amongst the human race, that he was indefatigable in his attentions to the poor cottagers of his neighborhood; and that he suffered severely from an attack of opthalmia, which was originated in one of his benevolent visits. Nearly the first of Shelley's poems was his "Queen Mab," in which (having in vain struggled to devote himself to metaphysics apart from poetry), he blended his metaphysical speculation with his poetical aspirations. The following quotations are taken from that poem, in which his wonderful command of language is well shown:—

"There's not one atom of yon earth
But once was living man;
Nor the minutest drop of rain,
That hangeth in its thinnest cloud,
But flowed in human veins;

And from the burning plains
Where Lybian monsters yell,
From the most gloomy glens
Of Greenland's sunless clime,
To where the golden fields
Of fertile England spread
Their harvest to the day,
Thou canst not find one spot
Whereon no city stood.

How strange is human pride!
I tell thee that those living things,
To whom the fragile blade of grass,
That springeth in the morn
And perishes ere noon.

In an unbounded world;
I tell thee that those viewless beings.
Whose mansion is the smallest particle
Of the impassive atmosphere,
Think, feel, and live, like man:
That their affections and antipathies,
Like his, produce the laws
Ruling their mortal state;
And the minutest throb.

That through their frame diffuses
The slightest, faintest motion,
Is fixed and indispensable
As the majestic laws
That rule yon rolling orbs.

How bold the flight of passion's wandering wing,
How swift the step of reason's firmer tread,
How calm and sweet the victories of life.
How terrorless the triumph of the grave!
How powerless were the mightiest monarch's arm,
Vain his loud threat and impotent his frown!
How ludicrous the priest's dogmatic roar!
The weight of his exterminating curse,
How light! and his affected charity,
To suit the pressure of the changing times,
What palpable deceit!—but for thy aid,
Religion! but for thee, prolific fiend,
Who peoplest earth with demons, hell with men,
And heaven with slaves!

Thou taintest all thou look'st upon!—The stare,
Which on thy cradle beamed so brightly sweet,
Were gods to the distempered playfulness
Of thy untutored infancy: the trees,
The grass, the clouds, the mountains, and the sea,

All living things that walk, swim, creep, or fly,
Were gods: the sun had homage, and the moon
Her worshipper. Then thou becam'st a boy,
More daring in thy frenzies: every shape,
Monstrous or vast, or beautifully wild,
Which, from sensation's relics, fancy culls;
The spirits of the air, the shuddering ghost,
The genii of the elements, the powers
That give a shape to nature's varied works,
Had life and place in the corrupt belief
Of thy blind heart—yet still thy youthful hands
Were pure of human blood. Then manhood gave
Its strength and ardor to thy frenzied brain;
Thine eager gaze scanned the stupendous scene,
Whose wonders mocked the knowledge of thy pride.

Their everlasting and unchanging laws
Reproached thine ignorance.
Awhile thou stood'st
Baffled and gloomy; then thou did'st sum up
The elements of all that thou did'st know.

The changing seasons, winter's leafless reign,
The budding of the heaven-breathing trees,
The eternal orbs that beautify the night,
The sunrise, and the setting of the moon,
Earthquakes and wars, and poisons and disease,
And all their causes, to an abstract point,
Converging, thou did'st bend, and called it God;
The self-sufficing, the omnipotent,
The merciful, and the avenging God!

Who, prototype of human misrule, sits
High in Heaven's realm, upon a golden throne,
Even like an earthly king: and whose dread work,
Hell gapes forever for the unhappy slaves
Of fate, whom he created in his sport,
To triumph in their torments when they fell!

Earth heard the name; earth trembled, as the smoke
Of his revenge ascended up to Heaven,
Blotting the constellations: and the cries
Of millions, butchered in sweet confidence,
And unsuspecting peace, even when the bonds
Of safety were confirmed by wordy oaths,

Sworn in his dreadful name, rung through the land;
Whilst innocent babes writhed on thy stubborn spear,
And thou did'st laugh to hear the mother's shriek
Of maniac gladness, as the sacred steel
Felt cold in her torn entrails!

Religion! thou wert then in manhood's prime;
But age crept on: one God would not suffice

For senile puerility; thou fram'dst
A tale to suit thy dotage, and to glut
Thy misery-thirsting soul, that the mad fiend
Thy wickedness had pictured might afford
A plea for sating the unnatural thirst
For murder, rapine, violence, and crime,
That still consumed thy being, even when
Thou heard'st the step of fate:—that flames might light
Thy funeral scene, and the shrill horrent shrieks
Of parents dying on the pile that burned
To light their children to thy paths, the roar
Of the encircling flames, the exulting cries
Of thine apostles, loud commingling there,
Might sate thy hungry ear
Even on the bed of death!

But now contempt is mocking thy gray hairs;
Thou art descending to the darksome grave,
Unhonored and unpitied, but by those
Whose pride is passing by like thine, and sheds
Like thine, a glare that fades before the sun
Of truth, and shines but in the dreadful night
That long has lowered above the ruined world."

Speaking of the Atheist's martyrdom in answer to the spirit of "Ianthe," Shelley makes his fairy say:—

"There is no God!
Nature confirms the faith his death-groan sealed.
Let heaven and earth, let man's revolving race,
His ceaseless generations, tell their tale;

Let every part depending on the chain
That links it to the whole, point to the hand
That grasps its term! Let every seed that falls
In silent eloquence unfold its store
Of argument. Infinity within,

Infinity without, belie creation;
The exterminate spirit it contains
Is nature's only God: but human pride
Is skilful to invent most serious names
To hide its ignorance.

The name of God
Has fenced about all crime with holiness,
Himself the creature of his worshippers,
Whose names and attributes and passions change,
Seeva, Buddh, Foh, Jehovah, Goa, or Lord,
Even with the human dupes who build his shrines.
Still serving o'er the war-polluted world
For desolation's watch-word; whether hosts
Stain his death-blushing chariot wheels, as on
Triumphantly they roll, whilst Brahmins raise
A sacred hymn to mingle with the groans;
Or countless partners of his powers divide
His tyranny to weakness: or the smoke
Of burning towns, the cries of female helplessness,
Unarmed old age, and youth, and infancy,
Horribly massacred, ascend to heaven
In honor of his name; or, last and worst,
Earth groans beneath religion's iron age,
And priests dare babble of a God of peace,
Even whilst their hands are red with guiltless blood,
Murdering the while, uprooting every germ
Of truth, exterminating, spoiling all,
Making the earth a slaughter-house."

"Ianthe's" spirit, however, asks still further, and the ghost of Ahasuerus having been summoned, the question is repeated, "Is there a God?"

"Ahasuerus. —Is there a God? ay, an Almighty God,
And vengeful as Almighty! Once his voice
Was heard on earth: earth shuddered at the sound,

The fiery-visaged firmament expressed
Abhorrence, and the grave of nature yawned
To swallow all the dauntless and the good
That dared to hurl defiance at his throne,
Girt as it was with power. None but slaves
Survived,—cold-blooded slaves, who did the work
Of tyrannous omnipotence: whose souls
No honest indignation ever urged
To elevated daring, to one deed
Which gross and sensual self did not pollute.
These slaves built temples for the omnipotent fiend,
Gorgeous and vast: the costly altars smoked
With human blood, and hideous moans rung
Through all the long-drawn aisles. A murderer heard
His voice in Egypt, one whose gifts and arts
Had raised him to his eminence in power,
Accomplice of omnipotence in crime,
And confidant of the all-knowing one.

These were Jehovah's words:
"From an eternity of idleness,
God, awoke: in seven days toil made earth
From nothing; rested, and created man.
I placed him in a paradise, and there
Planted the tree of evil, so that he
Might eat and perish, and my soul procure
Wherewith to sate its malice, and to turn,
Even like a heartless conqueror of the earth,
All misery to my fame. The race of men,
Chosen to my honor, with impunity,
May sate the lusts I planted in their heart.
Here I command thee hence to lead them on,
Until, with hardened feet, their conquering troops
Wade on the promised soil through woman's blood,

And make my name be dreaded through the land.
Yet ever burning flame and ceaseless woe
Shall be the doom of their eternal souls,
With every soul on this ungrateful earth,
Virtuous or vicious, weak or strong, —even all
Shall perish, to fulfil the blind revenge
Which you, to men, call justice, of their God."

The murderer's brow
Quivered with horror.
God omnipotent!
Is there no mercy? must our punishment
Be endless? will long ages roll away,
And see no 'term? Oh! wherefore hast thou made
In mockery and wrath this evil earth?
Mercy becomes the powerful—be but just:
O God! repent and save.

"One way remains!
I will beget a son, and he shall bear
The sins of all the world: he shall arise
In an unnoticed corner of the earth,

And there shall die upon a cross, and purge
The universal crime; so that the few
On whom my grace descends, those who are marked
As vessels to the honor of their God,
May credit this strange sacrifice, and save
Their souls alive. Millions shall live and die
Who ne'er shall call upon their Saviour's name,
But, unredeemed, go to the gaping, grave.
Thousands shall deem it an old woman's tale,
Such as the nurses frighten babes withal.
These in a gulph of anguish and of flame
Shall curse their reprobation endlessly.
Yet tenfold pangs shall force them to avow,

Even on their beds of torment, where they howl,

My honor, and the justice of their doom.

What then avail their virtuous deeds, their thoughts

Of purity, with radiant genius bright,

Or lit with human reason's earthly ray?

Many are called, but few I will elect.

Do thou my bidding, Moses!"

In his poem of "Rosalind and Helen," the poet indulges in the following prophecy, which he puts in the mouth of Helen:—

"Fear not the tyrants shall rule forever,

Or the priests of the bloody faith;

They stand on the brink of that mighty river,

Whose waves they have tainted with death.

It is fed from the depths of a thousand dells,

Around them it foams, and rages, and swells;

And their swords and their sceptres I floating see,

Like wrecks on the surge of eternity."

Beside the poems mentioned, Shelley wrote "The Cenci," "Alastor," "Prometheus Unbound," and many others, including a beautiful little ode to a "Skylark," and the well-known "Sensitive Plant."

Shelley was a true and noble man—no poet was ever warmed by a more genuine and unforced aspiration.—De Quincey says, "Shelley would, from his earliest manhood, have sacrificed all that he possessed for any comprehensive purpose of good for the race of man. He dismissed all insults and injuries from his memory. He was the sincerest and most truthful of human creatures.

"If he denounced marriage as a vicious institution, *that* was but another phase of the partial lunacy which affected him: for to no man were purity and fidelity more essential elements in the idea of real love. Again, De Quincey speaks of Shelley's "fearlessness, his gracious nature, his truth, his purity from all flesh-liness of appetite, his freedom from vanity, his diffusive love and tenderness." This testimony is worth much, the more especially when we remember that it is from the pen of Thomas de Quincey, who, while truthfully acknowledging the man, hesitates not to use polished irony, rough wit, and covert sneering, when dealing with the man's uttered thinkings.

"That Shelley understood the true mission of a poet, and the true nature of poetry, will appear from the following extract from one of his prose essays:—"Poetry," he says, "is the record of the best and happiest moments of the happiest and best minds. We are aware of evanescent visitations of thought and feeling, sometimes associated with place and person, sometimes regarding our own mind alone, and always arising unforeseen, and departing unbidden, but elevating andd delightful beyond all expression. Poets are not only subject to these experiences, as spirits of the most refined organization, but they can color all they combine with the evanescent lines of this ethereal world; a word, a trait in the representation of a scene or passion will touch the enchanted cord, and reanimate in those who have ever experienced these emotions, the sleeping, the cold, the buried image of the past. Poetry thus makes immortal all that is best and most beautiful in the world; it arrests the vanishing apparitions which haunt the interlunations of life, and veiling them, or in language or in form, sends them forth among mankind, bearing sweet news of kindred joy to those with whom their sisters abide—abide, because there is no portal of expression from the caverns of the spirit which they inhabit into the universe of things."

Shelley's beautiful imagery and idealistic drapery is sometimes so accumulated in his poems, that it is difficult to follow him in his thinkings. In his verse he wishes to stand high as a philosophical reasoner, and this, together with his devotion to the cause, which even men of De Quincey's stamp call "Insolent Infidelity," has prevented Shelley from becoming so popular as he might have been.

Shelley lived a life of strife, passed his boyhood and youth in struggling to be free—misunderstood and misinterpreted: and when at last in his manhood happier circumstances were gathering around him, a blast of wind came, and the waves of the sea washed away one who was really and truly "a man and a poet."

On Monday. July 8th, 1822, being then in his 29th year, Shelley was returning from Leghorn to his home at Lerici, in a schooner-rigged boat of his own, with one friend and an English servant; when the boat had reached about four miles from the shore, the storm suddenly rose, and the wind suddenly shifted. From excessive smoothness, all at once the sea was foaming, and breaking, and getting up in a heavy swell. The boat is supposed to have filled to leeward, and (carry-ins: two tons of ballast) to have sunk instantaneously—all on board were drowned. The body of Shelley was washed on shore eight days afterwards, near Via Reggio, in an advanced state of decomposition, and was therefore burned on a funeral pyre in the presence of Leigh Hunt, Lord Byron, Mr. Trelawney, and a Captain Shenley.

Thus died Shelley in the mid day of life, and ere the warm sun of that mid-day could dispel the clouds that had gathered round the morning of his career. The following comparison made between the personal appearance of Shelley and of Byron, by Gilfillan, has been called by De Quincey "an eloquent parallel," and we therefore conclude the present number by quoting it:—

"In the forehead and head of Byron there is more massive power and breadth: Shelley has a smooth, arched, spiritual expression; wrinkle there seems none on his brow; it is as if perpetual youth had there dropped its freshness. Byron's eye seems the focus of pride and lust: Shelley's is mild, pensive, fixed on you, but seeing you through the mist of his own idealism. Defiance curls on Byron's nostril, and sensuality steps his full large lips. The lower features of Shelley's face are frail, feminine, flexible.—Byron's head is turned upwards as if having risen proudly above his contemporaries, he were daring to claim kindred, or demand a contest with a superior order of beings. Shelley's is half bent, in reverence and humility, before some vast vision seen by his own eye alone. Misery erect, and striving to cover its retreat under an aspect of contemptuous fury, is the permanent and pervading expression of Byron's countenance. Sorrow, softened and shaded away by hope and habit, lies like a 'holier day' of still moonshine upon that of Shelley. In the portrait of Byron, taken at the age of nineteen, you see the unnatural age of premature passion; his hair is young, his dress is youthful, but his face is old. In Shelley you see the eternal child, none the less that his hair is grey, and that sorrow seems half his immortality."

"I."

CLAUD ARIAN HELVETIUS

If France, at the present day, has not reason to be proud of its "leading man," it has in former times produced those minds that shed lustre upon the country, and who, by their literature, add immortality to its renown. During the eighteenth century, when religious persecution and intolerance were rampant throughout Europe, France furnished men to check oppression and expose superstition, while others followed to lay the foundation of excellence and greatness in the examination and cultivation of its true source—the mind. Heivetius sought to direct men's attention to self-examination, and to show how many disputes might be avoided if each person understood *what* he was disputing about. "Helvetius on the Mind" is a work that ought to be read widely, and studied attentively, especially by "rising young men," as it is one of those *Secular* works too rarely found among our literature.

Claud Arian Helvetius was born in Paris in the year 1715. After his preparatory studies, he was sent to the College of Louis le Grand, having for his tutor the famous Poree, who bestowed additional attention upon Heivetius, perceiving in him great talent and genius. Early in life Heivetius formed the friendship of some of the leading minds of France, Montesquieu being his intimate friend. Voltaire, too, sought his correspondence when at the age of twenty-three, calling him his "Young Apollo," and his "Son of Parnassus." The first literary attempts of Helvetius consisted of poetry— "Epistles on Happiness," which appeared as a posthumous production, with the "lavish commendations" of Voltaire. After ten years' thought and study Helvetius in 1758, published a work entitled "De L'Esprit," which brought upon him a great amount of persecution. The Parliament of Paris condemned it, and Helvetius was removed from the office he held of "Maitre d'Hotel to the Queen." Voltaire remarks:—"it is a little extraordinary that they should have persecuted, disgraced, and harassed, a much respected philosopher of our days, the innocent, the good Helvetius, for having said that if men had been without hands they could not have built houses, or worked in tapestry. Apparently those who have condemned this proposition, have a secret for cutting stones and wood, and for sewing with the feet.... I have no doubt that they will soon condemn to the galleys the first who shall have the insolence to say, that a man cannot think without his head; for, some bachelor will tell him, the soul is a pure spirit, the head is nothing but matter: God can place the soul in the nails, as well as in the skull, therefore I proscribe you as impious."

During the persecution raised against him, Helvetius visited England in 1764. In 1765 he visited Prussia, being well received by Frederick, in whose place he lodged. Voltaire strongly advised Helvetius to leave France in these words:—"In your place, I should not hesitate a moment to sell all that I have in France; there are some excellent estates in my neighborhood, and there you might cultivate in peace the arts you love." About this period Hume became acquainted with Helvetius, whom he styles, in writing to Dr. Robertson, "a very fine genius and worthy man." In 1765, Helvetius returned from Prussia, and retired to his estate at Vore. The sight of misery much affected him; and when relieving distress, he enjoined strict secrecy. Sometimes, when told he relieved those undeserving his aid, he would say, "If I were a king I would correct them, but as I am only rich and they are poor, I do my duty in relieving them." An attack of gout in the head and stomach terminated his life in December, 1771, in the fifty-sixth year of his age.

In "De L'Esprit, or, Essays on the Mind," chap. I.. Helvetius makes the following remarks on the "Mind considered in itself":—

"We hear every day disputes with regard to what ought to be called the Mind; each person delivers his thoughts, but annexes different ideas to the word; and thus the debate is continued, without understanding each other. In order, therefore, to enable us to give a just and precise idea of the word Mind, and its different acceptations, it is necessary first to consider the Mind in itself. We consider the Mind either as the effect of the faculty of thinking, and in this sense the Mind is no more than an assemblage of our thoughts, or, we consider it as the very faculty of thinking. But in order to understand what is meant by the Mind, in the latter acceptation, we ought previously to know the productive causes of our ideas. Man has two faculties; or, if I may be allowed the expression, two passive powers whose existence is generally and distinctly acknowledged. The one is the faculty of receiving the different impressions caused by external objects, and is called Physical Sensibility. The other is the faculty of preserving the impressions caused by those objects, called Memory; and Memory is nothing more than a continued, but weakened sensation.—Those faculties which I consider as the productive causes of our thoughts, and which we have in common with beasts, would produce but a very small number of ideas, if they were not assisted by certain external organizations. If Nature, instead of hands and flexible fingers, had terminated our wrist with the foot of a horse, mankind would doubtless have been totally destitute of art, habitation, and defence against other animals. Wholly employed in the care of procuring food, and avoiding the beasts of prey, they would have still continued wandering in the forests, like fugitive flocks. It is therefore evident that, according to this supposition, the police would never have been carried in any society to that degree of perfection, to which it is now arrived. There is not a nation now existing, but, with regard to the action of the mind, must not have continued very inferior to certain savage nations, who have not two hundred different ideas, nor two hundred words to express those ideas; and whose language must consequently be reduced, like that of animals, to five or six different sounds or cries, if we take from it the words bow, arrow, nets, etc., which suppose the use of hands. From whence I conclude, that, without a certain exterior organization, sensibility and memory in us would prove two sterile faculties. We ought to examine if these two faculties, by the assistance of this organization, have in reality produced all our thoughts. But; before we examine this subject, I may possibly be asked whether these two faculties are modifications of a spiritual or a material substance? This question, which has formerly been so often debated by philosophers, and by some persons revived in our time, does not necessarily fall within the limits of my work.—-What I have to offer, with regard to the Mind, is equally conformable to either of these hypothesis. I shall therefore only observe that, if the church had not fixed our belief in respect to this particular, and we had been obliged by the light of reason alone to acquire a knowledge of the thinking, principle, we must have granted, that neither opinion is capable of demonstration; and consequently that, by weighing the reasons on both sides, balancing the difficulties, and determining in favor of the greater number of probabilities, we should form only conditional judgments. It would be the fate of this problem, as it hath been of many others, to be resolvable only by the assistance of the calculation of probabilities."

Helvetius, on the question "whether genius ought to be considered as a natural gift, or as an effect of education," says:—

"I am going to examine in this discourse what the mind receives from nature and education; for which purpose it is necessary first, to determine what is here meant by the word Nature. This word may raise in our minds a confused idea of a being or a force that has endued us with all our senses: now the senses are the sources of all our ideas. Being deprived of our senses, we are deprived of all the ideas relative to them: a man born blind has for this reason no idea of colors; it is then evident that, in this signification, genius ought to be considered as a gift of nature. But, if the word be taken in a different acceptation, and we suppose that among the men well formed and endued with all their senses, without any perceivable defect of their organization, nature has made such a remarkable difference, and formed such an unequal distribution of the intellectual powers, that one shall be so organized as to be stupid, and the other be a man of genius, the question will become more delicate. I confess that, at first, we cannot consider the great inequality in the minds of men, without admitting that there is the same difference between them as between bodies, some of which are weak and delicate, while others are strong and robust. What can here occasion such variations from the uniform manner wherein nature operates? This reasoning, it is true, is founded only on analogy. It is like that of the astronomers who conclude that the moon is inhabited, because it is composed of nearly the same matter as our earth.—How weak soever this reasoning may be, it must yet appear demonstrative; for, say they, to what cause can be attributed the great disproportion of intellects observable between people who appear to have had the same education! In order to reply to this objection, it is proper first to inquire, whether several men can, strictly speaking, have the same education; and for this purpose to fix the idea included in the word Education. If by education we merely understand that received in the same places, and under the same masters; in this sense the education is the same with an infinite number of men. But, if we give to this word a more true and extensive signification, and in general comprehend everything that relates to our instruction; then I say, that nobody receives the same education; because each individual has, for his preceptors, if I may be allowed to say so, the form of government under which he lives, his friends, his mistresses, the people about him, whatever he reads, and in short chance; that is, an infinite number or events, with respect to which our ignorance will not permit us to perceive their causes, and the chain that connects them together. Now, this chance has a greater share in our education than is imagined. It is this places certain objects before us, and in consequence of this, occasions more happy ideas, and sometimes leads to the greatest discoveries. To give some examples: it was chance that conducted Galileo into the gardens of Florence, when the gardeners were working the pumps: it was that which inspired those gardeners, when, not being able to raise the water above the height of 32 feet, to ask him the cause, and by that question piqued the vanity of the philosopher, put in action by so casual a question, that obliged him to make this natural effect the subject of his thoughts, till, at last, by discovering the weight of the air, he found the solution of the problem. In the moment when the peaceful soul of Newton was employed by no business, and agitated by no passion, it was also chance that, drawing him under an apple tree, loosened some of the fruit from the branches, and gave that philosopher the first idea of his system on gravitation: it was really this incident that afterwards made him turn his thoughts to inquire whether the moon does not gravitate towards the earth with the same force as that with which bodies fall on its surface? It is then to chance that great geniuses are frequently obliged for their most happy thoughts. How many great minds are confounded among the people of moderate capacities for want of a certain tranquillity of soul, the question of a gardener, or the fall of an apple!"

Of the "exclusive qualities of the Mind and Soul," Helvetius observes:—

"My view in the preceding chapters was to affix clear ideas to the several qualities of the mind, I propose in this to examine if there are talents that must necessarily exclude each other? This question, it is said, is determined by facts; no person is, at the same time, superior to all others in many different kinds of knowledge. Newton is not reckoned among the poets, nor Milton among the geometricians: the verses of Leibnitz are bad. There is not a man who, in a single art, as poetry, or painting, has succeeded in all the branches of it. Corneille and Racine have done nothing in comedy comparable to Molière: Michael Angelo has not drawn the pictures of Albani, nor Albani painted those of Julius Romano. The genius of the greatest men appears then to be confined within very narrow limits. This is, doubtless, true: but I ask, what is the cause? Is it time, or is it wit, which men want to render themselves illustrious in the different arts and sciences? The progress of the human mind, it is said, ought to be the same in all the arts and sciences: the operations of the mind are reduced to the knowledge of the resemblances and differences that subsist between various objects. It is then by observation that we obtain, in all the different kinds of study, the new and general ideas on which our superiority depends. Every great physician, every great chemist, may then become a great geometrician, a great astronomer, a great politician, and the first, in short, in all the sciences This fact being stated, it will doubtless be concluded, that it is the short duration of human life that forces superior minds to limit themselves to one kind of study. It must, however, be confessed, that there are talents and qualities possessed only by the exclusion of some others. Among mankind some are filled with the love of glory, and are not susceptible of any other of the passions: some may excel in natural philosophy, civil law, geometry, and, in short, in all the sciences that consist in the comparison of ideas. A fondness for any other study can only distract or precipitate them into errors. There are other men susceptible not Only of the love of glory, but an infinite number of other passions: these may become celebrated in different kinds of study, where the success depends on being moved. Such is, for instance, the dramatic kind of writing: but, in order to paint the passions, we must, as I have already said, feel them very warmly: we are ignorant both of the language of the passions and of the sensations they excite in us, when we have not experienced them. Thus ignorance of this kind always produces mediocrity. If Fontenelle had been obliged to paint the characters of Rhadamistus, Brutus, or Cataline, that great man would certainly have fallen much below mediocrity.... Let a man, for instance, like M. de Fontenelle, contemplate, without severity, the wickedness of mankind; let him consider it, let him rise up against crimes without hating the criminals, and people will applaud his moderation; and yet, at the same instant, they will accuse him of being too lukewarm in friendship. They do not perceive, that the same absence of the passions, to which he owes the moderation they commend, must necessarily render him less sensible of the charms of friendship."

The "abuse of words" by different schools of philosophers is thus ably pointed out:—

"Descartes had before Locke observed that the Peripatetics, intrenching themselves behind the obscurity of words, were not unlike a blind man, who, in order to be a match for his clear-sighted antagonist, should draw him into a dark cavern. 'Now,' added he, 'if this man can introduce light into the cavern, and compel the Peripatetics to fix clear ideas to their words, the victory is his own. In imitation of Descartes and Locke, I shall show that, both in metaphysics and morality, the abuse of words, and the ignorance of their true import, is a labyrinth in which the greatest geniuses have lost themselves; and, in order to set this particular in a clear light, instance, in some of those words which have given rise to the longest and sharpest disputes among philosophers: such, in metaphysics, are Matter, Space, and Infinite. It has at all times been alternately asserted that Matter felt, or did not feel, and given rise to disputes equally loud and vague. It was very late before it came into the disputants! heads to ask one another, what they were disputing about, and to annex a precise idea to the word Matter. Had they at first fixed the meaning of it, they would have perceived, if I may use the expression, that men were the creators of Matter; that Matter was not a being; that in nature there were only individuals to which the name of Body had been given; and that this word Matter could import no more than the collection of properties common to all bodies. The meaning of this word being determined, all that remained was to know, whether extent, solidity, and impenetrability, were the only properties common to all bodies; and whether the discovery of a power, such for instance as attraction, might not give rise to a conjecture that bodies had some properties hitherto unknown, such as that of sensation, which, though evident only in the organized members of animals, might yet be common to all individuals! The question being reduced to this, it would have appeared that if, strictly speaking, it is impossible to demonstrate that all bodies are absolutely insensible, no man, unless instructed by a particular revelation, can decide the question otherwise than by calculating and comparing the verisimilitude of this opinion with that of the contrary...."

Instructed by the errors of great men who have gone before us, we should be sensible that our observations, however multiplied and concentrated, are scarcely sufficient to form one of those partial systems comprehended in the general system; add that it is from the depth of imagination that the several systems of the universe have hitherto been drawn; and, as our informations of remote countries are always imperfect, so the informations philosophers have of the system of the world are also defective. With a great genius and a multitude of combinations, the products of their labors will be only fictions till time and chance shall furnish then? with a general fact, to which all others may be referred.

"What I have said of the word Matter, I say also of Space. Most of the philosophers have made a being of it; and the ignorance of the true sense of the word has occasioned long disputes. They would have been greatly shortened by annexing a clear idea to this word; for then the sages would have agreed that Space, considered in bodies, is what we call extension; that we owe the idea of a void, which partly composes the idea of Space, to the interval seen betwixt two lofty mountains; an interval which, being filled only by air, that is, by a body which at a certain distance makes no sensible impression on us, must have given us an idea of a vacuum; being nothing more than a power of representing to ourselves mountains separated from each other, and the intervening distances not being filled by other bodies. With regard to the idea of Infinite, comprehended also within the idea of Space, I say that we owe this idea of Infinite only to the power which a man standing on a plain has of continually extending its limits, the boundary of his imagination not being determinable: the absence of limits is therefore the only idea we can form of Infinite. Had philosophers, previously to their giving any opinion on this subject, determined the signification of the word Infinite, I am inclined to believe they would have adopted the above definition, and not spent their time in frivolous disputes. To the false philosophy of former ages, our gross ignorance of the true signification of words is principally owing; as the art of abusing them made up the greatest part of that philosophy. This art, in which the whole science of the schools consisted, confounded all ideas; and the obscurity it threw on the expressions, generally diffused itself over all the sciences, especially morality."

The following remarks show Helvetia's notions of the "love of glory": —

"By the word Strong-Passion, I mean a passion the object of which is so necessary to our happiness, that without the possession of it life would be insupportable. This was Omar's idea of the passion, when he said, 'Whoever thou art, that lovest liberty, desirest to be wealthy without riches, powerful without subjects, a subject without a master, dare to condemn death: kings will then tremble before thee, whilst thou alone shalt fear no person.' .... It was the passion of honor and philosophic fanaticism alone that could induce Timicha, the Pythagorean, in the midst of torture, to bite off her tongue, that she might not expose herself to reveal the secrets of her sect. Cato, when a child, going with his tutor to Sylla's palace, at seeing the bloody heads of the proscribed, asked with impatience the name of the monster who had caused so many Roman citizens to be murdered. He was answered, it was Sylla: 'How,' says he, 'does Sylla murder thus, and is Sylla still alive?' 'Yes,' it was replied, 'the very name of Sylla disarms our citizens.' 'Oh! Rome,' cried Cato, 'deplorable is thy fate, since within the vast compass of thy walls not a man of virtue can be found, and the arm of a feeble child is the only one that will oppose itself against tyranny!' Then, turning towards his governor, 'Give me,' said he, 'your sword; I will conceal it under my robe, approach Sylla, and kill him. Cato lives, and Rome is again free.' If the generous pride, the passion of patriotism and glory, determine citizens to such heroic actions, with what resolution and intrepidity do not the passions inspire those who aim at distinction in the arts and sciences, and whom Cicero calls the peaceable heroes? It is from a desire of glory that the astronomer is seen, on the icy summits of the Cordileras, placing his instruments in the midst of snows and frost; which conducts the botanist to the brinks of precipices in quest of plants; which anciently carried the juvenile lovers of ihe sciences into Egypt, Ethiopia, and even into the Indies, for visiting the most celebrated philosophers, and acquiring from their conversation the principles of their doctrine. How strongly did this passion exert itself in Demosthenes, who, for perfecting his pronunciation, used every day to stand on the sea-shore, and with his mouth full of pebbles harangue the agitated waves! It was from the same desire of glory that the young Pythagoreans submitted to a silence of three years, in order to habituate themselves to recollection and meditation; it induced Democritus to shun the distractions of the world, and retire among the tombs, to meditate on those valuable truths, the discovery of which, as it is always very difficult, is also very little esteemed; in fine, it was this that prompted Heraclitus to cede to his younger brother the throne of Ephesus, to which he had the right of primogeniture, that he might give himself up entirely to philosophy; which made the Athletic improve his strength, by denying himself the pleasures of love; it was also from a desire of popular applause that certain ancient priests renounced the same pleasures, and often, as Boindin pleasantly observes of them, without any other recompense for their continence than the perpetual temptation it occasions,... 'The cause,' says Cardinal Richelieu, 'why a timorous mind perceives an impossibility in the most simple projects, when to an elevated mind the most arduous seems easy, is, because, before the latter the mountains sink, and before the former mole-hills are metamorphosed into mountains.'"

The different motives that influence our conduct are thus stated:—

"A mother idolizes her son; 'I love him,' says she, 'for his own sake.' However, one might reply, you take no care of his education, though you are in no doubt that a good one would contribute infinitely to his happiness; why, therefore, do not you consult some men of sense about him, and read some of the works written on this subject? 'Why, because,' says she, 'I think I know as much of this matter as those authors and their works.' But how did you get this confidence in your own understanding? Is it not the effect of your indifference? An ardent desire always inspires us with a salutary distrust of ourselves. If we have a suit at law of considerable consequence, we visit counsellors and attorneys, we consult a great number, and examine their advice. Are we attacked by any of those lingering diseases, which incessantly place around us the shades and horrors of death? We seek physicians, compare their opinions, read physical books, we ourselves become little physicians. Such is the conduct prompted by a warm interest. With respect to the education of children, if you are not influenced in the same manner, it is because you do not love your son as well as yourself. 'But,' adds the mother, 'what then should be the motive of my tenderness?' Among fathers and mothers, I reply, some are influenced by the desire of perpetuating their name in their children; they properly love only their names; others are fond of command, and see in their children their slaves. The animal leaves its young when their weakness no longer keeps them in dependence; and paternal love becomes extinguished in almost all hearts, when children have, by their age or station, attained to independence. 'Then,' said the poet Saadi, 'the father sees nothing in them but greedy heirs,' and this is the cause, adds some poet, of the extraordinary love of the grandfather for his grandchildren; he considers them as the enemies of his enemies. There are, in short, fathers and mothers, who make their children their playthings and their pastime. The loss of this plaything would be insupportable to them; but would their affliction prove that they loved the child for itself? Everybody knows this passage in the life of M. de Lauzun: he was in the Bastile; there, without books, without employment, a prey to lassitude and the horrors of a prison, he took it in his head to tame a spider. This was the only consolation he had left in his misfortune. The governor of the Bastile, from an inhumanity common to men accustomed to see the unhappy, crushed the spider. The prisoner felt the most cutting grief, and no mother could be affected by the death of a son with a more violent sorrow. Now whence is derived this conformity of sentiments for such different objects? It is because, in the loss of a child, or in the loss of the spider, people frequently weep for nothing but for the lassitude and want of employment into which they fall. If mothers appear in general more afflicted at the death of a child than fathers employed in business, or given up to the pursuit of ambition, it is not because the mother loves her child more tenderly, but because she suffers a loss more difficult to be supplied. The errors, in my opinion, are, in this respect, very frequent; people rarely cherish a child for its own sake. That paternal love of which so many men make a parade, and by which they believe themselves so warmly affected, is most frequently nothing more than an effect, either of a desire of perpetuating their names, or of pride of command...... Do you not know that Galileo was unworthily dragged to the prison of the Inquisition, for having maintained that the sun is placed in the centre, and does not move around the earth; that his system first offended the weak, and appeared directly contrary to that text of Scripture—'Sun, stand thou still?' However, able divines have since made Galileo's principles agree with those of religion. Who has told you, that a divine more happy or more enlightened than you, will not remove the contradiction, which you think you perceive between your religion, and the opinion you resolve to condemn! Who forces you by a precipitate censure to expose, if not religion, at least its ministers, to the hatred excited by persecution? Why, always borrowing the assistance of force and terror, would you impose silence on men of genius, and deprive mankind of the useful knowledge they are capable of dispensing? You obey, you say, the dictates of religion. But it commands you to distrust yourselves, and to love your neighbor. If you do not act in conformity to these principles, you are then not actuated by the spirit of God. But you say, by whom then are we inspired? By laziness and pride. It is laziness, the enemy of thought, which makes you averse to those opinions, which you cannot, without study and some fatigue of attention, unite with the principles received in the schools; but which being proved to be philosophically true, cannot be theologically false. It is pride, which is ordinarily carried to a greater height in the bigot than in any other person, which makes him detest in the man of genius the benefactor of the human race, and which exasperates him against the truths discovered by humility. It is then this laziness and this pride, which, disguising themselves under the appearance of zeal, render them the persecutors of men of learning; and which in Italy, Spain, and Portugal, have forged chains, built gibbets, and held the torch to the piles of the Inquisition. Thus the same pride, which is so formidable in the devout fanatic, and which in all religions makes him persecute, in the name of the Most High, the men of genius, sometimes arms against them the men in power. After the example of those Pharisees, who treated as criminals the persons who did not adopt all their decisions, how many viziers treat, as enemies to the nation, those who do not blindly approve their conduct!"

J. W.

FRANCES W. D'ARUSMONT

The previous issues of this publication contain notices of the lives and writings of men of eminence in the world of Freethought. This number is devoted to a review of the career and works of a most talented and accomplished lady—a Freethinker and Republican. As a proof—if any proof were needed—that women, if adequately educated, are equally capable with men to become teachers and reformers, the works of the subject of present notice afford abundant evidence. The efforts now being made to procure an adjustment of the laws relating to women, whereby they will be protected in their property, and consequently improved in their social position, deserve the support of all classes; When females become independent, there will be less ignorance among women and more happiness among men.

Frances Wright, afterwards Madame D'Arusmont, was a native of Dundee. She was born on the 6th of September, 1795. She came of a wealthy family, who had been extensive holders of city property from the year 1500. Her father was a man of considerable literary attainments, and to his active antiquarian researches and donations the British Museum is indebted for many rare and valuable coins and medals. He died young, as also his wife, leaving three children—two girls and a boy. Frances was then but two years and a half old. At the wish of her grandfather, General Duncan Campbell, she was taken to England, and reared as a ward of Chancery, under the guardianship of a maternal aunt. She grew to be very tall in person, erect, and of a commanding figure; large eyes, and magnificent head, with a face somewhat masculine, but well formed, and decidedly handsome. Her brother was sent to India, at the age of fifteen, as a cadet in the East India Company's service, and was killed on the passage out in an encounter with a French vessel. Her sister passed her life with her, and died in Paris in 1831.

At an early age, Miss Wright gave evidence of great intellectual ability. The education she received was of a very superior kind. She diligently applied herself to the various branches of science, and to the study of ancient and modern letters and the arts, being impelled by a strong desire for knowledge. At the age of nineteen, she published her first work, "A Few Days in Athens." Her attention was early drawn to the sufferings of the lower classes, and on reflection she became convinced that some great vice lay at the foundation of the whole of human practice: She determined to endeavor to discover, and assist in removing it. She read Bocca's "History of the American Revolution," and resolved to visit that country, it appearing to her young imagination as the land of freedom and hope.—After having familiarised herself with the government and institutions of America, she sailed for New York 1818. She returned to England in 1820, and published a large volume, entitled "Views of Society and Manners in America." It was dedicated to Jeremy Bentham, and had a large sale. The work being translated into most of the continental languages, she became known to the prominent reformers of Europe.

In 1821, she made her first visit to Paris, and was there introduced to General Lafayette, who, having previously read her work on America, invited her to that city. A republican in all her views and hopes, she was highly appreciated by Lafayette and other eminent supporters of the liberal party in France.—She remained in Paris until 1824, when she returned to the United States, and immediately undertook a project for the abolition of slavery upon a plan somewhat different from any that then engaged the attention of philanthropists. For this purpose she purchased two thousand acres of land at Chickasaw Bluffe, (now Memphis, Tennessee), intending to make a good farm rather than a cotton plantation. She then purchased several slave families, gave them their liberty, and removed them to the farm, residing there herself to direct their labor. Commencing this novel undertaking with all that enthusiasm for which she was remarkable, she continued the experiment some three years and a half, when her health gave way, and, suffering under severe sickness, she made a voyage to Europe for her recovery. During her absence, the farm got involved in difficulties by the influence of her enemies; and finally, the whole project falling through, the negroes were sent off to Hayti at her expense.—She gave much time and money to the carrying forward of this experiment; and though it was a failure, it strikingly exhibited her strong sympathy and benevolence for an oppressed and degraded class of beings. Returning from Europe, she went to New Harmony (Indiana) to assume the proprietorship of a periodical the Harmony Gazette, which had been published under the direction of Robert Dale Owen. In 1828, leaving Mr. Owen in charge of the paper, she began a lecturing tour through the Union; and probably no man, and certainly no *woman*, ever met with such furious opposition. Her views, as announced in her paper, had made her generally known, and, being somewhat new and radically "anti-theological," brought down upon her head the rancor of religious bigotry. As no church or hall would be opened for her, she lectured in theatres; and her ability and eloquence drew great audiences. On one occasion, while preparing to lecture in a theatre at Baltimore, she was threatened with the destruction of her life if she attempted to speak. She calmly replied, that she thought she knew the American people, and for every riotous fanatic that might annoy her, a hundred good citizens would protect her, and she was not afraid to place herself in their hands. She judged rightly. She went to the theatre, which was crammed from pit to ceiling, and lectured to an admiring and enthusiastic audience. In other cities she was not always so fortunate; more or less rioting occurred, while the press, almost without exception, denounced her in the bitterest terms. Subsequently, her paper was removed to New York. Some years afterwards, she again made a lecturing tour, but this time she spoke on subjects of a political nature, and met with a better reception. In addition to lecturing, she conducted a political magazine, entitled the Manual of American Principles, and was also engaged with Mr. Kneeland in editing the Boston Investigator. She wrote a great deal, and upon many subjects. Among her many works is a tragedy called "Altorf," which was performed on the stage, the principal character being sustained by Mr. James Wallack. Her last work, of any considerable size, was entitled "England the Civiliser," published in London in 1847.

Madame D'Arusmont died suddenly in Cincinnati, on Tuesday, December 14, 1852, aged fifty-seven. She had been for sometime unwell, in consequence of a fall upon the ice the previous winter, which broke her thigh, and probably hastened her decease; but the immediate cause of her death was the rupture of a blood vessel. She was aware of her situation, knew when she was dying, and met her last hour with perfect composure. A daughter, her only child, survives her.

In a small work entitled "Observations on Religion and Civilization," are given the following "Definitions of Theology and Religion: in the words and in the things signified. Origin and Nature of Theology:" —

"Theology from the Greek *theos, logos*, renders distinct the meaning of the subject it attempts to treat.—*Theos*, God, or Gods, unseen beings and unknown causes. *Logos*, word, talk—or, if we like to employ yet more familiar and expressive terms, prattle or chatter. *Talk, or prattle, about unseen beings or unknown causes*, The idleness of the subject, and inutility—nay, absolute insanity of the occupation, sufficiently appears in the strict etymological meaning of the word employed to typify them. The danger, the mischief, the cruelly immoral, and, if I may be permitted to coin a word for the occasion, the *unhumanizing* tendencies both of the subject and the occupation, when and where these are (as they have for the most part ever been throughout the civilized world) absolutely protected by law and upheld by government, sufficiently appear also from the whole page of history. Religion, from the Latin *religio, religio*, renders with equal distinctness the things signified. *Religo*, to tie over again, to bind fast; *religio*, a binding together, a bond of union. The importance of the great reality, here so accurately shadowed out, appears sufficiently in the etymological signification of the word. Its utility will be evident if we read, with intelligence, the nature, the past history, the actual condition, and the future destiny of man. But now, taking these two things in the most strict etymological sense of the words which express them, it will readily be distinguished that the first is a necessary creation of the *human intellect* in a certain stage of inquiry; the second, a necessary creation of the *human soul* (by which I understand both our intellectual and moral faculties taken conjointly) in any and every state of human civilization. Theology argues, in its origin, the first awakening of human attention to the phenomena of nature, and the first crude efforts of human ingenuity to expound them. While man sees the sun and stars without observing either their diurnal or their annual revolutions; while he receives upon his frame the rain and the wind, and the varying elements, without observing either their effects upon himself or upon the field of nature around him, he is as the brute which suffers and enjoys without inquiring why it experiences light or darkness, pain or pleasure. When first he puts, in awkward language, to himself or to his fellow, the question *why does such an effect follow such a cause*? he commences his existence, if not as a reasonable being, (a state at which he has not yet arrived) at least *as a being capable of reason.* The answer to this first inquiry of awakening intelligence is, of course, such as his own circumscribed observation supplies.—It is, in fine, in accordance with the explanation of the old nurse to the child, who, asking, when startled by a rolling peal of thunder—'what makes that noise' was fully satisfied by the reply: 'my darling, it is God Almighty overhead moving his furniture.' Man awakening to thought, but still unfamiliar with the concatenation of natural phenomena, inevitably conceives of some huge being, or beings, bestriding the clouds and whirlwind, or wheeling the sun and the moon like chariots through the blue vault. And so again, fancy most naturally peoples the gloom of the night with demons, the woods and the waters with naiads and dryads, elves and fairies, the church-yard with ghosts, and the dark cave and the solitary cot with wizards, imps and old witches. Such, then, is theology in its origin; and, in all its stages, we find it varying in grossness according to the degree of ignorance of the human mind; and, refining into verbal subtleties and misty metaphysics in proportion as that mind exchanges, in its progress from darkness to light, the gloom of ignorance for the mass of terror."

The nature of belief in the unknowable, and the dire consequences arising from fanaticism, are ably depicted in the following passages, selected from Lecture IV., on "Religion:"—

"Admitting religion to be the most important of all subjects, its truths must be the most apparent; for we shall readily concede, both that a thing true, must be always of more or less importance—and that a thing essentially important, must always be indisputably true. Now, again, I conceive we shall be disposed to admit, that exactly in proportion to the indisputability of a truth, is the proof it is capable of affording; and that, exactly in proportion to the proof afforded, is our admission of such truth and belief in it. If, then, religion be the most important subject of human inquiry, it must be that also which presents the most forcible, irrefragable, and indisputable truths to the inquirer.—It must be that on which the human mind can err the least, and where all minds must be the most agreed. If religion be at once a science, and the most true of all sciences, its truths must be as indisputable as those in any branch of the mathematics—as apparent to all the senses as those revealed by the chemist or observed by the naturalist, and as easily referred to the test of our approving or disapproving sensations, as those involved in the science of morals.... Is religion a science? Is it a branch of knowledge? Where are the *things known* upon which it rests? Where are the accumulated facts of which it is compounded? What are the human sensations to which it appeals? Knowledge is compounded of *things known*. It is an accumulation of facts gleaned by our senses, within the range of material existence, which is subject to their investigation.... Now let us see where, in the table of knowledge, we may class religion. Of what part or division of nature, or material existence, does it treat? What bodies, or what properties of tangible bodies, does it place in contact with our senses, and bring home to the perception of our faculties? It clearly appertains not to the table of human knowledge, for it treats not of objects discoverable within the field of human observation. 'No,' will you say? 'but its knowledge is superhuman, unearthly—its field is in heaven.' My friends, the knowledge which is not human, is of slippery foundation to us human creatures. Things *known*, constitute knowledge; and here is a science treating of things unseen, unfelt, uncomprehended! Such cannot be *knowledge*. What, then, is it? Probability? possibility? theory? hypothesis? tradition? written? spoken? by whom? when? where? Let its teachers—nay, let all earth reply! But what confusion of tongues and voices now strike on the ear! From either Indies, from torrid Africa, from the frozen regions of either pole, from the vast plains of ancient Asia, from the fields and cities of European industry, from the palaces of European luxury, from the soft chambers of priestly ease, from the domes of hierarchal dominion, from the deep cell of the self-immolated monk, from the stony cave of the self-denying anchorite, from the cloud-capt towers, spires, and minarets of the crescent and the cross, arise shouts, and hosannas, and anathemas, in the commingled names of Brama, and Veeshnu, and Creeshna, and Juggernaut; heavenly kings, heavenly queens, triune deities, earth-born gods, heaven-born prophets, apotheosized monarchs, demon-enlightened philosophers, saints, angels, devils, ghosts, apparitions, and sorceries! But, worse than these sounds which but stun the ear and confound the intellect, what sights, oh! human kind! appal the heart! The rivers of earth run blood! Nation set against nation! Brother against brother! Man against the companion of his bosom! and that soft companion, maddened with the frenzy of insane remorse for imaginary crimes? fired with the rage of infatuated bigotry, or subdued to diseased helplessness and mental fatuity, renounces kindred, flies from social converse, and pines away a useless or mischievous existence in sighings and tremblings, spectral fears, uncharitable feelings and bitter denunciations! Such are thy doings, oh! religion! Or, rather, such are thy doings, oh! man! While standing in a world so rich in sources of enjoyment, so stored with objects of real inquiry and attainable knowledge, yet shutting thine eyes, and, worse, thine heart, to the tangible things and sentient creatures around thee, and winging thy diseased imagination beyond the light of the sun which gladdens thy world, and contemplation of the objects which are here to expand thy mind and quicken the pulses of thy heart!... I will pray ye to observe how much of our positive misery originates in our idle speculations in matters of faith, and in our blind, our fearful forgetfulness of facts—our cold, heartless, and, I will say, *insane* indifference to visible causes of tangible evil, and visible sources of tangible happiness. Look to the walks of life, I beseech ye—look into the public prints—look into your sectarian churches—look into the bosoms of families—look into your own bosoms, and those of your fellow beings, and see how many of our disputes and dissensions, public and private—how many of our unjust actions—how many of our harsh judgments—how many of our uncharitable feelings—spring out of our ignorant ambition to rend the veil which wraps from our human senses the knowledge of things unseen, and from our human faculties the conception of causes unknown? And oh! my fellow beings! do not these very words *unseen* and *unknown*, warn the enthusiast against the profanity of such inquiries, and proclaim to the philosopher their futility? Do they not teach us that religion is no subject for instruction, and no subject for discussion? Will they not convince us that as beyond the horizon of our observation we can know nothing, so within that horizon's the only safe ground for us to meet in public?... Every day we see sects splitting, creeds new modelling, and men forsaking old opinions only to quarrel about their opposites.

"I see three Gods in one, says the Trinitarian, and excommunicates the Socinian, who sees a God-head in unity. I see a heaven but no hell, says the Universalist, and disowns fellowship with such as may distinguish less. 'I see a heaven and hell also, beyond the stars,' said lately the Orthodox friend, and expelled his shorter-sighted brethren from the sanctuary. I seek them both in the heart of man, said the more spiritual follower of Penn, and straightway builded him up another temple, in which to quarrel with his neighbor, who perhaps only employs other words to express the same ideas. For myself, pretending to no insight into these mysteries, possessing no means of intercourse with the inhabitants of other worlds, confessing my absolute incapacity to see either as far back as a first cause, or as far forward as a last one, I am content to state to you, my fellow creatures, that all my studies, reading, reflection, and observation, have obtained for me no knowledge beyond the sphere of our planet, our earthly interests and our earthly duties; and that I more than doubt whether, should you expend all your time and all your treasure in the search, you will be able to acquire any better information respecting unseen worlds and future events than myself."

The philosophical romance, "A Few Days in Athens," though the first of Miss Wright's works, and written when she was very young, displays considerable power and eloquence. It is the most pleasing of all her writings. It is intended to portray the doctrines of Epicurus, and gives a picture of the Gargettian, in the "Gardens of the Academy," surrounded by his pupils, calculated to counteract many of the popular and erroneous notions entertained of that philosopher's teachings. The following dialogue between Epicurus and his favorite, Theon, will afford the readers of the "Half-Hours" an opportunity of judging how far Miss Wright has conveyed a truthful idea of Epicurus's ethical philosophy:—

"On leaving you, last night," said Theon, "I encountered Cleanthes. He came from the perusal of your writings, and brought charges against them which I was unprepared to answer."

"Let us hear them, my son; perhaps, until you shall have perused them yourself, we may assist your difficulty."

"First, that they deny the existence of the Gods."

"I see but one other assertion that could equal that in folly," said Epicurus.

"I knew it," exclaimed Theon, triumphantly, "I knew it was impossible. But where will not prejudice lead men, when even the uptight Cleanthes is capable of slander?"

"He is utterly incapable of it," said the Master; "and the inaccuracy, in this case, I rather suspect to rest with you than with him. To *deny* the existence of the Gods would indeed be presumption in a 'philosopher; a presumption equalled only by that of him who should *assert* their existence."

"How!" exclaimed the youth, with a countenance in which astonishment seemed to suspend every other expression.

"As I never saw the Gods, my son," calmly continued the Sage, "I cannot *assert* their existence; and that I never saw them, is no reason for my *denying* it."

"But do we believe nothing except that of which we have ocular demonstration?"

"Nothing, at least, for which we have not the evidence of one or more of our senses; that is, when we believe on just grounds, which I grant, taking men collectively, is very seldom."

"But where would this spirit lead us! To impiety!—to Atheism!—to all, against which I felt confidence in defending the character and philosophy of Epicurus!"

"We will examine presently, my son, into the meaning of the terms you have employed. When you first entered the Garden your mind was unfit for the examination of the subject you have now started: it is no longer so; and we will therefore enter upon the inquiry, and pursue it in order."

"Forgive me if I express—if I acknowledge," said the youth, slightly recoiling from his instructor, "some reluctance to enter on the discussion of truths, whose very discussion would seem to argue a doubt, and"—

"And what then!"

"That very doubt were a crime."

"If the doubt of any truth shall constitute a crime, then the belief of the same truth should constitute a virtue."

"Perhaps a duty would rather express it!" "When you charge the neglect of any duty as crime, or account its fulfilment a virtue, you suppose the existence of a power to neglect or fulfil; and it is the exercise of this power, in the one way or the other which constitutes the merit or demerit. Is it not so?"

"Certainly."

"Does the human mind possess the power to believe or disbelieve, at pleasure, any truths whatsoever."

"I am not prepared to answer: but I think it does, since it possesses always the power of investigation."

"But, possibly, not the will to exercise the power. Take care lest I beat you with your own weapons. I thought this very investigation appeared to you a crime?"

"Your logic is too subtle," said the youth, "for my inexperience."

"Say, rather, my reasoning too close. Did I bear you down with sounding words and weighty authorities, and confound your understanding with hair-drawn distinctions, you would be right to retreat from the battery."

"I have nothing to object to the fairness of your deductions," said Theon. "But would not the doctrine be dangerous that should establish our inability to help our belief; and might we not stretch the principle, until we asserted our inability to help our actions?"

"We might, and with reason. But we will not now traverse the ethical *pons asinorum* of necessity—the most simple and evident of mortal truths, and the most darkened, tortured, and belabored by moral teachers. You inquire if the doctrine we have essayed to establish, be not dangerous. I reply—not, if it be true.—Nothing is so dangerous as error—nothing so safe as truth. A dangerous truth would be a contradiction in terms, and an anomaly in things."

"But what is a truth?" said Theon.

"It is pertinently asked. A truth I consider to be an ascertained fact; which truth would be changed to an error, the moment the fact, on which it rested, was disproved."

"I see, then, no fixed basis for truth."

"It surely has the most fixed of all—the nature of things. And it is only an imperfect insight into that nature which occasions all our erroneous conclusions, whether in physics or morals."

"But where, if we discard the Gods and their will, as engraven on our hearts, are our guides in the search after truth?"

"Our senses and our faculties as developed in and by the exercise of our senses, are the only guides with which I am acquainted. And I do not see why, even admitting a belief in the Gods, and in a superintending Providence, the senses should not be viewed as the guides provided by them, for our direction and instruction. But here is the evil attendant on an ungrounded belief, whatever be its nature. The moment we take one thing for granted, we take other things for granted; we are started in a wrong road, and it is seldom that we gain the right one, until we have trodden back our steps to the starting place. I know but of one thing that a philosopher should take for granted; and that only because he is forced to it by an irresistible impulse of his nature; and because, without doing so, neither truth nor falsehood could exist for him. He must take for granted the evidence of his senses; in other words, he must believe in the existence of things, as they exist to his senses. I *know* of no other existence, and can therefore *believe* in no other: although, reasoning from analogy, I may *imagine* other existences to be.—This, for instance, I do as respects the Gods. I see around me, in the world I inhabit, an infinite variety in the arrangement of matter—a multitude of sentient beings, possessing different kinds and varying grades of power and intelligence—from the worm that crawls in the dust, to the eagle that soars to the sun, and man who marks to the sun its course. It is possible, it is moreover probable, that, in the worlds which I see not—in the boundless infinitude and eternal duration of matter, beings may exist, of every countless variety, and varying grades of intelligence, inferior and superior to our own, until we descend to a minimum and rise to a maximum, to which the range of our observation affords no parallel, and of which our senses are inadequate to the conception. Thus far, my young friend, 1 believe in the Gods, or in what you will of existences removed from the sphere of my knowledge. That you should believe, with positiveness, in one unseen existence or another, appears to me no crime, although it may appear to me unreasonable; and so, my doubt of the same should appear to you no moral offence, although you might account it erroneous. I fear to fatigue your attention, and will, therefore, dismiss, for the present, these abstruse subjects."

"But we shall both be amply repaid for their discussion, if this truth remain with you—that an opinion, right or wrong, can never constitute a moral offence, nor be in itself a moral obligation. It may be mistaken; it may involve an absurdity, or a contradiction.—It is a truth; or it is an error: it can never be a crime or a virtue." —[Chapter xiv.]

Miss Wright was a poetess, as well as a politician and writer on ethics. In her "Fourth of July" address, delivered in the New Harmony Hall, in 1828, in commemoration of the American Independence, is the following:—

> *"Is there a thought can fill the human mind*
> *More pure, more vast, more generous, more refined*
> *Than that which guides the enlightened patriot's toil?*
> *Not he whose view is bounded by his soil—*
> *Not he whose narrow heart can only shrine*
> *The land, the people that he calleth mine—*
> *Not he who, to set up that land on high,*
> *Will make whole nations bleed, whole nations die—*
> *Not he who, calling that land's rights his pride,*
> *Trampleth the rights of all the earth beside.*

No! He it is, the just, the generous soul,
Who owneth brotherhood with either pole,
Stretches from realm to realm his spacious mind,
And guards the weal of all the human kind—
Holds freedom's banner o'er the earth unfurl'd,
And stands the guardian patriot of a world!"

J. W.

EPICURUS

Epicurean. — One who holds the principles of Epicurus —
Luxurious, contributing to luxury.

Epicurism — The principles of Epicurus — Luxury, sensual
enjoyment, gross pleasure.

The words with which this page is headed may be found in the current and established dictionaries of the present day; and it shall be our task to show that never was slander more foul, calumny more base, or libel more cowardly, than when it associated the words luxury and sensuality with the memory of the Athenian Epicurus. The much-worn anecdote of the brief endorsed "The Defendant has no case, abuse the Plaintiffs Solicitor," will well apply here. The religionists had no case, the Epicurean Philosophy was impregnable as far as theological attacks were concerned, and the theologians have, therefore, constantly and vehemently abused its founder; so that, at last, children have caught the cry as though it were the enunciation of a tact, and have grown into men believing that Epicurus was a sort of discriminating hog, who wallowed in the filth which some have miscalled pleasure.

Epicurus was born in the early part of the year 344, B. C, the third year of the 109th Olympiad, at Gargettus, in the neighborhood of Athens. His father, Neocles, was of the Ægean tribe. Some allege that Epicurus was born in the island of Samos; but, according to others, he was taken there when very young by his parents, who formed a portion of a colony of Athenian citizens, sent to colonize Samos after its subjugation by Pericles. The father and mother of Epicurus were in very humble circumstances; his father was a schoolmaster, and his mother, Chærestrata, acted as a kind of priestess, curing diseases, exorcising ghosts, and exercising other fabulous powers. Epicurus has been charged with sorcery, because he wrote several songs for his mother's solemn rites. Until eighteen, he remained at Samos and the neighboring isle of Teos; from whence he removed to Athens, where he resided until the death of Alexander, when, disturbances arising, he fled to Colophon. This place, Mitylene, and Lampsacus, formed the philosopher's residence until he was thirty-six years of age; at which time he founded a school in the neighborhood of Athens. He purchased a pleasant garden, where he taught his disciples until the time of his death.

We are told by Laertius, "That those disciples who were regularly admitted into the school of Epicurus, lived together, not in the manner of the Pythagoreans, who cast their possessions into a common stock; for this, in his opinion, implied mutual distrust rather than friendship; but upon such a footing of friendly attachment, that each individual cheerfully supplied the necessities of his brother."

The habits of the philosopher and his followers were temperate and exceedingly frugal, and formed a strong contrast to the luxurious, although refined, manners of the Athenians. At the entrance of the garden, the visitor of Epicurus found the following inscription:—"The hospitable keeper of this mansion, where you will find pleasure the highest good, will present you with barley cakes and water from the spring. These gardens will not provoke your appetite by artificial dainties, but satisfy it with natural supplies. Will you not, then, be well entertained?" And yet the owner of the garden, over the gate of which these words were placed, has been called "a glutton" and "a stomach worshipper!"

From the age of thirty-six until his decease, he does not seem to have quitted Athens, except temporarily. When Demetrius besieged Athens, the Epicureans were driven into great difficulties for want of food; and it is said that Epicurus and his friends subsisted on a small quantity of beans which he possessed, and which he shared equally with them.

The better to prosecute his studies, Epicurus lived a life of celibacy. Temperate and continent himself, he taught his followers to be so likewise, both by example and precept. He died 273 B. C, in the seventy-third year of his age; and, at that time, his warmest opponents seem to have paid the highest compliments to his personal character; and, on reading his life, and the detailed accounts of his teachings, it seems difficult to imagine what has induced the calumny which has been heaped upon his memory.

We "cannot quote from his own works, in his own words, because, although he wrote very much, only a summary of his writings has come to us uninjured; but his doctrines have been so fully investigated and treated on, both by his opponents and his disciples, that there is no difficulty or doubt as to the principles inculcated in the school of Epicurus.

"The sum of his doctrine concerning philosophy, in general, is this:— Philosophy is the exercise of reason in the pursuit and attainment of a happy life; whence it follows, that those studies which conduce neither to the acquisition nor the enjoyment of happiness are to be dismissed as of no value. The end of all speculation ought to be, to enable men to judge with certainty what is to be chosen, and what to be avoided, to preserve themselves free from pain, and to secure health of body, and tranquillity of mind. True philosophy is so useful to every man, that the young should apply to it without delay, and the old should never be weary of the pursuit; for no man is either too young or too old to correct and improve his mind, and to study the art of happiness. Happy are they who possess by nature a free and vigorous intellect, and who are born in a country where they can prosecute their inquiries without restraint: for it is philosophy alone which raises a man above vain fears and base passions, and gives him the perfect command of himself. As nothing ought to be dearer to a philosopher than truth, he should, pursue it by the most direct means, devising no actions himself, nor suffering himself to be imposed upon by the fictions of others, neither poets, orators, nor logicians, making no other use of the rules of rhetoric or grammar, than to enable him to speak or write with accuracy and perspicuity, and always preferring a plain and simple to an ornamented style. Whilst some doubt of everything, and others profess to acknowledge everything, a wise man will embrace such tenets, and only such as are built upon experience, or upon certain and indisputable axioms."

The following is a summary of his Moral Philosophy:—

"The end of living, or the ultimate good, which is to be sought for its own sake, according to the universal opinion of mankind, is happiness; yet men, for the most part, fail in the pursuit of this end, either because they do not form a right idea of the nature of happiness, or because they do not make use of proper means to attain it. Since it is every man's interest to be happy through the whole of life, it is the wisdom of every one to employ philosophy in the search of felicity without delay; and there cannot be a greater folly, than to be always beginning to live.

"The happiness which belongs to man, is that state in which he enjoys as many of the good things, and suffers as few of the evils incident to human nature as possible; passing his days in a smooth course of permanent tranquillity. A wise man, though deprived of sight or hearing, may experience happiness in the enjoyment of the good things which yet remain; and when suffering torture, or laboring under some painful disease, can mitigate the anguish by patience, and can enjoy, in bis afflictions, the consciousness of bis own constancy. But it is impossible that perfect happiness can be possessed without the pleasure which attends freedom from pain, and the enjoyment of the good things of life. Pleasure is in its nature good, as pain is in its nature evil; the one is, therefore, to be pursued, and the other to be avoided, for its own sake.—Pleasure, or pain, is not only good, or evil, in itself, but the measure of what is good or evil, in every object of desire or aversion; for the ultimate reason why we pursue one thing, and avoid another, is because we expect pleasure from the former, and apprehend pain from the latter. If we sometimes decline a present pleasure, it is not because we are averse to pleasure itself, but because we conceive, that in the present instance, it will be necessarily connected with a greater pain. In like manner, if we sometimes voluntarily submit to a present pain, it is because we judge that it is necessarily connected with a greater pleasure. — Although all pleasure is essentially good, and all pain essentially evil, it doth not thence necessarily follow, that in every single instance the one ought to be pursued, and the other to be avoided; but reason is to be employed in distinguishing and comparing the nature and degrees of each, that the result may be a wise choice of that which shall appear to be, upon the whole, good. That pleasure is the first good, appears from the inclination which every animal, from its first birth, discovers to pursue pleasure, and avoid pain; and is confirmed by the universal experience of mankind, who are incited to action by no other principle than the desire of avoiding pain, or obtaining pleasure. There are two kinds of pleasure: one consisting in a state of rest, in which both body and mind are undisturbed by any kind of pain; the other arising from an agreeable agitation of the senses, producing a correspondent emotion in the soul. It is upon the former of these that the enjoyment of life chiefly depends. Happiness may therefore be said to consist in bodily ease, and mental tranquillity, When pleasure is asserted to be the end of living, we are not then to understand that violent kind of delight or joy which arises from the gratification of the senses and passions, but merely that placid state of mind, which results from the absence of every cause of pain or uneasiness. Those pleasures, which arise from agitation, are not to be pursued as in themselves the end of living, but as means of arriving at that stable tranquillity, in which true happiness consists. It is the office of reason to confine the pursuit of pleasure within the limits of nature, in order to the attainment of that happy state, in which the body is free from every kind of pain, and the mind from all perturbation. This state must not, however, be conceived to be perfect in proportion as it is inactive and torpid, but in proportion as all the functions of life are quietly and pleasantly performed. A happy life neither resembles a rapid torrent, nor a standing pool, but is like a gentle stream, that glides smoothly and silently along.

"This happy state can only be obtained by a prudent care of the body, and a steady government of the mind. The diseases of the body are to be prevented by temperance, or cured by medicine, or rendered tolerable by patience. Against the diseases of the mind, philosophy provides sufficient antidotes. The instruments which it employs for this purpose are the virtues; the root of which, whence all the rest proceed, is prudence. This virtue comprehends the whole art of living discreetly, justly, and honorably, and is, in fact, the same thing with wisdom. It instructs men to free their understandings from the clouds of prejudice; to exercise temperance and fortitude in the government of themselves: and to practice justice towards others. Although pleasure, or happiness, which is the end of living, be superior to virtue, which is only the means, it is every one's interest to practice all the virtues; for in a happy life, pleasure can never be separated from virtue.

"A prudent man, in order to secure his tranquillity, will consult his natural disposition in the choice of his plan of life. If, for example, he be persuaded that he should be happier in a state of marriage than in celibacy, he ought to marry; but if he be convinced that matrimony would be an impediment to his happiness, he ought to remain single. In like manner, such persons as are naturally active, enterprising, and ambitious, or such as by the condition of their birth are placed in the way of civil offices, should accommodate themselves to their nature and situation, by engaging in public affairs; while such as are, from natural temper, fond of leisure and retirement, or, from experience or observation, are convinced that a life of public business would be inconsistent with their happiness, are unquestionably at liberty, except where particular circumstances call them to the service of their country, to pass their lives in obscure repose.

"Temperance is that discreet regulation of the desires and passions, by which we are enabled to enjoy pleasures without suffering any consequent inconvenience. They who maintain such a constant self-command, as never to be enticed by the prospect of present indulgence, to do that which will be productive of evil, obtain the truest pleasure by declining pleasure. Since, of desires some are natural and necessary; others natural, but not necessary; and others neither natural nor necessary, but the offspring of false judgment; it must be the office of temperance to gratify the first class, as far as nature requires: to restrain the second within the bounds of moderation; and, as to the third, resolutely to oppose, and, if possible, entirely repress them.

"Sobriety, as opposed to inebriety and gluttony, is of admirable use in teaching men that nature is satisfied with a little, and enabling them to content themselves with simple and frugal fare. Such a manner of living is conducive to the preservation of health: renders a man alert and active in all the offices of life; affords him an exquisite relish of the occasional varieties of a plentiful board, and prepares him to meet every reverse of fortune without the fear of want.

"Continence is a branch of temperance, which prevents the diseases, infamy, remorse, and punishment, to which those are exposed, who indulge themselves in unlawful amours. Music and poetry, which are often employed as incentives to licentious pleasure are to be cautiously and sparingly used.

"Gentleness, as opposed to an irrascible temper, greatly contributes to the tranquillity and happiness of life, by preserving the mind from perturbation, and arming it against the assaults of calumny and malice. A wise man, who puts himself under the government of reason, will be able to receive an injury with calmnese, and to treat the person who committed it with lenity; for he will rank injuries among the casual events of life, and will prudently reflect that he can no more stop the natural current of human passions, than he can curb the stormy winds. Refractory servants in a family should be chastised, and disorderly members of a state punished without wrath.

"Moderation, in the pursuit of honors or riches, is the only security against disappointment and vexation. A wise man, therefore, will prefer the simplicity of rustic life to the magnificence of courts. Future events a wise man will consider as uncertain, and will, therefore, neither suffer himself to be elated with confident expectation, nor to be depressed by doubt and despair: for both are equally destructive of tranquillity. It will contribute to the enjoyment of life, to consider death as the perfect termination of a happy life, which it becomes us to close like satisfied guests, neither regretting the past, nor anxious for the future.

"Fortitude, the virtue which enables us to endure pain, and to banish fear, is of great use in producing tranquillity. Philosophy instructs us to pay homage to the gods, not through hope or fear, but from veneration of their superior nature. It moreover enables us to conquer the fear of death, by teaching us that it is no proper object of terror; since, whilst we are, death is not, and when death arrives, we are not: so that it neither concerns the living nor the dead. The only evils to be apprehended are bodily pain, and distress of mind. Bodily pain it becomes a wise man to endure with patience and firmness; because, if it be slight, it may easily be borne; and if it be intense, it cannot last long. Mental distress commonly arises not from nature, but from opinion; a wise man will therefore arm himself against this kind of suffering, by reflecting that the gifts of fortune, the loss of which he may be inclined to deplore, were never his own, but depended upon circumstances which he could not command. If, therefore, they happen to leave him, he will endeavor, as soon as possible, to obliterate the remembrance of them, by occupying his mind in pleasant contemplation, and engaging in agreeable avocations.

"Justice respects man as living in society, and is the common bond without which no society can subsist. This virtue, like the rest, derives its value from its tendency to promote the happiness of life. Not only is it never injurious to the man who practices it, but nourishes-in his mind calm reflections and pleasant hopes; whereas it is impossible that the mind in which injustice dwells, should not be full of disquietude.—Since it is impossible that iniquitous actions should promote the enjoyment of life, as much as remorse of conscience, legal penalties, and public disgrace, must increase its troubles, every one who follows the dictates of sound reason, will practice the virtues of justice, equity, and fidelity. In society, the necessity of the mutual exercise of justice, in order to the common enjoyment of the gifts of nature, is the ground of those laws by which it is prescribed. It is the interest of every individual in a state to conform to the laws of justice; for by injuring no one, and rendering to every man his due, he contributes his part towards the preservation of that society, upon the perpetuity of which his own safety depends. Nor ought any one to think that he is at liberty to violate the rights of his fellow citizens, provided he can do it securely; for he who has committed an unjust action can never be certain that it will not be discovered; and however successfully he may conceal it from others, this will avail him little, since he cannot conceal it from himself. In different communities, different laws may be instituted, according to the circumstances of the people who compose them. Whatever is thus prescribed is to be considered as a rule of justice, so long as the society shall judge the observance of it to be for the benefit of the whole. But whenever any rule of conduct is found upon experience not to be conducive to the public good, being no longer useful, it should no longer be prescribed.

"Nearly allied to justice are the virtues of beneficence, compassion, gratitude, piety, and friendship.—He who confers benefits upon others, procures to himself the satisfaction of seeing the stream of plenty spreading around him from the fountain of his beneficence; at the same time, he enjoys the pleasure of being esteemed by others. The exercise of gratitude, filial affection, and reverence for the gods, is necessary, in order to avoid the hatred and contempt of all men. Friendships are contracted for the sake of mutual benefit; but by degrees they ripen into such disinterested attachment, that they are continued without any prospect of advantage. Between friends there is a kind of league, that each will love the other as himself. A true friend will partake of the wants and sorrows of his friend, as if they were his own; if he be in want, he will relieve him; if he be in prison, he will visit him; if he be sick, he will come to him; nay-situations may occur, in which he would not scruple to die for him. It cannot then be doubted, that friendship is one of the most useful means of procuring a secure, tranquil, and happy life."

No man will, we think, find anything in the foregoing summary to justify the foul language used against Epicurus, and his moral philosophy; the secret is in the physical doctrines, and this secret is, that Epicurus was actually, if not intentionally, an Atheist. The following is a summary of his physical doctrine:—

"Nothing can ever spring from nothing, nor can anything ever return to nothing. The universe always existed, and will always remain; for there is nothing into which it can be changed. There is nothing in Nature, nor can anything be conceived, besides body and space. Body is that which possesses the properties of bulk, figure, resistance, and gravity: it is this alone which can touch or be touched. Space is the region which is, or may be, occupied by body, and which affords it an opportunity of moving freely. That there are bodies in the universe is attested by the senses. That there is also space is evident; since otherwise bodies would have no place in which to move or exist, and of their existence and motion we have the certain proof of perception. Besides these, no third nature can be conceived; for such a nature must either have bulk and solidity, or want them; that is, it must either be body or space: this does not, however, preclude the existence of qualities, which have no subsistence but in the body to which they belong.

"The universe, consisting of body and space, is infinite, for it has no limits. Bodies are infinite in multitude; space is infinite in magnitude. The term above, or beneath, high or low, cannot be properly applied to infinite space. The universe is to be conceived as immoveable, since beyond it there is no place into which it can move; and as eternal and immutable, since it is neither liable to increase nor decrease, to production nor decay. Nevertheless, the parts of the universe are in motion, and are subject to change.

"All bodies consist of parts, of which they are composed, and into which they may be resolved; and these parts are either themselves simple principles, or may be resolved into such. These first principles, or simple atoms, are divisible by no force, and, therefore, must be immutable. This may also be inferred from the uniformity of Nature, which could not be preserved if its principles were not certain and consistent. The existence of such atoms is evident, since it is impossible that anything which exists should be reduced to nothing. A finite body cannot consist of parts infinite, either in magnitude or number; divisibility of bodies *ad infinitum*, is therefore conceivable. All atoms are of the same nature, or differ in no essential qualities—From their different effects upon the senses, it appears, however, that they differ in magnitude, figure, and weight. Atoms exist in every possible variety of figure—round, oval, conical, cubical, sharp, hooked, etc. But in every shape, they are, on account of their solidity, infrangible, or incapable of actual division.

"Gravity must be an essential property of atoms; for since they are perpetually in motion, or making an effort to move, they must be moved by an internal impulse, which may be called gravity.

"The principle of gravity, that internal energy which is the cause of all motion, whether simple or complex, being essential to the primary corpuscles or atoms, they must have been incessantly and from eternity in actual motion."

Epicurus, who boasts that he was an inquirer and a philosopher in his thirteenth year, was scarcely likely to bow his mind to the mythology of his country. The man who, when he was but a schoolboy, insisted upon an answer to the question, "Whence came chaos?" could hardly be expected to receive as admitted facts the fabulous legends as to Jupiter and the other gods. His theology is, however, in some respects, obscure, and unintelligible; for while he zealously opposed the popular fables, which men misname God-ideas, he at the same time admitted the existence of material gods, whom he placed in the intervals between the infinite worlds, where they passed a life undisturbed by aught, and enjoyed a happiness which does not admit of augmentation. These inactive gods play a strange part in the system of Epicurus; and it is asserted by many that these extraordinary conceptions of Deity were put forward by the philosopher to screen him from the consequences attaching to a charge of Atheism. Dr. Heinrich Ritter, who does not seem very friendly disposed towards Epicurus, or his philosophy, repudiates this notion, and argues Epicurus was not in truth an Atheist, and alleges that it was a mere pretence on his part; and that from his very theory of knowledge the existence of gods could be deduced. This has been much litigated, (vide Electric Review for 1806, p. 606.) It is quite evident that Epicurus neither regarded "the gods" in the capacity of Creators, controllers, or rulers, so that his Theism (if it be Theism) twas not of a very superstitious character. The God who neither created man, nor exercised any influence whatever over his actions or thinkings, could have but little to do with man at all.

If we attempt to review the whole of the teachings of Epicurus, we and they are defective and imperfect in many respects, and necessarily so. We say necessarily so, because the imperfect science of the day limited the array of facts presented to the philosopher, and narrowed the base upon which he was to erect his system. We must expect, therefore, to find the structure weak in many points, because it was too large for the foundation; but we are not, therefore, to pass it on one side, and without further notice; it should rather be our task to lay good, wide, and sure foundations, On which to build up a system, and develope a method, really having, for its end, the happiness of mankind. We live 2000 years later than the Athenian philosopher.—In those 2000 years many facts have been dragged out of "the circle of the unknown and unused." Astronomy, geology, physiology, psychology—all except theology are belter understood. Men pretend they are searching after happiness, and where do they try to find it? Not here amongst the known, but in the possible hereafter amongst the unknowable. How do they try to find it? Not by the aid of the known, not by the light of facts, gathered in years of toil, and sanctified by the blood of some of the noblest of truth's noble martyrs; no—but in the darkness of the unknown and unknowable; in the next world. Question the men who fly to theology for happiness, and they will tell you that the most learned of the theologians sum up their knowledge in the word "incomprehensible." Is it wonderful that their happiness is somewhat marred "here" by quarrels as to the true definition of "hereafter?" G. H. Lewes says, of the Epicurean philosophy, "that the attempt failed because the basis was not broad enough. The Epicureans are therefore to be regarded as men who ventured on a great problem, and failed because they only saw part of the truth." And we might add that Christianity, and every other religious "anity," fails, because the professors expect to obtain happiness in the next life, and neglect to work for it in the present one.

Epicurus says, no life can be pleasant except a virtuous life; and he charges you to avoid whatever maybe calculated to create disquiet in the mind, or give pain to the body. The Rev. Habbakuk Smilenot, of little Bethel, says that all pleasure here, is vanity and vexation in the hereafter; and he charges you to continually worry and harass your mind with fears that you may be condemned to hell, and doubts whether you will be permitted to enter heaven. Which is the best, the philosophy of Epicurus, or the theology of Smilenof?

G. H. Lewes says:—"Epicureanism, in leading man to a correct appreciation of the moral end of his existence, in showing him how to be truly happy, has to combat with many obstructions which hide from him the real road of life. These obstructions are his illusions, his prejudices, his errors, his ignorance. This ignorance is of two kinds, as Victor Cousin points out; ignorance of the laws of the external world, which creates absurd superstitions, and troubles the mind with false fears and false hopes. Hence the necessity of some knowledge of physics." (We can scarcely blame Epicurus that he was not in advance of his time, as far as the physical sciences are concerned, and therefore imparted an imperfect system of physics. We must, with our improved knowledge, ourselves remove the obstruction.) "The second kind of ignorance is that of the nature of man. Socrates had taught men to regard their own nature as the great object of investigation; and this lesson Epicurus willingly gave ear to.—But man does not interrogate his own nature out of simple curiosity, or simple erudition; he studies his nature in order that he may improve it; he learns the extent of his capacities, in order that he may properly direct them. The aim, therefore, of all such inquiries must be happiness."

We may add that the result of all such inquiries will be happiness, if the inquirer will but base his investigation and experiments upon facts. Let him understand that, as he improves the circumstances which surround him, so will he advance himself, becoming happier, and making his fellows happy also. Remember the words of Epicurus, and seek that pleasure for yourself which appears the most durable, and attended with the greatest pleasure to your fellow men.

"I"

ZENO, THE STOIC

In the previous number we gave a short sketch of the opinions of Epicurus. In this we shall deal with the founder of a rival sect—the Stoics. Amongst the disciples and students in the Stoic schools have been many illustrious names, and not the least worthy is the name with which we are now dealing.

Zeno was born at Cittius, a small maritime town in the Island of Cyprus. This place having been originally peopled by a colony of Phoenicians, Zeno is sometimes called a Phoenician; but at the period when he flourished, it was chiefly inhabited by Greeks. The date of his birth is uncertain, but must have been about the year B.C. 362. His father was a merchant, and Zeno appears to have been, in the early part of his life, engaged in mercantile pursuits. He received a very liberal education from his father, whom, we are told, perceived in his son a strong inclination for philosophical studies, and who purchased for Zeno the writings of the Socratic philosophers; which were studied with avidity, and which undoubtedly exercised a considerable influence over his future thinkings. When about thirty years of age, he made a trading voyage from Cittius to Athens, with a very valuable cargo of Phoenician purple, but was unfortunately shipwrecked on the coast of Greece, and the whole of his freight destroyed. It is supposed that this severe loss, which must have considerably reduced his means, materially influenced Zeno, and induced him to embrace the tenets of the Cynics, whose leading principle was a contempt of riches. We are told that upon is first arrival in Athens, he went into the shop of a bookseller, and took up, by accident, a volume of the "Commentaries of Xenophon." Alter reading a few pages, Zeno was so much delighted with the work, that he asked the bookseller to direct him where he might meet such men as the author? Crates, the Cynic philosopher, passed by at the time, and the bookseller said, "Follow that man!" He did so, and after listening to several of his discourses, was so pleased with the doctrines of the Cynics, that he became a disciple. He did not long remain attached to the Cynic school—their peculiar manners were too gross for him; and his energetic and inquiring mind was too much cramped by that indifference to all scientific investigation which was one of their leading characteristics. He therefore sought instruction elsewhere, and Stilpo, of Megara, became his teacher, from whom he acquired the art of disputation, in which he afterwards became so proficient. The Cynics were displeased at his following other philosophy, and we are told that Crates attempted to drag him by force out of the school of Stilpo, on which Zeno said, "You may seize my body, but Stilpo has laid hold of my mind." The Megaric doctrine was, however, insufficient. Zeno was willing to learn all that Stilpo could teach, but having learned all, his restless and insatiable appetite for knowledge required more, and after an attendance of several years upon the lectures of Stilpo, he passed over to the expositors of Plato, Xenocrates, and Polemo. The latter philosopher appears to have penetrated Zeno's design in attending the various schools—*i.e.*, to collect materials from various quarters for a new system of his own; and when he came to the school, Polemo said, "I am no stranger, Zeno, to your Phoenician arts; I perceive that your design is to creep slily into my garden, and steal away my fruit." After twenty years of study, having mastered the tenets of the various schools, Zeno determined to become the founder of a sect himself. In accordance with this determination, he opened a school in a public portico, called the Painted Porch, from the pictures of Polygnotus, and other eminent painters, with which it was adorned. This portico became famous in Athens, and was called (Stoa)—-the Porch. From this Stoa the school derived its name, the students being called the Stoics. Zeno was a subtle reasoner, and exceedingly popular. He taught a strict system of morals and exhibited a pleasing picture of moral discipline in his own life. As a man, his character appears deserving of the highest respect. He became exceedingly respected and revered at Athens for the probity and severity of bis life and manners, and consistency thereof with his doctrine. He possesed so large a share of public esteem that the Athenians decreed him a golden crown, and on account of his approved integrity, deposited the keys of their citadel in his hands. Antigouus Gonates, King of Macedon, was a constant attendant at his lectures whilst at Athens, and when that monarch returned, he earnestly invited Zeno to his court. During the philosopher's lifetime, the Athenians erected a statue of brass as a mark of the estimation in which they held him.

Zeno lived to the extreme age of ninety-eight, when, as he was leaving, his school one day, he fell and broke his finger. The consciousness of his infirmity afflicted him so much, that he exclaimed, "Why am I thus importuned? Earth, I obey thy summons!" and immediately going home, he put his affairs in order, and strangled himself. In person, Zeno was tall and slender; his brow was furrowed with thought; and this, with his long and close application to study, gave a tinge of severity to his aspect. Although of a feeble constitution, he preserved his health by his great abstemiousness, his diet consisting of figs, bread, and honey. He was plain and modest in his dress and habits and very frugal in all his expenses, showing the same respect for the poor as for the rich, and conversing as freely with the slave as he did with the king. Independent in spirit, he broke off all communication with his friend Democharis, because that person had offered to procure a gratuity for Zeno from the King of Macedon. His system appears to have been little more than a collection from his various lessons of whatever was most in unison with his peculiar habit of thought, and an attempt to reconcile and combine in one system the various elements of different theories. Taking from so many schools various portions of their doctrine, he seems to have provoked the antagonism of many of his contemporaries, and several philosophers of learning and ability employed their eloquence to diminish the growing influence of the new school. Towards the close of his life, he found a powerful antagonist in the person of Epicurus, and the Epicureans and Stoics have since treated each other as rival sects. Zeno's school appears to have been generally a resort for the poor, and it was a common joke amongst his adversaries, that poverty was the charm for which he was indebted for his scholars. The list of his disciples, however, contains the names of some very rich and powerful men, who may have regarded the Stoic theory as a powerful counter-agent to the growing effeminacy of the age. After Zeno's death, the Athenians, at the request of Antigonus, erected a monument to his memory, in the Ceramicura.

From the particulars which have been related concerning Zeno, it will not be difficult to perceive what kind of influence his circumstances and character must have had upon his philosophical system. If his doctrines be diligently compared with the history of his life, it will appear, that having attended upon many eminent preceptors, and being intimately conversant with their opinions, he compiled, out of their various tenets, an heterogeneous system, on the credit of which he assumed to himself the title of the founder of a new sect.... The dialectic arts which Zeno learned in the school of Diodorus Chronus, he did not fail to apply to the support of his own system, and to communicate to bis followers. As to the moral doctrine of the Cynic sect, to which Zeno strictly adhered to the last, there can be no doubt that he transferred it almost without alloy, into his own school. In morals, the principal difference between the Cynics and the Stoics was, that the former disdained the cultivation of nature, the latter affected to rise above it. On the subject of physics, Zeno received his doctrine through the channel of the Platonic school, as will fully appear from a careful comparison of their respective systems. The Stoic philosophy, being in this manner of heterogeneous origin, it necessarily partook of the several systems of which it was composed. The idle quibbles, jejune reasonings, and imposing sophisms, which so justly exposed the schools of the dialectic philosophers to ridicule, found their way into the Porch, where much time was wasted, and much ingenuity thrown away, upon questions of no importance. Cicero censures the Stoics for encouraging in their schools a barren kind of disputation, and employing themselves in determining trifling questions, in which the disputants can have no interest, and which, at the close, leave them neither wiser nor better. And that this censure, is not, as some modern advocates for Stoicism have maintained, a mere calumny, but grounded upon fact, sufficiently appears from what is said by the ancients, particularly by Sextus Empiricus, concerning the logic of the Stoics. Seneca, who was himself a Stoic, candidly acknowledges this. It may, perhaps, be thought surprising that philosophers, who affected so much gravity and wisdom, should condescend to such trifling occupations. But it must be considered, that, at this time, a fondness for subtle disputations so generally prevailed in Greece, that excellence in the arts of reasoning and sophistry was a sure path to fame. The Stoics, with whom vanity was unquestionably a ruling passion, were ambitious for this kind of reputation. Hence it was that they engaged with so much vehemence in verbal contests, and that they largely contributed towards the confusion, instead of the improvement, of science, by substituting vague and ill-defined terms in the room of accurate conceptions. The moral part of the Stoical philosophy, in like manner, partook of the defects of its origin. It may be as justly objected against the Stoics as the Cynics, that they assumed an artificial severity of manners, and a tone of virtue above the condition of a man. Their doctrine of moral wisdom was an ostentatious display of words, in which little regard was paid to nature and reason. It professed to raise human nature to a degree of perfection before unknown; but its real effect was, merely to amuse the ear, and captivate the fancy, with fictions which can never be realized.... The extravagancies and absurdities of the Stoical philosophy may also be in some measure ascribed to the vehement contests which subsisted between Zeno and the Academics on the one hand, and between him and Epicurus on the other. For, not only did these disputes give rise to many of the dogmas of Stoicism, but led Zeno and his followers, in the warmth of controversy, to drive their arguments to the utmost extremity, and to express themselves with much greater confidence than they would probably otherwise have done. This is, perhaps, the true reason why so many extravagant notions are ascribed to the Stoics, particularly upon the subject of morals. Whilst Epicurus taught his followers to seek happiness in tranquillity, Zeno imagined his wise man, not only free from all sense of pleasure, but void of all passions and emotions, and capable of being happy in the midst of torture. That he might avoid the position taken by the Epicureans, he had recourse to a moral institution, which bore indeed the lofty front of wisdom, but which was elevated far above the condition and powers of human nature. The natural disposition of Zeno, and his manner of life, had, moreover, no inconsiderable influence in fixing the peculiar character of his philosophy. By nature severe and morose, and constitutionally inclined to reserve and melancholy, he early cherished this habit by submitting to the austere ami rigid discipline of the Cynics. Those qualities which he conceived to be meritorious in himself, and which he found to conciliate the admiration of mankind, he naturally transferred to his imaginary character of a wise or perfect man.

In order to form an accurate judgment concerning the doctrine of the Stoics, besides a careful attention to the particulars already enumerated, it will be necessary to guard with the utmost caution against two errors, into which several writers have fallen. Great care should be taken, in the first place, not to judge of the doctrine of the Stoics from words and sentiments, detached from the general system, but to consider them as they stand, related to the whole train of premises and conclusions.... The second caution is, not to confound the genuine doctrines of Zeno, and other ancient fathers of this sect, with the glosses of the later Stoics.... Out of the many proofs of this change, which might be adduced, we shall select one, which is the more worthy of notice, as it has occasioned many disputes among the learned. The doctrine we mean is that concerning fate. This doctrine, according to Zeno and Chrysippus, implies an eternal and immutable series of causes and effects, within which all events are included, and to which the Deity himself is subject: whereas, the later Stoics, changing the term fate into the Providence of God, discoursed with great plausibility on this subject, but still in reality retained the ancient doctrine of universal fate. From this example, a judgment may be formed concerning the necessity of using some caution, in appealing to the writings of Seneca, Antoninus, and Epictetus, as authorities, in determining what were the original doctrines of the Stoic philosophers.

Concerning philosophy in general, the doctrine of the Stoics was, that wisdom consists in the knowledge of things divine and human; that philosophy is such an exercise of the mind as produces wisdom; that in this exercise consists the nature of virtue; and consequently, that virtue is a term of extensive meaning, comprehending the right employment of the mind in reasoning, in the study of nature, and in morals. The wisdom of the Stoics is either progressive, through several stages; or perfect, when every weakness if subdued, and every error corrected, without the possibility of a relapse into folly, or vice, or of being again enslaved by any passion, or afflicted by any calamity. With Socrates and the Cynics, Zeno represented virtue as the only true wisdom; but being disposed to extend the pursuits of his wise man into the regions of speculation and science, he gave, after his usual manner, a new signification to an old term, and comprehended the exercise of the understanding in the search of truth, as well as the government of the appetites and passions, under the general term, virtue. The great importance of the united exercise of the intellectual and active powers of the mind, are thus beautifully asserted by the philosophical emperor:—"Let every one endeavor so to think and act, that his contemplative and active faculties may at the same time be going on towards perfection. His clear conceptions, and certain knowledge, will then produce within him an entire confidence in himself, unperceived perhaps by others, though not affectedly concealed, which will give a simplicity and dignity to his character; for he will at all times be able to judge, concerning the several objects which come before him, what is their real nature, what place they hold in the universe, how long they are by nature fitted to last, of what materials they are composed, by whom they may be possessed, and who is able to bestow them, or take them away." The sum of the definitions and rules given by the Stoics concerning logic is this:—Logic is either rhetorical or dialectic. Rhetorical logic is the art of reasoning and discoursing on those subjects which require a diffuse kind of declamation. Dialectic is the art of close argumentation in the form of disputation or dialogue. The former resembles an open, the latter, a closed hand.—Rhetoric is of three kinds, deliberative, judicial, and demonstrative. The dialectic art is the instrument of knowledge, as it enables a man to distinguish truth from error, and certainty from bare probability. This art considers things as expressed by words, and words themselves. External things are perceived by a certain impression, made either upon some parts of the brain, or upon the percipient faculty, which may be called an image, since it is impressed upon the mind, like the image of a seal upon wax.

This image is commonly accompanied with a belief of the reality of the thing perceived; but not necessarily, since it does not accompany every image, but those only which are not attended with any evidence of deception. Where only the image is perceived by itself, the thing is apprehensible; where it is acknowledged and approved as the image of some real thing, the impression is called apprehension, because the object is apprehended by the mind as a body is grasped by the hand. Such apprehension, if it will bear the examination of reason, is knowledge; if it is not examined, it is mere opinion; if it will not bear this examination, it is misapprehension. The senses, corrected by reason, give a faithful report; not by affording a perfect apprehension of the entire nature of things, but by leaving no room to doubt of their reality. Nature has furnished us with these apprehensions, as the elements of knowledge, whence further conceptions are raised in the mind, and a way is opened for the investigations of reason. Some images are sensible, or received immediately through the senses; others rational, which are perceived only in the mind. These latter are called notions, or ideas. Some images are probable, to which the mind assents without hesitation; others improbable, to which it does not readily assent; and others doubtful, where it is not entirely perceived, whether they are true or false. True images are those which arise from things really existing, and agree with them. False images, or phantasms, are immediately derived from no real object. Images are apprehended by immediate perception, through the senses, as when we see a man; consequentially, by likeness, as when from a portrait we apprehend the original; by composition, as when, by compounding a horse and man, we acquire the image of a Centaur; by augmentation, as in the image of a Cyclops; or by diminution, as in that of a pigmy. Judgment is employed either in determining, concerning particular things, or concerning general propositions. In judging of things we make use of some one of our senses, as a common criterion or measure of apprehension, by which we judge whether a thing is, or is not; or whether or not it exists with certain properties; or we apply to the thing, concerning which a judgment is to be formed, some artificial measure, as a balance, a rule, etc., or we call in other peculiar measures to determine things not perceptible by the senses. In judging of general propositions, we make use of our pre-conceptions, or universal principles, as *criteria*, or measures of judgment. The first impressions from the senses produce in the mind an involuntary emotion; but a wise man afterwards deliberately examines them, that he may know whether they be true or false, and assents to, or rejects them, as the evidence which offers itself to his understanding appears sufficient or insufficient. This assent, or approbation, will indeed be as necessarily given, or withheld, according to the ultimate state of the proofs which are adduced, as the scales of a balance will sink or rise, according to the weights which are placed upon them; but while the vulgar give immediate credit to the reports of the senses, wise men suspend their assent, till they have deliberately examined the nature of things, and carefully estimated the weight of evidence. The mind of man is originally like a blank leaf, wholly without characters, but capable of receiving any. The impressions which are made upon it, by means of the senses, remain in the memory, after the objects which occasioned them are removed; a succession of these continued impressions, made by similar, objects, produces experience; and hence arises permanent notions, opinions, and knowledge. Even universal principles are originally formed by experience from sensible images. All men agree in their common notions or preconceptions; disputes only arise concerning the application of these to particular cases.

Let us pass on to the Stoical doctrine concerning nature. According to Zeno and his followers, there existed from eternity a dark and confused chaos, in which was contained the first principles of all future beings. This chaos being at length arranged, and emerging into variable forms, became the world, as it now subsists. The world, or nature, is that whole which comprehends all things, and of which all thing are parts and members. The universe, though one whole, contains two principles, distinct from elements, one passive, the other active. The passive principle is pure matter without qualities; the active principle is reason, or God. This is the fundamental doctrine of the Stoics concerning nature....The Stoical system teaches, that both the active and passive principles in nature are corporeal, since whatever acts or suffers must be so. The efficient cause, or God, is pure ether, or fire, inhabiting the exterior surface of the heavens, where every thing which is divine is placed. This ethereal substance, of divine fire, comprehends all the vital principles by which individual beings are necessarily produced, and contains the forms of things, which from the highest regions of the universe, are diffused through every other part of nature. Seneca, indeed, calls God incorporeal reason; but by this term he can only mean to distinguish the divine ethereal substance from gross bodies; for, according to the Stoics, whatever has a substantial existence is corporeal; nothing is incorporeal, except that infinite vacuum which surrounds the universe; even mind and voice are corporeal, and, in like manner, Deity. Matter, or the passive principle, in the Stoical system, is destitute of all qualities, but ready to receive any form, inactive, and without motion, unless moved by some external cause. The con =trary principle, or the ethereal operative fire, being active, and capable of producing all things from matter, with consummate skill, according to the forms which it contains, although in its nature corporeal, considered in opposition to gross and sluggish matter, or to the elements, is said to be immaterial and spiritual. For want of carefully attending to the preceding distinction, some writers have been so far imposed upon, by the bold innovations of the Stoics in the use of terms, as to inter from the appellations which they sometimes apply to the Deity, that they conceived him to be strictly and properly incorporeal. The truth appears to be, that, as they sometimes spoke of the soul of man, a portion of the Divinity, as an exceedingly rare and subtle body, and sometimes as a warm or fiery spirit,* so they spoke of the Deity as corporeal, considered as distinct from the incorporeal vacuum, or infinite space; but as spiritual, considered in opposition to gross and inactive matter. They taught, indeed, that God is underived, incorruptible, and eternal, possessed of intelligence, good and perfect, the efficient cause of all the peculiar qualities or forms of things; and the constant preserver and governor of the world; and they described the Deity under many noble images, and in the most elevated language. The hymn of Cleanthes, in particular, is justly admired for the grandeur of its sentiments, and the sublimity of its diction. But if in reading these descriptions, we hastily associate with them modern conceptions of Deity, and neglect to recur to the leading principles of the sect, we shall be led into fundamental misapprehensions of the true doctrine of Stoicism. For according to this sect. God and matter are alike underived and eternal, and God is the former of the universe in no other sense than as he has been the necessary efficient cause, by which motion and form have been impressed upon matter.

What notions the Stoics entertained of God sufficiently appears from the single opinion of his finite nature; an opinion which necessarily followed from the notion that he is only a part of a spherical, and therefore a finite universe. On the doctrine of divine providence, which was one of the chief points upon which the Stoics disputed with the Epicureans, much is written, and with great strength and elegance, by Seneca, Epictetus, and other later Stoics. But we are not to judge of the genuine and original doctrine of this sect from the discourses of writers who had probably corrupted their language on this subject, by visiting the Christian school. The only way to form an accurate judgment of their opinions concerning Providence, is to compare their popular language upon this head with their general system, and explain the former consistently with the fundamental principles of the latter.

If this be fairly done, it will appear that the agency of Deity is, according to the Stoics, nothing more than the active motion of a celestial ether, or fire, possessed of intelligence, which at first gave form to the shapeless mass of gross matter, and being always essentially united to the visible world by the same necessary agency, preserves its order and harmony.

The Stoic idea of Providence is, not that of a being, wholly independent of matter, freely directing and governing all things, but that of a necessary chain of causes and effects, arising from the action of a power, which is itself a part of the existence which it regulates, and which equally with that existence is subject to the immutable law of necessity. Providence, in the Stoic creed, is only another name for absolute necessity, or fate, to which God and matter, or the universe, which consists of both, is immutably subject. The rational, efficient, and active principle in nature, the Stoics called by various names: Nature, fate, Jupiter, God.

"What is nature," says Seneca, "but God; the divine reason, inherent in the whole universe, and in all its parts? or you may call him, if you please, the author of all things."

And again: "Whatever appellations imply celestial power and energy, may be justly applied to God; his names may properly be as numerous as his offices," The term nature, when it is at all distinguished in the Stoic system from God, denotes not a separate agent, but that order of things which is necessarily produced by his perpetual agency. Since the active principle of nature is comprehended within the world, and with matter makes one whole, it necessarily follows that God penetrates, pervades, and animates matter, and the things which are formed from it; or, in other words, that he is the soul of the universe.

The universe is, according to Zeno and his followers, "a sentient and animated being." Nor was this a new tenet, but, in some sort, the doctrine of all antiquity. Pythagoras, Heraclitus, and after these, Zeno, taking it for granted that there is no real existence which is not corporeal, conceived nature to be one whole, consisting of a subtle ether and gross matter, the former the active, the latter the passive principle, as essentially united as the soul and body of man that is, they supposed God, with respect to nature, to be, not a co-existing, but an informing principle.

Concerning the second principle in the universe, matter, and concerning the visible world, the doctrine of the Stoics is briefly this:—Matter is the first essence of all things, destitute of, but capable of receiving, qualities. Considered universally, it is an eternal whole, which neither increases nor decreases. Considérée! with respect to its parts, it is capable of increase or diminution, of collision and separation, and is perpetually changing. Bodies are continually tending towards dissolution; matter always remains the same. Matter is not infinite, but finite, being circumscribed by the limits of the world; but its parts are infinitely divisible. The world is spherical in its form; and is surrounded by an infinite vacuum. The action of the divine nature upon matter first produced the element of moisture, and then the other elements, fire, air, and earth, of which all bodies are composed. Air and fire have essential levity, or tend towards the exterior surface of the world; earth and water have essential gravity, or tend towards the centre. All the elements are capable of reciprocal conversion; air passing into fire, or into water; earth into air and water; but there is this essential difference among the elements, that fire and air have within themselves a principle of motion, while water and earth are merely passive.... The world, including the whole of nature, God and matter, subsisted from eternity, and will for ever subsist; but the present regular frame of nature had a beginning, and will have an end. The parts tend towards a dissolution, but the whole remains immutably the same. The world is liable to destruction from the prevalence of moisture, or of dryness; the former producing a universal inundation, the latter a universal conflagration. These succeed each other in nature as regularly as winter and summer. When the universal inundation takes place, the whole surface of the earth is covered with water, and all animal life is destroyed; after which, nature is renewed and subsists as before, till the element of fire, becoming prevalent in its turn, dries up all the moisture, converts every substance into its own nature, and at last, by a universal conflagration, reduces the world to its pristine state. At this period, all material forms are lost in one chaotic mass: all animated nature is re-united to the Deity, and nature again exists in its original form, as one whole, consisting of God and matter. From this chaotic state, however, it again emerges, by the energy of the efficient principle, and gods, and men, and all the forms of regulated nature, are renewed, and to be dissolved and renewed in endless succession. The above is collated from Ritter, Enfield, and Lewes, as a specimen of one of the earlier phases of Freethought. Freethought as then expressed had many faults and flaws, but it has grown better every day, extending and widening its circle of utterance, and we hope that it will continue to do so.

"I."

MATTHEW TINDAL

It is easy to mark the progress of the age by recurring to the history of past Freethinkers. Bishops, established and dissenting, are now repeating the parts the old Deiste played. *They* were sadly treated for setting the example, modern divines follow with applause.

Matthew Tindal was an example of this. He labored to establish religion on the foundation of Reason and Nature. It was to be expected that Christians would be pleased at efforts which would have no effect but to strengthen its foundations. The effort was met by reprobation, and resented as an injury. It is but a just retaliation that believers should now have to establish in vain that evidence they once denounced.

Matthew Tindal was an English Deistical writer, who was born at Beer-Terres, in Devonshire, 1656.—His father, it appears, was a clergyman, who held the living of Beer-Terres, presented to him by the University of Cambridge, in the time of the Civil Wars.—Young Matthew was educated at Oxford, where at twenty-eight he took the degree of LL.D. Matthew Tindal, LL. D., was early tossed about by the winds of doctrine. First he embraced Romanism: afterwards he became a Protestant. Then politics interested him, and he engaged in controversy on the side of William III. He was appointed Commissioner of a Court for Trying Foreigners. In 1693 he published an essay on the Law of Nations When fifty-four, in 1710, he entered so vigorously into theological controversy, arising out of Trinitarian criticism, that his marked satire led to his books being condemned by the House of Commons, and burnt by the hangman. He resented this indignity by a spirited attack on the dominant priestly party in his "High Church Catechism," and he also wrote in defence of philosophical necessity. But his most notable work was the performance of his old age, his "Christianity as Old as the Creation: or, the Gospel, a Republication of the Religion of Nature." This was produced in his seventy-third year. He was attacked in Reply by Bishop Waterland. It is generally agreed that in point of good spirit and good temper the Bishop was far inferior to the Deist. Dr. Conyers Middleton, says Thomas Cooper, in his brief sketch of Tindal, appeared in defence of Tindal in a "Letter to Dr. Waterland," whom he condemned for the shallowness of his answer to Tindal, and boldly and frankly admitted that the Freethinker was right in asserting that the Jews borrowed some of their ceremonies and customs from Egypt; that allegory was, in some cases, employed in the Scriptures, where common readers took the relation for fact; and, that the Scriptures are *not* of "absolute and universal inspiration." The following sentence, which will be found in this "Letter" of Dr. Conyers Middleton, does honor to his name:—"If religion consists in depreciating moral duties and depressing natural reason; if the duty of it be to hate and persecute for a different way of thinking where the best and wisest have never agreed—then. I declare myself an Infidel, and to have no share in that religion." Matthew Tindal died at his house in Coldbath Fields, of the stone, 1773, aged seventy-seven. * Rysbrach, the famous statuary, took a model of him.

> * *Julian Hibbert gives 1656-7: Dr. Beard, 1556; Thomas*
> *Cooper, 1657, as the year of Tindal's birth. All agree that*
> *he died 1733—he was therefore seventy-six or seventy-seven*
> *at the time of his death.*

Tindal opens his great work thus:—"The author makes no apology for writing on a subject of the last importance; and which, as far as I can find, has no where been so fully treated: he builds nothing on a thing so uncertain as tradition, which differs in most countries; and of which, in all countries, the bulk of mankind are incapable of judging; but thinks he has laid down such plain and evident rules, as may enable men of the meanest capacity, to distinguish between religion and superstition; and has represented the former in every part so beautiful, so amiable, and so strongly affecting, that they, who in the least reflect, must be highly in love with it; and easily perceive, that their duty and happiness are inseparable."

The character of the performance will be seen from a few of the propositions he maintains:—

"That God, at all times, has given mankind sufficient means of knowing whatever he requires of them.

"That the religion of nature consists in observing those things, which our reason, by considering the nature of God and man, and the relation we stand in to him, and one another, demonstrates to be our duty; and that those things are plain; and likewise what they are.

"That the perfection and happiness of all rational beings, supreme as well as subordinate, consist in living up to the dictates of their nature.

"That God requires nothing for his own sake; no, not the worship we are to render him, nor the faith we are to have in him.

"That the not adhering to those notions reason dictates, concerning the nature of God, has been the occasion of all superstition, and those innumerable mischiefs, that mankind, on the account of religion, have done either to themselves, or one another.

"The bulk of mankind, by their reason, must be able to distinguish between religion and superstition; otherwise they can never extricate themselves from that superstition they chance to be educated in."

Tindal deals with the question of the obscurity of Revelation in these terms, sufficiently salient to alarm the very proper divines of that day:—

"Had God, from time to time, spoken to all mankind in their several languages, and his words had miraculously conveyed the same ideas to all persons; yet he could not speak more plainly than he has done by the things themselves, and the relation which reason shows there is between them. Nay, since it is impossible in any book, or books, that a particular rule could be given for every case, we must even then have had recourse to the light of nature to teach us our duty in most cases; especially considering the numberless circumstances which attend us, and which, perpetually varying, may make the same actions, according as men are differently affected by them, either good or bad. And I may add, that most of the particular rules laid down in the gospel for our direction, are spoken after such figurative a manner, that except we judge of their meaning, not merely by the letter, but by what the law of nature antecedently declares to be our duty, they are apt to lead us wrong. And if precepts relating to morality are delivered after an obscure manner, when they might have been delivered otherwise; what reason can you assign, for its being so, but that infinite wisdom meant to refer us to that law for the explaining them? Sufficient instances of this nature I shall give you hereafter, though I must own, I cannot carry this point so far as a learned divine, who represents the Scriptures more obscure (which one would think impossible) than even the fathers. He tells us, 'that a certain author (viz., Flaccus Illyricus) has furnished us with one-and-fifty reasons for the obscurity of the Scriptures;' adding, 'I think I may truly say that the writing of the prophets and apostles abound with tropes, and metaphors, types, and allegories, parables, and dark speeches; and are as much, nay, much more unintelligible in many places, than the writings of the ancients.' It is well this author, who talks of people being stark Bible-mad, stopped here; and did not with a celebrated wit * cry, 'The truly illuminated books are the darkest of all.' The writer above mentioned supposes it impossible, that God's will should be fully revealed by books; 'except,' says he, 'it might be said perhaps without a figure, that even the world itself could not contain the books which should be written.' But with submission to this reverend person, I cannot help thinking, but that (such is the divine goodness) God's will is so clearly and fully manifested in the Book of Nature, that he who runs may read it."

Dean Swift — "Tale of a Tub."

In the next extract we make, we find Tindal quoting two striking passages from Lord Shaftesbury, followed by an acute vindication of the integrity of the Law of Nature over the Scriptures:—

"Had the heathen distinguished themselves by creeds made out of spite to one another, and mutually persecuted each other about the worship of their gods, they would soon have made the number of their votaries as few as the gods they worshipped; but we don't find (except in Egypt, that mother-land of superstition) that they ever quarrelled about their gods; though their gods sometimes quarrelled, and fought about their votaries. By the universal liberty that was allowed by the ancients, 'Matters (as a noble author observes) were so balanced, that reason had fair play; learning and science flourished; wonderful was the harmony and temper which arose from these contrarieties. Thus superstition and enthusiasm were mildly treated; and being let alone, they never raged to that degree as to occasion bloodshed, wars, persecutions, and devastations; but a new sort of policy has made us leap the bounds of natural humanity, and out of a supernatural charity, has taught us the way of plaguing one another most devoutly. It has raised an antipathy, that no temporal interest could ever do, and entailed on us a mutual hatred to all eternity. And savage zeal, with meek and pious semblance, works dreadful massacre; and for heaven's sake (horrid pretence) makes desolate the earth.' And further, Shaftesbury observes, 'The Jupiter of Strangers, was, among the ancients, one of the solemn characters of divinity, the peculiar attribute of the supreme deity; benign to mankind, and recommending universal love, mutual kindness, and benignity between the remotest and most unlike of the human race. Such was the ancient heathen charity and pious duty towards the whole of mankind; both those of different nations and different worship. But, good God! how different a character do bigots give us of the Deity, making him an unjust, cruel, and inconsistent Being; requiring all men to judge for themselves, and act according to their consciences; and yet authorizing some among them to judge for others, and to punish them for not acting according to the consciences of those judges, though ever so much against their own. These bigots thought they were authorized to punish all those that differ with them in their religious worship, as God's enemies; but had they considered that God alone could discern men's hearts, and alone discover whether any, by conscientiously offering him a wrong worship, could become his enemies; and that infinite wisdom best knew how to proportion the punishment to the fault, as well as infinite power how to inflict it; they would, surely, have left it to God to judge for himself, in a cause which immediately related to himself; and where they were not so much as parties concerned, and as likely to be mistaken as those they would punish. Can one, without horror, think of men's breaking through all the rules of doing as they would be done unto, in order to set themselves up for standards of truth for God as well as man? Do not these impious wretches suppose, that God is not able to judge for himself; at least, not able to execute his own judgment? And that, therefore, he has recourse, forsooth, to their superior knowledge or power; and they are to revenge his injuries, root out his enemies, and restore his lost honor, though with the destruction of the better part of mankind? But, to do the propagators of these blasphemous notions justice, they do not throw this load of scandal on the law of Nature, or so much as pretend from thence to authorize their execrable principles; but endeavor to support them by traditional religion; especially by mis-interpreted texts from the Old Testament; and thereby make, not only natural and revealed religion, but the Old and New Testament (the latter of which requires doing good both to Jews and Gentiles) contradict each other. But to return; if what the light of Nature teaches us concerning the divine perfections, when duly attended to, is not only sufficient to hinder us from falling into superstition of any kind whatever; but, as I have already shown, demonstrates what God, from his infinite wisdom and goodness, can, or cannot command; how is it possible that the law of Nature and grace can differ? How can it be conceived, that God's laws, whether internally, or externally revealed, are not at all times the same, when the author of them is, and has been immutably the same forever?'"

The following passage exhibits the judicious mixture of authority and argument for which our author is remarkable. The quotation is a good illustration of Tindal's best manner. He is replying to Dr. Samuel Clark:—

"It cannot be imputed to any defect in the light of nature, that the pagan world ran into idolatry, but to their being entirely governed by priests, who pretended communication with their gods, and to have thence their revelations, which they imposed on the credulous as divine oracles: whereas the business of the Christian dispensation was to destroy all those traditional revelations; and restore, free from all idolatry, the true primitive, and natural religion, implanted in mankind from the creation. The Dr. (Clark) however, seems afraid, lest he had allowed too much to the light of nature, in relation to the discovery of our duty both to God and man; and not left room for revelation to make any addition; he therefore supposes, 'there are some duties, which nature hints at only in general.'—But, if we cannot, without highly reflecting on the wisdom and goodness of God, suppose that he has not, at all times, given the whole rational creation a plain rule for their conduct, in relation to those duties they owe to God, themselves, and one another; must we not suppose reason, and religion (that rule of all other rules) inseparable; so that no rational creature can be ignorant of it, who attends to the dictates of his own mind; I mean, as far as it is necessary for him to know it! An ignorant peasant may know what is sufficient for him, without knowing as much as the learned rector of St. James's. Though the Dr. says, 'the knowledge of the law of nature is, in fact, by no means universal;' yet he asserts, that 'man is plainly in his own nature an accountable creature;' which supposes that the light of nature plainly, and undeniably, teaches him that law, for breach of which he is naturally accountable; and did not the Dr. believe this law to be universal, he could not infer a future judgment from the conscience *all* men have of their actions, or the judgment they pass on them in their own minds whereby 'They that have not any law, are a law unto themselves; their consciences bearing witness, and their thoughts accusing, or excusing one another;' which is supposing but one law, whether that law be written on paper, or in men's hearts only; and that all men by the judgment they pass on their own actions, are conscious of this law. And, the apostle Paul, though quoted by the Dr., is so far from favoring his hypothesis of any invincible ignorance, even in the wisest and best of the philosophers, that he, by saying, The Gentiles, that have not the law, do by nature the things contained in the law, makes the law of nature and grace to be the same: and supposes the reason why they were to be punished, was their sinning against light and knowledge. That which may be known of God was manifest in them, and when they knew God, they glorified him not as God. And they were likewise guilty of abominable corruptions, not ignorantly, but knowing the judgment of God, that they who do such things are worthy of death.

"Had the Dr. but considered this self-evident proposition, that there can be no transgression where there is no law; and that an unknown law is the same as no law; and consequently, that all mankind, at all times, must be capable of knowing all (whether more or less) that God requires, it would have prevented his endeavoring to prove, that, till the gospel dispensation, mankind were entirely, and unavoidably ignorant of their duty in several important points; and thus charging the light of nature with undeniable defects. I think it no compliment to external revelation, though the Dr. designed it as the highest, to say, it prevailed, when the light of nature was, as he supposes, in a manner extinct; since then an irrational religion might as easily obtain, as a rational one. The Dr., to prove that revelation has supplied the insufficiency, and undeniable defects of the light of nature, refers us to Phil., iv., 1, which he introduces after this pompous manner:—'Let any man of an honest and sincere mind consider, whether that practical doctrine has not, even in itself, the greatest marks of a divine original, wherein whatsoever things are true, whatsoever things are honest, whatsoever things are just, whatsoever things are pure, whatsoever things are lovely, whatsoever things are of good report, if there be any virtue, it there be anything praiseworthy; all these, and these only, are earnestly recommended to man's practice.' I would ask the Dr., how he can know what these are, which are thus alone earnestly recommended to man's practice; or, why they have, in themselves, the greatest marks of a divine original; but from the light of nature? Nay, how can the Dr. know there are defects in the light of nature, but from that light itself? which supposes this light is all we have to trust to; and consequently, all the Dr. has been doing, on pretence of promoting the honor of revelation, is introducing universal scepticism. And I am concerned, and grieved, to see a man, who had so great a share of the light of nature, employing it to expose that light, of which before he had given the highest commendation; and which can have no other effect, than to weaken even his own demonstration, drawn from that light, for the being of a God. I shall mention but one text more, which, had not the Dr. thought it highly to his purpose, for showing the insufficiency of the light of nature, he would not have ushered it in after this most solemn manner:—'When men have put themselves into this temper and frame of mind, let them try if they can any longer reject the evidence of the gospel. If any man will do his will, he shall know of the doctrine; whether it be of God.' Is it not strange, to see so judicious a divine write after such a manner, as if he thought the best way to support the dignity of revelation, was to derogate from the immutable and eternal law of nature? and while he is depressing it, extol revelation for those very things it borrows from that law? in which, though he asserts there are undeniable defects, yet he owns that God governs all his own actions by it, and expects that all men should so govern theirs.

"But, I find the Dr.'s own brother, the Dean of Sa-rum, is entirely of my mind, as to those texts the Dr. quotes—viz., Rom. ii., 14, and Phil, iv., 8. As to the first—viz., Rom. ii., 14, he says, 'The apostle supposes, that the moral law is founded in the nature and reason of things: that every man is endued with such powers and faculties of mind, as render him capable of seeing, and taking notice of this law; and also with such a sense and judgment of the reasonableness and fitness of conforming his actions to it, that he cannot but in his own mind acquit himself when he does so; and condemn himself when he does otherwise.' And as to the second—viz., Phil, iv., 8, where the same apostle recommends the practice of Virtue, upon the fore-mentioned principles of comeliness and reputation.—'These principles,' says he, 'if duly attended to, were sufficient to instruct men in the whole of their duty towards themselves, and towards each other. And they would also have taught them their duty towards God, their Creator and Governor, if they had diligently pursued them. For according as the apostle expresses it, Rom. i., 20, the invisible things of God from the creation of the world are clearly seen, being understood by the things that are made, even his eternal power and Godhead. The same fitness and decency that appears in men's regular behavior towards each other, appears also in their behavior towards God. And this, likewise, is founded in the nature and reason of things; and is what the circumstances and condition they are in do absolutely require. Thus we see therein moral virtue, or good consists, and what the obligation to it is from its own native beauty and excellency.'"

One more example of Tindal's style will show how skilfully and cogently he forced, the great authorities of his day to bear Witness to the truth of his leading proposition, the natural antiquity of all the reasonable precepts of the Bible: —

"The most accurate Dr. Barrow gives this character of the Christian religion, 'That its precepts are no other than such as physicians prescribe for the health of our bodies; as politicians would allow to be needful for the peace of the state; as Epicurean philosophers recommend for the tranquillity of our minds, and pleasures of our lives; such as reason dictates, and daily shows conducive to our welfare in all respects; which consequently, were there no law enacting them, we should in wisdom choose to observe, and voluntarily impose them on ourselves; confessing them to be fit matters of law, and most advantageous and requisite to the good, general and particular, of mankind.'

"That great and good man Dr. Tillotson says, 'That all the precepts of Christianity are reasonable and wise, requiring such duties as are suitable to the light of nature, and do approve themselves to the best reason of mankind; such as have their foundation in the nature of God, and are an imitation of the divine excellencies; such as tend to the perfection of human nature, and to raise the minds of men to the highest pitch of goodness and virtue. They command nothing that is unnecessary, they omit nothing that may tend to the glory of God, or the welfare of men, nor do they restrain us in anything, but what is contrary to the regular inclinations of nature, or to our reason, and true interest; they forbid us nothing but what is base and unworthy to serve our humors and passions, to make ourselves fools and beasts. In a word, nothing but what tends to our private harm, or prejudice, or to public disorder and confusion.'

"The late Dean of Canterbury, in a sermon preached in defence of Christianity, says, * 'What can be a more powerful incentive to obedience, than for a rational creature clearly to discern the equity, the necessity, the benefit, the decency and beauty of every action he is called to do, and thence to be duly sensible how gracious a master he serves; one that is so far from loading him with fruitless, arbitrary, and tyrannical impositions, that each command abstracted from his command who issues it, is able to recommend itself; and nothing required but what every wise man would choose of his accord: and cannot, without being his own enemy, wish to be exempted from?' And this character of Christianity he makes to be essential to its being from God, and therefore must make it the same with natural religion, which has this character impressed on it.

"'There was none of the doctrines of our Saviour (says the late Archbishop of York) ** calculated for the gratification of men's idle curiosities, the busying and amusing them with airy and useless speculations; much less were they intended for an exercise of our credulity, or a trial how far we could bring our reason to submit to our faith; but as on the one hand they were plain and simple, and such as by their agreeable-ness to the rational faculties of mankind, did highly recommend themselves to our belief; so on the other hand they had an immediate relation to practice, and were the general principles and foundation, on which all human and divine virtues were naturally to be superstructed.'

* Boyle's Lect., p. 26,

** Sermon before the Queen on Christmas Day, 1724.

"Does not every one see, that if the religion of nature had been put instead of Christianity, these descriptions would have exactly agreed with it? The judicious Dr. Scot affirms, 'God never imposes laws on us pro imperio, as arbitrary tests and trials of our obedience. The great design of them (says he,) is to do us good, and direct our actions to our own interest. This, if we firmly believe, will infinitely encourage our obedience; for when I am sure God commands me nothing but what my own health, ease, and happiness requires; and that every law of his is both a necessary and sovereign prescription against the diseases of my nature, and he could not prescribe less than he has, without being defective in his care of my recovery and happiness; with what prudence and modesty can I grudge to obey him?'

"Nay, the most considerate men, even among the Papists, do not scruple to maintain there's nothing in religion but what is moral. The divines of Port Royal for instance, say, 'All the precepts, and all the mysteries that are expressed in so many different ways in the holy volumes, do all centre in this one commandment of loving God with all our heart, and in loving our neighbors as ourselves: for the Scripture (it is St. Austin who says it) forbids but one only thing, which is concupiscence, or the love of the creature; as it commands but one only thing, which is charity, and the love of God. Upon this double precept is founded the whole system of the Christian religion; and it is unto this, say they, according to the expression of Jesus Christ, that all the ancient law and the prophets have reference; and we may add also, all the mysteries, and all the precepts of the new law; for love, says St. Paul, is the fulfilling of the law.' And these divines likewise cite a remarkable passage of St. Austin on this subject, viz., 'He that knows how to love God, and to regulate his life by that love, knows all that the Scripture propounds to be known.' And might add the authority of a greater man, and a Papist too, * who says, 'Religion adds nothing to natural probity, but the consolation of doing that for love and obedience to our Heavenly Father, which reason itself requires us do in favor of virtue.'"

* *Archbishop of Cambray: Lettres sur la Religion,*

p. 258, a Paris.

Tindal was a solid, rather than a brilliant writer: but he perfectly knew what he was about; and the work from which we quote, was well conceived and carefully executed. His ground was skilfully chosen, his arguments were placed on an eminence where his friends could see them, and where his enemies could not assail them. Dr. Leland, in his view of Deistical writers, is quite in a rage with him, because he discredits Book Revelation, to set up Nature's Revelation. His real offence was, that he did prove that Nature was the only source of truth and reason—the criterion by which even Divine Revelation must be judged. He carried men back to the gospel of nature, by the side of which the gospel of the Jewish fishermen did not show to advantage. Tindal did put something in the place of that which he was supposed desirous of removing. How unwilling Christians of that day were to admit of improvement in religion, is shown by the number of attacks Tindal's work sustained. The Bishop of London published a "Second Pastoral Letter" against it; Dr. Thomas Burnet "confuted" it; Mr. Law "fully" answered it; Dr. Stebbing "obviated the principal objections" in it. "The same learned and judicious writer," observes Leland, a second time entered the lists, in "answer to the fourteenth chapter of a book, entitled 'Christianity as Old as the Creation.'" Mr. Balgny issued a "Second Letter to a Deist," occasioned by Tindal's work. Mr. Anthony O'Key gave a short view of the whole controversy. Dr. Foreter, Dr. John Conybeare, "particularly engaged public attention" as Dr. Tindal's antagonists. Mr. Simon Brown produced a "solid and excellent" answer; and Dr. Leland, with many blushes, tells us that he himself issued in Dublin, in 1773, two volumes, taking a wider compass than the other answers.

"Christianity as Old as the Creation" is a work which Freethinkers may yet consult with advantage, as a repertory of authorities no longer accessible to the readers of this generation. What these authorities allege will be found to have intrinsic value, to be indeed lasting testimonies in favor of Rationalism. In passing in review the noble truths, Tindal insists that it is impossible not to wonder at the policy, or rather want of policy displayed by Christians. Tindal is an author whom they might be proud of, if they were really in love with reason. Tindal's opponents have shown how instinctively the children of faith distrust the truths of Nature. After all the "refutations," and "confutations" and answers made to the great Deist, Tin-dal's work has maintained its ground, and the truths he so ably and spiritedly vindicated, have spread wider since and taken deeper root.

J. W.

DAVID HUME

Lord Brougham has rendered service not only to "Letters," but also to Freethought, by his admirable "Lives," incomparably the best we have, of Voltaire, Rousseau, Hume, Gibbon, etc. From Lord Brougham we learn (whose life in this sketch we follow) that David Hume, related to the Earl of Hume's family, was born in Edinburgh, in April, 1711. Refusing to be made a lawyer, he was sent, in 1734, to a mercantile house in Bristol. The "desk" not suiting the embryo historian's genius, we find him in 1737 at La Flèche, in Anjou, writing his still-born "Treatise on Human Nature;" which in 1742, in separate Essays, attracted some notice. Keeper and companion to the Marquis of Annandale in 1745, private secretary to General St. Clair in 1747, he visited on embassy the courts of Vienna and Turin. While at Turin he completed his "Inquiry Concerning the Human Understanding," the "Treatise on Human Nature" in a new form. Returned to Scotland, he published his "Political Discourses" in 1752, and the same year his "Inquiry Concerning the Principles of Morals." The "Essays, Moral and Metaphysical," are the form in which we now read these speculations. In 1752, Hume became librarian to the Faculty of Advocates. In 1754 he published the first volume of his "History of England." In 1755, appeared his "Natural History of Religion." In 1763 he accompanied the British ambassador to Paris. In 1765 he became *charge d'affaires*.

In 1766 he was appointed Under Secretary of State under Marshal Conway. In 1775 he was seized with a mortal disease, which he bore without any abatement of his cheerfulness; and on the 25th of August, "*le bon* David," as he was styled in Paris, died, to use his own words, having "no enemies—except all the Whigs, all the Tories, and all the Christians"—which was something to his honor, and a testimony of the usefulness of his life.

David Hume was the first writer who gave historical distinction to Great Britain. Lord John Russell remarked in a speech at Bristol, in October, 1854:—"We have no other 'History of England' than Hume's.... When a young man of eighteen asks for a 'History of England,' there is no resource but to give him Hume." Hume was the author of the modern doctrines of politics and political economy, which now rule the world of science. He was "the sagacious unfolder of truth, the accurate and bold discoverer of popular error." More than a sceptic, he was an Atheist. Such is Lord Brougham's judgment of him.

Hume carried Freethought into high places. In originality of thought, grace of style, and logical ability, he distanced all rival writers on religion in his time, and what is of no small importance, his life was as blameless as his intellect was unapproachable.

Our first extract from his writings is a felicitous statement of the *pro* and *con.*, on the questions of polygamous and single, marriages:—

"A man, in conjoining himself to a woman, is bound to her according to the terms of his engagement. In begetting children, he is bound, by all the ties of nature and humanity, to provide for their subsistence and education. When he has performed these two parts of duty, no one can reproach him with injustice or injury. And as the terms of his engagement, as well as the methods of subsisting his offspring, may be various, it is mere superstition to imagine that marriage can be entirely uniform, and will admit only of one mode or form. Did not human laws restrain the natural liberty of men, every particular marriage would be as different as contracts or bargains of any other kind or species. As circumstances vary, and the laws propose different advantages, we find, that in different times and places, they impose different conditions on this important contract. In Tonquin, it is usual for the sailors, when the ship comes into the harbor, to marry for the season; and, notwithstanding this precarious engagement, they are assured, it is said, of the strictest fidelity to their bed, as well as in the whole management of their affairs, from those temporary spouses. I cannot, at present, recollect my authorities; but I have somewhere read, that the Republic of Athens, having lost many of its citizens by war and pestilence, allowed every man to marry two wives, in order the sooner to repair the waste which had been made by these calamities. The poet Euripides happened to be coupled to two noisy vixens, who so plagued him with their jealousies and quarrels, that he became ever after a professed *woman hater*; and is the only theatrical writer, perhaps the only poet, that ever entertained an aversion to the sex.... The advocates for polygamy may recommend it as the only effectual remedy for the disorders of love, and the only expedient for freeing men from that slavery to the females which the natural violence of our passions has imposed upon us. By this means alone can we regain our right of sovereignty and, sating our appetite, re-establish the authority of reason in our minds, and, of consequence, our own authority in our families. Man, like a weak sovereign, being unable to support himself against the wiles and intrigues of his subjects, must play one faction against another, and become absolute by the mutual jealousy of the females. To divide and to govern is an universal maxim; and by neglecting it, the Europeans undergo a more grievous and a more ignominious slavery than the Turks or Persians, who are subjected indeed to a sovereign that lies at a distance from them, but in their domestic affairs rules with an uncontrollable sway. On the other hand, it may be urged with better reason, that this sovereignty of the male is a real usurpation, and destroys that nearness of rank, not to say equality, which nature has established between the sexes. We are, by nature, their lovers, their friends, their patrons. Would we willingly exchange such endearing appellations for the barbarous title of master and tyrant? In what capacity shall we gain by this inhuman proceeding? As lovers, or as husbands? The *lover* is totally annihilated; and courtship, the most agreeable scene in life, can no longer have place where women have not the free disposal of themselves, but are bought and sold like the meanest animal. The *husband* is as little a gainer, having found the admirable secret of extinguishing every part of love, except its jealousy. No rose without its thorn; but he must be a foolish wretch indeed, that throws away the rose and preserves only the thorn. But the Asiatic manners are as destructive to friendship as to love. Jealousy excludes men from all intimacies and familiarities with each other. No one dares bring his friend to his house or table, lest he bring a lover to his numerous wives. Hence, all over the East, each family is as much separate from another as if they were so many distinct kingdoms. No wonder then that Solomon, living like an Eastern prince, with his seven hundred wives, and three hundred concubines, without one friend, could write so pathetically concerning the vanity of the world. Had he tried the secret of one wife or mistress, a few friends, and a great many companions, he might have found lite somewhat more agreeable. Destroy love and friendship, what remains in the world worth accepting?"

Next we quote his famous statement of the principle of *utility* in morals:—

"There has been a controversy started of late much better worth examination, concerning the general foundation of morals; whether they be derived from reason or from sentiment; whether we attain the knowledge of them by a chain of argument and induction, or by an immediate feeling and finer internal sense; whether, like all sound judgment of truth and falsehood, they should be the name to every rational intelligent being; or whether like the perception of beauty and deformity, they be founded entirely on the particular fabric and constitution of the human species. The ancient philosophers, though they often affirm that virtue is nothing but conformity to reason, yet, in general, seem to consider morals as deriving their existence from taste and sentiment. On the other hand, our modern inquirers, though they also talk much of the beauty of virtue, and, deformity of vice, yet have commonly endeavored to account for these distinctions by metaphysical reasonings, and by deductions from the most abstract principles of the understanding. Such confusion reigned in these subjects, that an opposition of the greatest consequence could prevail between one system and another, and even in the parts of almost each individual system: and yet nobody, till very lately, was ever sensible of it. The elegant Lord Shaftesbury, who first gave occasion to remark this distinction, and who, in general, adhered to the principles of the ancients, is not, himself, entirely free from the same confusion.... In all determinations of morality, the circumstance of public utility, is ever principally in view; and wherever disputes arise, either in philosophy or common life, concerning the bounds of duty, the question cannot, by any means, be decided with greater certainty, than by ascertaining, on any side, the true interests of mankind. If any false opinion, embraced from appearances, has been found to prevail; as soon as farther experience and sounder reasoning have given us juster notions of human affairs, we retract our first sentiment, and adjust anew the boundaries of moral good and evil. Giving alms to common beggars is naturally praised; because it seems to carry relief to the distressed and indigent; but when we observe the encouragement thence arising to idleness and debauchery, we regard that species of charity rather as a weakness than a virtue. Tyrannicide, or the assassination of usurpers and oppressive princes, was highly extolled in ancient times; because it both freed mankind from many of these monsters, and seemed to keep the others in awe whom the sword or poniard could not reach. But history and experience having since convinced us, that this practice increases the jealousy and cruelty of princes, a Timoleon and a Brutus, though treated with indulgence on account of the prejudices of their times, are now considered as very improper models for imitation. Liberality in princes is regarded as a mark of beneficence. But when it occurs, that the homely bread of the honest and industrious is often thereby converted into delicious cakes for the idle and the prodigal, we soon retract our heedless praises. The regrets of a prince, for having lost a day, were noble and generous; but had he intended to have spent it in acts of generosity to his greedy courtiers, it was better lost than misemployed after that manner.... That justice is useful to society, and consequently that *part* of its merit, at least, must arise from that consideration, it would be a superfluous undertaking to prove. That public utility is the *sole* origin of justice, that reflections on the beneficial consequences of this virtue are the *sole* foundation of its merit; this proposition being more curious and important, will better deserve our examination and inquiry. Let us suppose that nature has bestowed on the human race such profuse abundance of all external conveniences, that, without any uncertainty in the event, without any care or industry on our part, every individual finds himself fully provided with whatever his most voracious appetite can want, or luxurious imagination wish or desire. His natural beauty, we shall suppose, surpasses all acquired ornaments; the perpetual clemency of the seasons renders useless all clothes or covering: the raw herbage affords him the most delicious fare; the clear fountain, the richest beverage. No laborious occupation required: no tillage: no navigation. Music, poetry, and contemplation, form his sole business: conversation, mirth, and friendship his sole amusement. It seems evident, that, in such a happy state, every other social virtue would flourish, and receive tenfold increase; but the cautious, jealous virtue of justice, would never once have been dreamed of. For what purpose make a partition of goods, where every one has already more than enough? Why give rise to property, where there cannot possibly be any injury? Why call this object *mine*, when, upon seizing of it by another, I need but stretch out my hand to possess myself of what is equally valuable? Justice, in that case, being totally useless, would be an idle ceremonial, and could never possibly have place in the catalogue of virtues. We see, even in the present necessitous condition of mankind, that, wherever any benefit is bestowed by nature in an unlimited abundance, we leave it always in common among the whole human race, and make no subdivisions of right and property. Water and air, though the most necessary of all objects, are not challenged as the property of individuals; nor can any man commit injustice by the most lavish use and enjoyment of these blessings. In fertile extensive countries, with few inhabitants, land is regarded on the same footing. And no topic is so much insisted on by those who defend the liberty of the seas, as the unexhausted use of them in navigation. Were the advantages procured by navigation as inexhaustible, these reasoners had never had any adversaries to refute; nor had any claims ever been advanced of a separate, exclusive dominion over the ocean.... Suppose a society to fall into such want of all common necessaries, that the utmost frugality and industry cannot preserve the greater number from perishing, and the whole from extreme misery. It will readily, I believe, be admitted that the strict laws of justice are suspended in such a pressing emergence, and give place to the stronger motives of necessity and self-preservation. Is it any crime, after a shipwreck, to seize whatever means or instrument of safety one can lay hold of, without regard to former limitations of properly? Or if a city besieged were perishing with hunger; can we imagine that men will see any means of preservation before them, and lose their lives from a scrupulous regard to what, in other situations, would be the rules of equity and justice? The use and tendency of that virtue is to procure happiness and security, by preserving order in society. But where the society is ready to perish from extreme necessity, no greater evil can be dreaded from violence and injustice; and every man may now provide for himself by all the means which prudence can dictate, or humanity permit. The public, even in less urgent necessities, opens granaries without the consent of proprietors; as justly supposing, that the authority of magistracy may, consistent with equity, extend so far. But were any number of men to assemble, without the tie of laws or civil jurisdiction; would an equal partition of bread in a famine, though effected by power and even violence, be regarded as criminal or injurious? Suppose, likewise, that it should be a virtuous man's fate to fall into the society of ruffians, remote from the protection of laws and government; what conduct must he embrace in that melancholy situation? He sees such a desperate rapaciousness prevail; such a disregard to equity, such contempt of order, such stupid blindness to future consequences, as must immediately have the most tragical conclusion, and must terminate in destruction to the greater number, and in a total dissolution of society to the rest. He, meanwhile, can have no other expedient than to arm himself, to whomever the sword he seizes, or the buckler may belong: to make provision of all means of defence and security: and his particular regard to justice being no longer of use to his own safety or that of others, he must consult the dictates of self-preservation alone, without concern for those who no longer merit his care and attention.... But perhaps the difficulty of accounting for these effects of usefulness, or its contrary, has kept philosophers from admitting them into their systems of ethics, and has induced them to employ any other principle, in explaining the origin of moral good and evil. But it is no just reason for rejecting any principle, confirmed by experience, that we cannot give a satisfactory account of its origin, nor are able to resolve it into other more general principles. And if we would employ a little thought on the present subject, we need be at no loss to account for the influence of utility, and deduce it from principles the most known and avowed in human nature.... Usefulness is agreeable, and engages our approbation. This is a matter of fact, confirmed by daily observation. But useful! For what? For somebody's interest, surely! Whose interest then? Not our own only; for our approbation frequently extends farther. It must therefore be the interest of those who are served by the character or action approved of; and these, we may conclude, however remote, are not totally indifferent to us. By opening up this principle, we shall discover one great source of moral distinctions."

The origin and mischiefs of Theistic influences is the subject of the following passage:—

"It must necessarily, indeed, be allowed, that in order to carry men's attention beyond the present course of things, or lead them into any inference concerning invisible intelligent power, they must be actuated by some passion which prompts their thought and reflection, some motive which urges their first inquiry. But what passion shall we here have recourse to, for explaining an effect of such mighty consequence? Not speculative curiosity, surely, or the pure love of truth. That motive is too refined for such gross apprehensions; and would lead men into inquiries concerning the frame of nature, a subject too large and comprehensive for their narrow capacities. No passions, therefore, can be supposed to work upon such barbarians, but the ordinary affections of human life; the anxious concern for happiness, the dread of future misery, the terror of death, the thirst of revenge, the appetite for food and other necessaries. Agitated by hopes and fears of this nature, especially the latter, men scrutinize, with a trembling curiosity, the course of future causes, and examine the various and contrary events of human life. And in this disordered scene, with eyes still more disordered and astonished, they see the first obscure traces of divinity.... We hang in perpetual suspense between life and death, health and sickness, plenty and want, which are distributed amongst the human species by secret and unknown causes, whose operation is oft unexpected, and always unaccountable. These *unknown causes*, then, become the constant object of hope and fear; and while the passions are kept in perpetual alarm by an anxious expectation of the events, the imagination is equally employed in forming ideas of those powers on which we have so entire a dependence. Could men anatomize nature, according to the most probable, at least the most intelligible philosophy, they would find that these causes are nothing but the particular fabric and structure of the minute parts of their own bodies and of external objects; and that by a regular and constant machinery, all the events are produced, about which they are so much concerned.... There is an universal tendency among mankind to conceive all beings like themselves, and to transfer to every object those qualities with which they are familiarly acquainted, and of which they are intimately conscious. We find human faces in the moon, armies in the clouds; and, by a natural propensity, it not corrected by experience and reflection, ascribe malice or good will to everything that hurts or pleases us. Hence the frequency and beauty of the *prosopopoia* in poetry; where trees, mountains, and streams are personified, and the inanimate parts of nature acquire sentiment and passion. And though these poetical figures and expressions gain not on the belief; they may serve, at least, to prove a certain tendency in the imagination, without which they could neither be beautiful nor natural. Nor is a river-god or hamadryad always taken for a mere poetical or imaginary personage, but may sometimes enter into the real creed of the ignorant vulgar; while each grove or field is represented as possessed of a particular genius or invisible power which inhabits and protects, it. Nay, philosophers cannot entirely exempt themselves from this natural frailty; but have oft ascribed to inanimate matter the horror of a *vacuum*, sympathies, antipathies, and other affections of human nature. The absurdity is not less, while we cast our eyes upwards; and, transferring, as is too usual, human passions and infirmities to the Deity, represent him as jealous and revengeful, capricious and partial, and, in short, a wicked and foolish man in every respect but his superior power and authority.—No wonder, then, that mankind, being placed in such an absolute ignorance of causes, and being at the same time so anxious concerning their future fortune, should immediately acknowledge a dependence on invisible powers, possessed of sentiment and intelligence. The *unknown causes* which continually employ their thought, appearing always in the same aspect, are all apprehended to be of the same kind or species. Nor is it long before we ascribe to them thought, and reason, and passion, and sometimes even the limbs and figures of men, in order to bring them nearer to a resemblance with ourselves.... It is remarkable, that the principles of religion have a kind of flux and reflux in the human mind, and that men have a natural tendency to rise from idolatry to Theism, and to sink again from Theism into idolatry. The vulgar—that is, indeed, all mankind, a few excepted—being ignorant and uninstructed, never elevate their contemplation to the heavens, or penetrate by their disquisitions into the secret structure of vegetable or animal bodies; so far as, to discover a Supreme Mind or Original Providence, which bestowed order on every part of nature. They consider these admirable works in a more confined and selfish view; and finding their own happiness and misery to depend on the secret influence, and unforeseen concurrence of external objects, they regard, with perpetual attention, the *unknown causes* which govern all these natural events, and distribute pleasure and pain, good and ill, by their powerful but silent operation. The unknown causes are still appealed to on every emergency; and in this general appearance or confused image, are the perpetual objects of human hopes and fears, wishes and apprehensions. By degrees, the active imagination of men, uneasy in this abstract conception of objects, about which it is incessantly employed, begins to render them more particular, and to clothe them in shapes more suitable to its natural comprehension. It represents them to be sensible, intelligent beings like mankind; actuated by love and hatred, and flexible by gifts and entreaties, by prayers and sacrifices. Hence the origin of religion: and hence the origin of idolatry or polytheism."

More has been written by theologians in endeavors to refute the following passage, than has ever been called forth by the wit of man before by the same number of words:—

"A miracle is a violation of the laws of nature; and as a firm and unalterable experience has established these laws, the proof against a miracle, from the very nature of the fact, is as entire as any argument from experience can possibly be imagined. Why is it more than probable that all men must die; that lead cannot, of itself, remain suspended in the air; that fire consumes wood, and is extinguished by water; unless it be that these events are found agreeable to the laws of nature, and there is required a violation of these laws, or, in other words, a miracle to prevent them? Nothing is esteemed a miracle, if it ever happen in the common course of nature. It is no miracle that a man, seemingly in good health, should die on a sudden; because such a kind of death, though more unusual than any other, has yet been frequently observed to happen. But it is a miracle that a dead man should come to life; because that has never been observed in any age or country. There must, therefore, be an uniform experience against every miraculous event, otherwise the event would not merit that appellation. And as an uniform experience amounts to a proof, there is here a direct and full proof, from the nature of the fact, against the existence of any miracle; nor can such a proof be destroyed, or the miracle rendered credible, but by an opposite proof which is superior. The plain consequence is (and it is a general maxim worthy of our attention,) 'That no testimony is sufficient to establish a miracle, unless the testimony be of such a kind that its falsehood would be more miraculous than the fact which it endeavors to establish. And even in that case there is a mutual destruction of arguments, and the superior only gives us an assurance suitable to that degree of force which remains after deducting the inferior.' When any one tells me that he saw a dead man restored to life, I immediately consider with myself whether it be more probable that this person should either deceive or be deceived, or that the fact which he relates should really have happened. I weigh the one miracle against the other; and according to the superiority which I discover, I pronounce my decision, and always reject the greater miracle. If the falsehood of his testimony would be more miraculous than the event which he relates; then, and not till then, can he pretend to command my belief or opinion.... There is not to be found, in all history, any miracle attested by a sufficient number of men, of such unquestioned good sense, education, and learning, as to secure us against all delusion in themselves; of such undoubted integrity, as to place them beyond all suspicion of any design to deceive others; of such credit and reputation in the eyes of mankind, as to have a great deal to lose in case of their being detected in any falsehood; and at the same time attesting facts, performed in such a public manner, and in so celebrated a part of the world, as to render the detection unavoidable; all which circumstances are requisite to give us a full assurance of the testimony of men.... One of the best attested miracles in all profane history, is that which Tacitus reports of Vespasian, who cured a blind man in Alexandria by means of his spittle, and a lame man by the mere touch of his foot; in obedience to a vision of the god Seraphis, who had enjoined them to have recourse to the emperor for these miraculous cures. The story may be seen in that fine historian; where every circumstance seems to add weight to the testimony, and might be displayed at large with all the force of argument and eloquence, if any one were now concerned to enforce the evidence of that exploded and idolatrous superstition. The gravity, solidity, age, and probity of so great an emperor, who through the whole course of his life, conversed in a familiar manner, with his friends and courtiers, and never affected those extraordinary airs of divinity assumed by Alexander and Demetrius. The historian, a contemporary writer, noted for candor and veracity, and, withal, the greatest and most, penetrating genius, perhaps of all antiquity; and so free from any tendency to credulity, that he even lies under the contrary imputation of Atheism and profaneness. The persons, from whose authority he related the miracle of established character for judgment and veracity, as we may-well presume; eye-witnesses of the fact, and confirming their testimony, after the Flavian family was despoiled of the empire, and could no longer give any reward as the price of a lie. *Utrumque, qui interfuere, nunc quoque memorant, postquam nullum mendacio pretium.* To which, if we add the public nature of the facts, as related, it will appear that no evidence can well be supposed stronger for so gross and so palpable a falsehood."

These extracts will give some idea of the grace, and power, and penetration of Hume. The society he kept, the abilities with which he was justly credited, the reputation his works deservedly won for him, made him a man of mark and influence in his day. Read by the learned, courted by statesmen, he taught gentlemen liberality, and governments toleration. The influence of Hume, silent and inappreciable to the multitude, has been of the utmost importance to the nation. His works have been studied by philosophers, politicians, and prelates. The writings of no Freethinker, except Voltaire, have maintained their ground with continually increasing reputation. Oddly enough, none of Hume's works were popular when they first appeared. In fact, his "Treatise on Human Nature" he had to reprint in the form of Essays, five years after its first publication. It then, for the first time, began to be bought; but not to any great extent. Five years later, he again made it re-appear, under the form of an "Inquiry Concerning the Human Understanding." It was not until this third publication that he "began to perceive symptoms of its coming into notice." The world has since made up for its negligence, by perpetual comment and solid appreciation. A king among thinkers, the clergy have in the provinces of politics and philosophical speculation to acknowledge allegiance to him, however they may rebel against his theological heresies.

J. W.

DR. THOMAS BURNET

It was only a very narrow accident which prevented Dr. Burnet, an ultra Freethinker in the Church of England, from becoming Archbishop of Canterbury at the death of Tillotson. A combination of clergymen were prepared to immolate themselves providing Burnet could be overthrown. They succeeded. Thomas Burnet kept the Charter House, in London, and his conscience—happier, perhaps, in this than if he had enjoyed the ecclesiastical preferment which King William seemed so anxious to give him. Amongst the clergy, Dr. Burnet was, with the single exception of Dean Swift, the greatest Freethinker of whom we can boast, who held an influential position in the Church. This position is sometimes claimed for Bishop Berkeley, a man of vast talents, a sincere Christian, although an innovator in philosophy.

Thomas Burnet was born in the year 1635. At the age of forty-five, he published the work, in Latin, with which his name is generally associated, "The Sacred Theory of the Earth: containing an account of the Original of the Earth, and of all the general changes which it has already undergone, or is to undergo, till the consummation of all Things." This book gives us an idea, formed by its author, of the origin of the world, and is remarkable as one of the first grand prophecies of geology; although of little value to us, it produced an impression upon the age by depicting the various strata of the mountainous regions, and comparing them in different countries, eliminating ideas of the nature of the vast changes we see in the universe, tracing the rise of most of the phenomena from the two elements, fire and water. Burnet thought that at one time the whole of matter was in a fluid state, revolving round a central sun, until the heavier particles sunk into the middle, and formed the stony strata which supports the earth, over which the lighter liquids coalesced until the heat of the sun effectually separated water from land. This is the foundation of a scheme which is elaborated in a poetic style, abounding in eloquent descriptions; in fact it is a philosophic prose poem of almost unalloyed beauty. In it there is some resemblance to the measured sentences of Shaftesbury, although unequal to that fine writer in soundness of judgment or practical usefulness. In 1691 an English translation was published.

By far the most interesting work to us of Burnet's (also written in Latin) is "Archæologia Philosophical or, an account of the Opinion of the Ancients on various Philosophical Problems." This work created great opposition by its free remarks on the Mosaic dispensation, although the writer in this, as in the case of his posthumous works, strongly protested against their being translated into the English language, as he was justly afraid of their influence on the minds of the laity, and from his high official station, with the influence his vast learning and his connection with Tillotson, and the Court gave him, he was, no doubt, apprehensive that the really religious champions of the Church of England would denounce him when exposed to the temptation of High Church preferment. Fragments of those works were translated by the clergy to prove to the unlearned what a dangerous character Thomas Burnet was. Charles Blount, writing to Gildon, says, "I have, according to my promise, sent you herewith the seventh and eighth chapters, as also the appendix, of the great and learned Dr. Burnet's book, published this winter in Latin, and by him dedicated to our most gracious Sovereign, King William..... As for the piece itself, I think it is one of the most ingenious I have ever read, and full of the most acute as well as learned observations. Nor can I find anything worthy an objection against him, as some of the censorious part of the world pretend; who would have you believe it a mere burlesque upon Moses, and destructive to the notion of original sin, wherefore by consequence (say they) there could be no necessity of a Redemption, which, however, I think no necessary consequence; but, for my part, either the great veneration I have for the doctor's extraordinary endowments, or else my own ignorance, has so far bribed me to his interests that I can, by no means, allow of any of those unjust reflections the wholesale merchants of credulity, as well as their unthinking retailers, make against him. It is true, in the seventh chapter he seems to prove that many parts of the Mosaic history of the creation appear inconsistent with reason, and in the eighth chapter the same appears no less inconsistent with philosophy; wherefore he concludes (as many fathers of the Church have done before him) that the whole rather seems to have been but a pious allegory." Dr. Burnet took the meaning of much of the Bible to be but a "pious allegory," and, as such, he strove to popularize it with the clergy. We do not believe that he intended to enlighten any but the clergy. He foresaw the "flood of fierce democracy," and, like other able men with vested rights in the ignorance of the people, he strove to temporize, to put off still further the day of Christianity's downfall. We place him in this biographical niche not because he dashed into the fray, like bold Hobbes or chivalrous Woolston, and took part in the battle of priestcraft because he thought it was right, but rather because he was a Freethinker in disguise, longing for Episcopal honors; yet, by one false step (the publishing of "Archæologia,") lost an archbishopric, and gave the authority of a great name to struggling opinion. His accession to our ranks was a brilliant accident. He died, at the age of eighty years, in 1715. After his demise, two works were translated (and published,) both expressive of his liberal views. The first, "On Christian Faith and Duties," throwing overboard the whole of the speculative tenets of the Bible, and giving practical effect to the morals taught in the New Testament, without striving to refute, or even apparently to disbelieve, their authority, but advising the clergy to treat them as a dead letter. The other posthumous treatise was, "On the State of the Dead and the Reviving," which shadows forth a scheme of Deism, inasmuch as Burnet here flatly contradicts the usual ideas of "hell torments" or "hell fire," while asserting the necessity of those "who have not been as good in this life as they ought to be" undergoing a probationary purification before they attained supreme happiness, yet, eventually, every human being would inhabit a heavenly elysium, where perennial pleasure would reign, and sorrow be forever unknown.

Those sentiments indicate a high degree of liberal culture, although they do not sufficiently embody our ideal of one of the great Freethinkers of the past. We should have preferred Burnet if he had systematically opposed the Church as Toland or Tindal, or if he had boldly entered the breach like William Whiston, whose singular talents and faithful honesty separated him alike from the Church, Dissent, and Deism, and left him shipwrecked on the world an able yet a visionary reformer. With more ability than Chubb, he resembled him in his weak policy; he chose to cut his sneers in slices, and served them up for a scholarly party rather than hazard the indignation of the ignorant amongst the clergy. We are, however, certain that although Thomas Burnet was deficient in many points where he might have done effective service, yet we honor him for the boldness with which he faced the scholars with his Latin works. He threw an apple of discord amongst their ranks which has served, in a constantly increasing manner, to divide and distract their attention. The result has been a constant internecine war in the Church, by which Freethought has largely profited.

We conclude our sketch of Dr. Burnet by quoting some extracts from the seventh chapter of the "Archæologia Philosophica," as translated by Charles Blount in the "Oracles of Reason," concerning Moses's description of Paradise and the original of things:—

"We have (says Burnet) hitherto made our inquiries into the originals of things, as well as after a true knowledge of Paradise amongst the ancients; yet still with reference to sacred writ, where it gave us any manner of light on the subject, but think it altogether unnecessary to define the place or situation of Paradise, since in respect to the theory of the earth, it is much the same thing where you place it, providing it be not on our modern earth. Now, if you inquire among the ancient fathers where the situation of it was, either they will have it to be none at all, or else obscure and remote from our understanding; some of them, indeed, term it an intelligible Paradise, but confined to no one particular place; whilst others, at the same time make it a sensible one, and here it is they first divided about it, etc.... Now, the history of Paradise, according to Moses, is this:—When God had, in six days, finished the creation of the world, the seventh day he rested from all manner of work. And here Moses relates particularly each day's operations: but for the story of mankind, as well male as female, of which he makes a particular treatise by himself. Wherefore, omitting the rest at present, let us consider the Mosaic doctrine upon those three subjects, viz., Adam, Eve, and the Garden of Eden, together with those things which are interwoven within them. As to the first man, Adam, Moses says he was formed not out of stones or dragon's teeth, as other Cosmists have feigned concerning their men, but out of the dust or clay of the earth, and when his body was formed, 'God *blew into his nostrils* the breath of life, and man was made a living soul.'

"But after another manner, and of another matter, was the woman built—viz., with one of Adam's small bones, for as Adam lay asleep, God took away one of his *ribs*, and out of that made Eve. So much for the forming of the first man and woman by the literal text. Moses has likewise given us a large account of their first habitation. He says that God made them in a certain famous garden in the East, and gave it to them as a farm to cultivate and to inhabit, which garden was a most delightful place, watered with four several fountains or rivers, planted with trees of every kind.... Amongst the trees, in the midst of the garden, stood two more remarkable than the rest; one was called the tree of life, the other the tree of death, or of the knowledge of good and evil.... God, upon pain of death, prohibits Adam and Eve from tasting the fruit of this tree; but it happened that Eve sitting solitary under this tree, without her husband, there came to her a serpent or adder, which (though I know not by what means or power) civilly accosted the woman (if we may judge of the thing by the event) in these words, or to this purpose:— *

> * We extract this portion not for its merits of buffoonery,
> but to show the real state of mind which could actuate a
> dignitary of the Church of England in writing it, as the
> eighth chapter is by far the most philosophical, but we wish
> to show Burnet's real sentiments.

"Serpent.—All hail, most fair one, what are you doing so solitary and serious under this shade?

"Eve.—I am contemplating the beauty of this tree.

"Serp.—'Tis truly an agreeable sight, but much pleasanter are the fruits thereof. Have you tasted them, my lady?

"Eve.—I have not, because God has forbidden us to eat of this tree.

"Serp.—What do I hear! What is that God that envies his creatures the innocent delights of nature? Nothing is sweeter, nothing more wholesome than this fruit: why, then, should he forbid it, unless in jest?

"Eve.—But he has forbid it us on pain of death.

"Serp.—Undoubtedly you mistake his meaning. This tree has nothing that would prove fatal to you, but rather something divine, and above the common order of nature.

"Eve.—I can give you no answer; but will go to my husband, and then do as he thinks fit.

"Serp.—Why should you trouble your husband over such a trifle! Use your own judgment.

"Eve.—Let me see—had I best use it or not? What 'can be more beautiful than this apple? How sweetly it smells! But it may be it tastes ill.

"Serp.—Believe me, it is a bit worthy to be eaten by the angels themselves; do but try, and if it tastes ill, throw it away.

"Eve.—Well, I'll try. It has, indeed, a most agreeable flavor. Give me another that I may carry it to my husband.

"Serp.—Very well thought on; here's another for you: go to your husband with it. Farewell, happy young woman. In the meantime I'll go my ways; let her take care of the rest.

"Accordingly, Eve gave the apple to the too uxorious Adam, when immediately after their eating of it, they became both (I don't know how) ashamed of their nakedness, and sewing fig leaves together, making themselves a sort of aprons, etc. After these transactions, God, in the evening, descended into the garden, upon which our first parents fled to hide themselves in the thickest of the trees, but in vain, for God called out, 'Adam, where art thou?' When he, trembling, appeared before God Almighty, and said, Lord, when I heard thee in this garden, I was ashamed because of my nakedness, and hid myself amongst the most shady parts of the thicket. Who told thee, says God, that thou wast naked? Have you eaten of the forbidden fruit? That woman thou gavest me brought it; 'twas she that made me eat of it. You have, says God, finely ordered your business, you and your wife. Here, you woman, what is this that you have done? Alas! for me, says Adam, thy serpent gave me the apple, and I did eat of it.

"This apple shall cost you dear, replied God, and not only you, but your posterity, and the whole race of mankind. Moreover, for this crime, I will curse and spoil the heavens, the earth, and the whole fabric of nature. But thou, in the first place, vile beast, shall bear the punishment of thy craftiness and malice. Hereafter shall thou go creeping on thy belly, and instead of eating apples, shall lick the dust of the earth. As for you, Mrs. Curious, who so much love delicacies, in sorrow-shall you bring forth your children. You shall be subject to your husband, and shall never depart from his side unless having first obtained leave. Lastly, as for you, Adam, because you have hearkened more to your wife than to me, with the sweat of your brow shall you obtain both food for her and her children. You shall not gather fruits which, as heretofore, grew of themselves, but shall reap the fruits of the earth with labor and trouble. May the earth be, for thy sake, accursed — hereafter grow barren. May she produce thistles, thorns, tares, with other hurtful and unprofitable herbs, and when thou hast here led a troublesome, laborious life, dust thou art, to dust shalt thou return......

"Great is the force of custom and a preconceived opinion over human minds. Wherefore, these short observations of the first originals of men or things, which we receive from Moses, are embraced without the least examination of them. But had we read the same doctrine in a Greek philosopher, or in a Rabbinical or Mahometan doctor, we should have stopped at every sentence with our mind full of objections and scruples. Now, this difference does not arise from the nature of the thing itself, but from the great opinion we have of the authority of the writer 'as being divinely inspired.' The author here defines his ideas in reference to fabulous writings, after which he proceeds in his inquiry. 'But out of what matter the first of mankind, whether, male or female, was composed, is not so easily known. If God had a mind to make a woman start from one of Adam's ribs, it is true it seems to be a matter not very proper; but, however, out of wood, stone, or any other being God can make a woman; and here, by the bye, the curious ask whether this rib was useless to Adam, and beyond the number requisite in a complete body. If not, when it was taken away, Adam would be a maimed person, and robbed of a part of himself that was necessary. I say necessary, for as much, as I suppose, that in the fabric of a human body nothing is superfluous, and that no one bone can be taken away without endangering the whole, or rendering it, in some measure, imperfect. But it, on the other side, you say this rib was really useless to Adam, and might be spared, so that you make him to have only twelve ribs on one side and thirteen on the other, they will reply that this is like a monster, as much as if the first man had been created with three feet, or three hands, or had had more eyes, or other members, than the use of a human body requires. But in the beginning we cannot but suppose that all things were made with all imaginable exactness.

"For my part, I do not pretend to decide this dispute, but what more perplexes me is, how, out of one rib, the whole mass of a woman's body could be built? For a rib does not, perhaps, equal the thousandth part of an entire body. If you answer that the rest of the matter was taken from elsewhere, certainly, then, Eve might much more truly be said to have been formed out of that borrowed matter, whatever it was, than out of Adam's rib. I know that the Rabbinical doctors solve this business quite another way, for they say the first man had two bodies, the one male, the other female, who were joined together, and that God having cloven them asunder, gave one side to Adam for a wife. Plato has, in his 'Symposium,' something very like this story, concerning his first man, Anoroginus, who was afterwards divided into two parts, male and female. Lastly, others conjecture that Moses gave out this original of woman to the end that he might inspire a mutual love between the two sexes, as parts of one and the same whole, so as more effectually to recommend his own institution of marriage.... But leaving this subject, I will hasten to something else.

"Now, the second article treats of God's, garden in Eden, watered with four rivers arising from the same spring.... Those rivers are, by Moses, called Pishon, Gishon, Hiddekal, and Perath, which the ancient authors interpret by Ganges, Nile, Tigris, and Euphrates. Nor do I truly think without some reason, for Moses seems to have proposed nothing more than the bringing four of the most celebrated rivers of the whole earth to the watering of his garden. Ah! but, say you, these four rivers do not spring from the same source, or come from the same place; 'tis true, nor any other four rivers that are named by the interpreters. Wherefore this objection will everywhere hold good, as well against the ancient as modern writers.—But although you should reduce these rivers to only two, as some do, to Tigris and Euphrates, yet neither have these two rivers the same fountain-head, but this is really and truly an evasion, instead of an explanation, to reduce, contrary to the history of Moses, a greater number of rivers to a smaller, only that they may the more conveniently be reduced to the same spring; for these are the words of Moses, 'But there comes a river out of Eden to water the garden, and from thence it divides itself into four branches, the name of the first is Pishon,' etc., whereby it is apparent that either in the exit or in the entrance of the garden there were four rivers, and that these four rivers did one and all proceed from the same fountain-head in Eden. Now, pray tell me in what part of the earth is this country of Eden, where four rivers arise from one and the same spring? But do not go about to say that only two came from that fountain of Eden, and that the other two arose from the Tigris or the Euphrates, where they split near the sea, and make, as it were, a bifrontic figure, since this does by no means answer the words of Moses. Besides, he mentions in the first place Pishon and Gishon, and afterwards Tigris and Euphrates as lesser rivers; whereas you, on the contrary, will have those to be derived from these last as rivers of an inferior order, which is a manifest distorting of the historical account. But to end all these difficulties concerning the channels of the rivers which watered Paradise, you will, perhaps, at last say, that the springs, as well as the courses of rivers, have been changed by the universal deluge: and that we cannot now be certain where it was they burst over the earth, and what countries they passed through. For my part I am much of your opinion, providing you confess there happened in the deluge such a disruption of the earth as we suppose there did. But from only an inundation of waters such a change could never happen. Besides, what geography will you have Moses to describe these rivers, ante-diluvian or post-diluvian'?—If the latter, there has happened no considerable alteration of the earth since the time of Moses and the flood. If the former, you then render Moses's description of the earth totally superfluous and unuseful to discover the situation of Paradise. Lastly, it is hard to conceive that any rivers, whether these or others, can have subsisted ever since the first beginning of the world; whether you have regard to their water or their channels. The channels of rivers are made by daily attrition; for if they had been made as ditches and furrows are, by earth dug out and heaped on each side, there would certainly have been seen everywhere great banks of earth. But we plainly see that this is only fortuitous; forasmuch as they often run through plains, and the river banks are no more than level with the adjacent fields; besides, whence could there be had water at the beginning of the world to fill these channels? If you say, that on the third day, when the great bed of the ocean was made, the smaller channels of the rivers were also: and as the greatest part of the waters of the abyss fell into the gulf of the seas, so the remaining part descended into these other channels, and therewith formed the primitive rivers. Admitting this, yet the waters would not only be as salt as those of the sea, but there would be no continual springs to nourish these rivers; insomuch as when the first stream of water had flown off, there being no fresh supplies of water to succeed it, these rivers would have been immediately dried up; I say because there were no perpetual springs; for whether springs proceed from rain, or from the sea, they could neither way have rose in so short a time; not from rain, for it had not as yet rained; neither was it possible, that in the short space of one day, the waters of the abyss should run down from the most inland places to the sea, and afterwards returning through ways that were never yet open to them, should strain themselves through the bowels of the earth, and ascend to the heads of their rivers. But of rivers we have said enough; let us now proceed to the rest.

"We have, in the third place, a very strange account of a serpent that talked with Eve, and enticed her to oppose God. I must confess, we have not yet known that this beast could ever speak, or utter any sort of voice, beside hissing. But what shall we think Eve knew of this business? If she had taken it for a dumb animal, the very speech of it would have so frightened her, that she would have fled from it. If, on the other side, the serpent had from the beginning been capable of talking and haranguing, and only lost his speech for the crime of having corrupted the faith of Eve, certainly Moses would have been far from passing over in silence this sort of punishment, and only mentioning the curse of licking the dust. Besides this, will you have the particular species of serpents, or all the beasts in Paradise, to have been imbued with the faculty of speaking, like the trees in Dodona's grove? If you say all, pray what offence had the rest been guilty of, that they also should lose the use of their tongues? If only the serpent enjoyed this privilege, how came it about that so vile an animal (by nature the most reverse and remote from man) should, before all his other fellow brutes, deserve to be master of so great a favor and benefit as that of speech?

"Lastly, since all discoursing and arguing includes the use of reason, by this very thing you make the serpent a rational creature. But I imagine you will solve this difficulty another way; for (say the sticklers for a literal interpretation) under the disguise of a serpent was hid the Devil, or an evil spirit, who, using the mouth and organs of this animal, spoke to the woman as though it were a human voice. But what testimony or what authority have they for this? The most literal reading of Moses, which they so closely adhere to, does not express anything of it; for what else does he seem to say, but that he attributes the seducing of Eve to the natural craftiness of the serpent, and nothing else? For these are Moses's words:—'Now the serpent was more cunning than any beast of the field that the Lord God had made.' Afterwards, continues he:—'The serpent said to the woman, yea, hath God said,' etc.—But besides, had Eve heard an animal, by nature dumb, speak through the means of some evil spirit, she would instantly have fled with horror from the monster.—When, on the contrary, she very familiarly received it; they argued very amicably together, as though nothing new or astonishing had taken place. Again, if you say that all this proceeded from the ignorance or weakness of a woman, it would on the other side have been but just, that some good angels should have succoured a poor, ignorant, weak woman; those just guardians of human affairs would not have permitted so unequal a conflict; for what if an evil spirit, crafty and knowing in business, had, by his subtlety, overreached a poor, weak, and silly woman, who had not as yet, either seen the sun rise or set, who was but newly born, and thoroughly inexperienced. Certainly, a person who had so great a price set upon her head, as the salvation of all mankind, might well have deserved a guard of angels. Aye, but perhaps (you will say) the woman ought to have taken care not to violate a law established on pain of death. 'The day you eat of it you shall surely die,', both you and yours; this was the law. Die! what does that mean, says the poor, innocent virgin, who as yet had not seen anything dead, no, not so much as a flower; nor had yet with her eyes or mind perceived the image of death—viz., sleep, or night? But what you add concerning his posterity and their punishment, that is not all expressed in the law. Now no laws are ever to so distorted, especially those that are penal. The punishment of the serpent will also afford no inconsiderable question, if the Devil transacted the whole thing under the form of a serpent; or if he compelled the serpent to do, or to suffer things, why did he (the serpent) pay for a crime committed by the Devil? Moreover, as to the manner and form of the punishment inflicted on the serpent, that from that time he should go creeping on his belly, it is not to be explained what that meant. Hardly any one will say, that prior to his catastrophe the serpent walked upright, like four footed beasts; and if, from the beginning, he crept on his belly like other snakes, it may seem ridiculous to impose on this creature as a punishment for one single crime, a thing which, by nature, he ever had before. But let this suffice for the woman and serpent; let us now go on to the trees. I here understand those two trees, which stood in the middle of the garden, the tree of life, and the tree of good and evil. The former so called, that it would give men a very long life, although, by what follows, we find our forefathers, prior to the flood, lived to very great ages, independent of the tree of life. Besides, if the longevity, or immortality of man had depended only upon one tree, or its fruit, what if Adam had not sinned? how could his posterity, diffused throughout the whole earth, have been able to come and gather fruit out of this garden, or from this tree? or how could the product of one tree have been sufficient for all mankind?"

Such is a condensed abstract of Dr. Burnet's seventh chapter of "Archæologia." The eighth chapter equals the above in boldness; but far exceeds it in breadth of logic and critical acumen, without, however, appearing so iconoclastic or so vulgar. The next chapter abounds in classical quotations, the Creation of the world and the Deluge is the theme on which so much is advanced, at a time when such language was greeted with the stake and the prison. We cannot calculate the effect of Burnet's works on the clerical mind; but this we do know, that since his day, there has progressed an internal revolution in the tenets of the church, which, in the last generation, gave birth to the neology, now so destructive of the internal peace of the churches. Neology has not come from Deism, for this power assails the outworks of Christianity; while the school of criticism is but a severe pruning knife of internal verbiage. Although the language quoted is harsh, the arguments common-place, which, although true, are now discarded by the educated Freethinker; yet if for no stronger language than this men were imprisoned only ten years ago, what must we say to the moral courage which could publish them 150 years ago? There must surely have been greater risks than in our day; and when a man dare hazard the highest power of the church for the duty of publishing unpopular sentiments, it is clearly our duty to; enshrine him as one of the guardians of that liberty of thought, and speech, which have won for us a freedom. we cherish and protect. Let the earth then lie lightly over the priest-Freethinker, Thomas Burnet.

A. C.

THOMAS PAINE

"The wise by some centuries before the crowd,
Must, by their novel systems, though correct,
Of course offend the wicked, weak, and proud,
Must meet with hatred, calumny, neglect."

Thomas Paine, "the sturdy champion of political and religious liberty," was born at Thetford, in the County of Norfolk, (Eng.,) 29th of January, 1737. Born of religious parents (his father being a Quaker, and his mother a member of the Church of England,) Paine received a religious education at Thetford Grammar School, under the Rev. William Knowles. At an early age he gave indications of his great talent, and found pleasure, when a boy, in studying poetical authors. His parents, however, endeavored to check his taste for poetry, his father probably thinking it would unfit him for the denomination to which *he* belonged. But Paine did not lose much time before experimenting in poetry himself. Hence we find him, when eight years of age, composing the following epitaph, upon a fly being caught in a spider's web:—

"Here lies the body of John Crow,
Who once was high, but now is low;
Ye brother Crows take warning all,
For as you rise, so you must fall."

At the age of thirteen, after receiving a moderate education in reading, writing, and arithmetic, Paine left school, to follow his father's trade (stay-making.) Although disliking the business, he pursued this avocation for nearly five years. When about twenty years of age, however, he felt—as most enterprising young men do feel—a desire to visit London, and enter into the competition and chances of a metropolitan life. His natural dislike to his father's business led him to abandon for a period his original occupation, and, after working some time with Mr. Morris, a noted stay-maker, in Long Acre, he resolved upon a seafaring adventure, of which he thus speaks:—

"At an early age, raw, adventurous, and heated with the false Heroism of a master [Rev. Mr. Knowles, Master of the Grammar School at Thetford] who had served in a man-of-war, I began my fortune, and entered on board the Terrible, Captain Death, from this adventure I was happily prevented by the affectionate and moral remonstrances of a good father, who from the habits of his life, being of the Quaker profession, looked on me as lost; but the impression, much as it affected me at the time, wore away, and I entered afterwards in the King of Prussia privateer, Captain Mender, and went with her to sea."

Sea life did not, as may be supposed, long satisfy a mind like Paine's. In April, 1759, after working nearly twelve months at Dover, we find him settled as master stay-maker at Sandwich; marrying, on September 27, Mary Lambert, daughter of an Exciseman of that place. But his matrimonial happiness was of short duration, his wife dying the following year.

Disgusted with the toil and inconvenience of his late occupation, Paine now renounced it forever, to apply himself to the profession of Exciseman. After fourteen months' study he obtained the appointment of supernumerary in the Excise, which he held, with intervals, till 1768, when he settled as Exciseman at Lewes, in Sussex, and married, 1771, Elizabeth Olive, daughter of a tobacconist, whose business he succeeded to. About this time Paine wrote several little pieces, in prose and verse, among which was the celebrated song on the "Death of General Wolfe," and "The Trial of Farmer Carter's Dog, Porter." The latter is a composition of "exquisite wit and humor."

In 1772 the Excise officers throughout the kingdom were dissatisfied with their salaries, and formed a plan to apply to Parliament for an increase. Paine being distinguished among them as a man of great talent, was solicited to draw up and state their case, which he did in a pamphlet entitled "The Case of the Salary of the Officers of Excise, and Thoughts on the Corruption arising from the Poverty of Excise Officers." Four thousand copies of this pamphlet were printed and circulated. Some time after this publication, Paine, being in the grocery business, was *suspected* of unfair practices, and was dismissed the Excise, after being in it twelve years. This *suspicion*, however, was never shown to be just. But to show how *very vigorous* the authorities were in *suppressing* smuggling, we will quote the following letter from Clio Rickman to the Editor of the Independent Whig, in October, 1807:—

"Sir,—If there are any characters more to be abhorred than others, it is those who inflict severe punishments against offenders, and yet themselves commit the same crimes.

"If any characters more than others deserve execration, exposure, and to be driven from among mankind, it is those governors of the people who break the laws they themselves make, and punish others for breaking.

"Suffer me, Mr. Editor, thus to preface the following fact; fact, I say, because I stand ready to prove it so.

"When Admiral Duncan rendezvoused in the Downs with his fleet, on the 8th of January, 1806, the Spider lugger, Daniel Falara, master, was sent to Guernsey to smuggle articles for the fleet, such as wine, spirits, hair powder, playing cards, tobacco, etc., for the supply of the different ships.

"At her arrival in the Downs, the ships' boats flocked round her to unload her and her contraband cargo. A Custom House extra boat, commanded by William Wallace, seeing the lugger, followed and took her; in doing which he did his duty.

"On his inspecting the smuggled articles with which she was laden, he found a number of cases directed to Admiral Duncan, the Right Honorable William Pitt, the heaven-born Minister of England, and to the Right Honorable Henry Dundas, Walmer Castle. In a few days, Wallace, the master of the Custom House cutter, received orders from Government to give the lugger and her smuggled cargo up, on penalty of being dismissed the service; and these cases of smuggled goods were afterwards delivered at the Prime Ministers, Mr. Pitt, at Walmer Castle.

"Mr. Editor, read what follows, and repress your indignation if you can.

"There are now in Deal jail fourteen persons for trifling acts of smuggling compared to the above of the Right Honorable William Pitt and the now Right Honorable Lord Melville.

"The former were poor, and knew not how to live, the latter were most affluently and splendidly supported by the people—that is, they were paupers upon the generous public, towards whom they thus scandalously and infamously conducted themselves.

"I am, Sir, your humble servant,

"Clio Rickman."

To those opponents of Thomas Paine who attach any weight to his dismissal from the Excise on suspicion of smuggling, we would mention the fact, that during Paine's service at Lewes, Mr. Jenner, the principal clerk in the Excise Office, London, wrote several letters from the Board of Excise, "thanking Mr. Paine for his assiduity in his profession, and for his information and calculations forwarded to the office." Shortly-after his dismissal, Mr. Paine and his wife, by mutual agreement, separated. Many tales have been put in circulation respecting the separation. Clio Rickman, in his "Life of Paine," has the following passage: —-

"That he did not cohabit with her from the moment they left the altar till the day of their separation, a space of three years, although they lived in the same house together, is an indubitable truth. It is also true, that no physical defect, on the part of Mr. Paine, can be adduced as a reason for such conduct.... Mr. Paine's answer, upon my once referring to this subject, was, 'It is nobody's business but my own: I had cause for it, but I will name it to no one.'.... This I can assert, that Mr. Paine always spoke tenderly and respectfully of his wife; and sent her several times pecuniary aid, without her knowing even whence it came."

In 1774 Paine left England, and arrived at Philadelphia a few months before the battle of Lexington. He made his appearance in the New World as editor of the Pennsylvanian Magazine; and it would appear that he then had in view the coming struggle, in which he took so prominent a part, for in his introduction to the first number of the above Magazine he states:—"Thus encompassed with difficulties, this first number of the Pennsylvanian Magazine entreats a favorable reception; of which we shall only say, that like the early snowdrop, it comes forth in a barren season, and contents itself with foretelling the reader that choicer flowers are preparing to appear." Upon the foreign supply of gunpowder being prohibited, he proposed a plan, in the Pennsylvanian Journal, of a saltpetre association for the voluntary supply of that article of destruction.

On the 10th of January, 1776, "Common Sense" was published, its circulation soon reaching 100,000 copies. The effect this remarkable pamphlet produced upon the minds of the American people, and the share it had in bringing to a successful issue the then pending struggle, may be gathered even from Paine's bitterest enemies. Mr. Cheetham, in his "Life of Paine," while endeavoring to damage the author of "Common Sense," admits the value of this pamphlet. He says:—"This pamphlet of forty octavo pages, holding out relief by proposing Independence to an oppressed and despairing people, was published in January, 1776; speaking a language which the colonists had felt, but not thought of. Its popularity, terrible in its consequences to the parent country, was unexampled in the history of the press. At first involving the colonists, in the crime of rebellion, and pointing to a road leading inevitably to ruin, it was read with indignation and alarm; but when the reader—and every one read it—recovering from the first shock, re-perused it, its arguments nourishing his feelings and appealing to his pride, re-animated his hopes, and satisfied his understanding that 'Common Sense,' backed by the resources and force of the colonies, poor and feeble as they were, could alone rescue them from the unqualified oppression with which they were threatened. The unknown author, in the moments of enthusiasm which succeeded, was an angel sent from heaven to save from all the horrors of slavery by his timely, powerful, and unerring councils, a faithful but abused, a brave but misrepresented people." Another of Paine's enemies and slanderers—Elkanah Watson—in a volume recently published, entitled "Men and Times of the Revolution," after speaking in very disparaging terms of Paine's appearance, habits, and disposition (which is proved false by the best of testimony,) admits the service rendered to America by "Common Sense." He says:—"Yet I could not repress the deepest emotions of gratitude towards him, as the instrument of Providence in accelerating the declaration of our Independence. He certainly was a prominent agent in preparing the public sentiment of America for that glorious event. The idea of Independence had not occupied the popular mind, and when guardedly approached on the topic, it shrunk from the conception, as fraught with doubt, with peril, and with suffering. In 1776 I was present at Providence, Rhode Island, in a social assembly of most of the prominent leaders of the State. I recollect that the subject of Independence was cautiously introduced by an ardent Whig, and the thought seemed to excite the abhorrence of the whole circle. A few weeks after, Paine's 'Common Sense' appeared, and passed through the continent like an electric spark. It everywhere flashed conviction, and aroused a determined spirit, which resulted in the Declaration of Independence, upon the 4th of July ensuing. The name of Paine was precious to every Whig heart, and had resounded throughout Europe." Other testimony could be given to Paine's influence in the American struggle for Independence; but after the two already mentioned from his opponents, it is unnecessary to give further proof.

In the same year that "Common Sense" appeared, Paine accompanied General Washington and his army, being with him in his retreat from Hudson River to the Delaware. Although great terror prevailed, Paine stood brave and undismayed, conscious he was advocating a just cause, and determined to bring it to a successful issue. He occupied himself in inspiring hope in the Americans, showing them their strength and their weakness. This object drew from his pen "The Crisis," a continuation of the "Common Sense," which was issued at intervals till the cessation of hostilities.

In 1777 Paine was unanimously, and unknown to himself, appointed Secretary in the Foreign Department, where he formed a close friendship with Dr. Franklin. He did not retain his office, however, long, as he refused to become a party to the fraudulent demands of a Mr. Silas Deane, one of the American Commissioners, then in Europe; and he resigned the office.

In 1780 he was chosen member of the American Philosophical Society, having previously received the degree of Master of Arts from the University of Philadelphia.

When the Independence of America was attained, and when oppression had received a severe and lasting check in that rising country, we find that Paine, so far from being satisfied with his success in the New World, began to look for a fresh field where he might render good service to the cause of right and freedom. Accordingly, in 1787. he visited Paris, his famous services to America giving him a welcome by those who knew the benefit arising from the establishment of human rights. His stay in Paris, at this time, was of short duration, as he returned to England after an absence of thirteen years, on September 3rd. After visiting his mother, and settling an allowance of nine shillings per week for her support, he resided for a short time at Rotherham, in Yorkshire, where an iron bridge was cast and erected upon a model of his invention, which obtained him great reputation for his mathematical skill.

The publication of "Mr. Burke's Reflections on the French Revolution" called from Paine his "Rights of Man," a book that created great attraction, and sold nearly a million and a half of copies. In politics Paine was clear and decided, and, from his moderation, what is called "sound." For the perusal of those who may not have read it, we give the following quotations, to show the principles upon which it is based: —

"Mr. Burke talks about what he calls an hereditary crown, as if it were some production of nature; or as if, like time, it had a power to operate, not only independently, but in spite of man; or as if it were a thing or a subject universally consented to. Alas! it has none of those properties, but is the reverse of them all. It is a thing in imagination, the property of which is more than doubted, and the legality of which in a few years will be denied. But, to arrange this matter in a clearer view than what general expressions can convey, it will be necessary to state the distinct heads under which (what is called) an hereditary crown, or, more properly speaking, an hereditary succession to the government of a nation, can be considered; which are, first, the right of a particular family to establish itself; secondly, the right of a nation to establish a particular family. With respect to the *first* of these heads, that of a family establishing itself with heredity powers on its own authority, and independent of the consent of a nation, all men will concur in calling it despotism: and it would be trespassing on their understanding to attempt to prove it. But the *second* head, that of a nation establishing a particular family with *hereditary powers*, does not present itself as despotism on the first reflection; but if men will permit a second reflection to take place, and carry that reflection forward but one remove out of their own persons to that of their offspring, they will then see that hereditary succession becomes in its consequences the same despotism to others, which they reprobated for themselves. It operates to preclude the consent of the succeeding generations; and the preclusion of consent is despotism. When the person who at any time shall be in possession of a government, or those who stand in succession to him, shall say to a nation, I hold this power in 'contempt' of you, it signifies not on what authority he pretends to say it. It is no relief, but an aggravation to a person in slavery, to reflect that he was sold by his parent; and as that which heightens the criminality of an act cannot be produced to prove the legality of it, hereditary succession cannot be established as a legal thing.... Notwithstanding the taxes of England amount to almost seventeen millions a year, said to be for the expenses of Government, it is still evident that the sense of the nation is left to govern itself by magistrates and jurors, almost at its own charge, on Republican principles, exclusive of the expense of taxes. The salaries of the judges are almost the only charge that is paid out of the revenue. Considering that all the internal government is executed by the people, the taxes of England ought to be the lightest of any nation in Europe; instead of which they are the contrary. As this cannot be accounted for on the score of civil government, the subject necessarily extends itself to the monarchical part..... If a law be bad, it is one thing to oppose the practice of it, but it is quite a different thing to expose its errors, to reason on its defects, and show cause why it should be repealed, or why another ought to be substituted in its place. I have always held it an opinion (making it also my practice) that it is better to obey a bad law, making use at the same time of every argument to show its errors and procure its repeal, than forcibly to violate it; because the precedent of breaking a bad law might weaken the force, and lead to a discretionary violation, of those which are good."

As may be supposed, such a work as "The Rights of Man," aiming directly at all oppression, regardless of party, could not be allowed to escape the Attorney-General's *answer*. Accordingly, we find a prosecution instituted against it. But instead of prosecuting the author, the publishers were selected. This drew from Paine a long Letter to the Attorney-General, suggesting the justice of *his* answering for the book he wrote. On the trial, Mr. (afterwards Lord) Erskine thus spoke of the author of "The Rights of Man:" — "The defendant's whole deportment previous to the publication has been wholly unexceptionable; he properly desired to be given up as the author of the book, if any inquiry should take place concerning it; and he is not affected in evidence, directly or indirectly, with any illegal or suspicious conduct, not even with uttering an indiscreet or taunting expression, nor with any one matter or thing inconsistent with the best subject in England."

On the 12th of September, 1792, Mr. Achilles Audibert came expressly to England, from the French Convention, to solicit Paine to attend and aid them, by his advice, in their deliberations. "On his arrival at Calais a public dinner was provided, a royal salute was fired from the battery, the troops were drawn out, and there was a general rejoicing throughout the town.... Paine was escorted to the house of his friend, Mr. Audibert, the Chief Magistrate of the place, where he was visited by the Commandant, and all the Municipal Officers in forms, who afterwards gave him a sumptuous entertainment in the Town Hall. The same honor was also paid him on his departure for Paris." Upon his arrival in Paris all was confusion. There were the King's friends mortified and subdued, the Jacobins split up into cavilling faction, some wishing a federative government, some desiring the King's death, and the death of all the nobility; while a portion were more discreet, wishing liberty without licentiousness, and having a desire to redress wrongs without revenge. These few accepted Paine as their leader, and renounced all connection with the Jacobin Club.

Paine, on all occasions, advocated the preservation of the King's life but his efforts were thwarted by the appointment, by Robespierre, of Barrere to office. So anxiously was Paine sought after, that both Calais and Versailles returned him as Deputy. To show how the author of "The Rights of Man" opposed all physical force where reason may be used, it is only necessary to state, that when the Letter of Dumourier reached Paris with the threat of restoring the King, Paine wrote a letter to the Convention, stating a plan for re-adjustment, and was taking it personally, when he was informed "that a decree had just been passed offering one hundred thousand crowns for Dumourier's head; and another, making it high treason to propose anything in his favor." Whilst Deputy for Calais, Paine was sought and admired by all classes. He dined every Friday, for a long period, with the Earl of Lauderdale and Dr. Moore; and so frequent were his visitors, that he set apart two mornings a week for his *levee* days. — He soon, however, changed his residence, preferring less formality and a more select circle. His "History of the French Revolution" we are deprived of by his imprisonment, which Gibbon thought would prove a great loss. The historian often applied for the MS., believing it to be of great worth. The opinion Paine held of the Revolution may be gathered from the following: —

"With respect to the Revolution, it was begun by good men, on good principles, and I have ever believed it would have gone on so, had not the provocative interference of foreign powers distracted it into madness, and sown jealousies among the leaders. The people of England have now two Revolutions, the American and the French before them. Their own wisdom will direct them what to *choose* and what to *avoid*, and in everything which relates to their happiness, combined with the common good of mankind, I wish them honor and success."

His speech against the death of the King, shows how far he was removed from party spirit or any feeling of revenge. Whilst he protested against the King being re-enthroned, he equally protested against his death, wishing him removed from the seat of his corruption, and placed in a more elevating atmosphere. — Entreating for the King's safety, he says: — "Let then the United States be the safeguard and the asylum of Louis Capet. There, hereafter, far removed from the miseries and crimes of royalty, he may learn, from the constant aspect of public prosperity, that the true system of government consists in fair, equal, and honora-able representation. In relating this circumstance, and in submitting this proposition, I consider myself as a citizen of both countries."

The policy pursued by Paine was not consonant with the views of Robespierre. Consequently, he was seized in the night and imprisoned in the Luxembourg eleven months, without any reason being assigned. The readers are doubtless aware of the many *Providential* escapes he had from the death for which he was seized. While in prison he wrote part of his "Age of Reason," (having commenced it just previous to his arrest) not Knowing one hour but he might be executed, and once being on the verge of death from fever. He knew the prejudice the "Age of Reason" would create, so he left its production to the latter part of his life, not wishing to make *that* an impediment to the good he sought to accomplish in the Political world.

After toiling in France to bring the Revolution to a *just* termination, and finding his efforts rendered abortive by that feeling which *former oppression had created*, he resolved to return to America, a country he saw thriving by a policy he wished to institute in France.

In 1802, Jefferson, then President of America, knowing his wish to return, wrote him the following letter: —

"You express a wish in your letter to return to America by a national ship. Mr. Dawson, who brings over the treaty, and who will present you with this letter, is charged with orders to the captain of the Maryland, to receive and accommodate you back if you can be ready to return at such a short warning. You will in general find us returned to sentiments worthy of former times; in these it will be your glory to have steadily labored, and with as much effect as any man living. That you may live long to continue your useful labors, and reap the reward in the thankfulness of nations, is my sin cere prayer.

"Accept the assurance of my high esteem and affectionate attachment,

"Thomas Jefferson."

But circumstances prevented Paine going by the Maryland. He sailed, however, on the 1st of September, 1802, in the London Pacquet. He had often previously arranged to return to America, but luckily, *Providence* prevented him. One ship that he intended to sail by, was searched by English frigates for Thomas Paine, and another sunk at sea, whilst at other times British frigates were cruising off the ports from which he was to sail, knowing him to be there.

So much religious misrepresentation has been circulated about Paine's life and death, that it becomes a duty to restate the *facts*. The manner of life Paine pursued may be gathered from the *reliable* testimony of Clio Rickman. He says, "Mr. Paine's life in London was a quiet round of philosophical leisure and enjoyment. It was occupied in writing, in a small epistolary correspondence, in walking about with me to visit different friends, occasionally lounging at coffeehouses and public places, or being visited by a select few. Lord Edward Fitzgerald, the French and American ambassadors, Mr. Sharp the engraver, Romney, the painter, Mrs. Wolstonecraft, Joel Barlow, Mr. Hull, Mr. Christie, Dr. Priestley, Dr. Towers, Colonel Oswald, the walking Stewart, Captain Sampson Perry, Mr. Tuffin, Mr. William Choppin, Captain De Stark, Mr. Home Tooke, etc., were among the number of his friends and acquaintances." His manner of living in France and America has already been noticed.

The perverted tales of Carver and Cheetham may be utterly disproved by referring to Clio Rickman's "Life of Paine." As his life, so was his death. When he became feeble and infirm (in Jan. 1809) he was often visited by those "good people" who so often intrude upon the domestic quiet of the afflicted. After the visit of an old woman, "come from the Almighty," (whom Paine soon sent back again) he was troubled with the Rev. Mr. Milledollar, and the Rev. Mr. Cunningham. The latter reverend said, "Mr. Paine, we visit you as friends and neighbors; you have now a full view of death, you cannot live long; and whoever does not believe in Jesus Christ, will assuredly be damned." "Let me," said Paine, "have none of your Popish stuff; get away with you; good morning, good morning." Another visitor was the Rev. Mr. Hargrove, with this statement:—"My name is Hargrove, Sir; I am minister of the new Jerusalem church; we, Sir, explain the scripture in its true meaning; the key has been lost these four thousand years, and we have found It." "Then," said Paine, in his own neat way, "it must have been very rusty." Shortly before his death, he stated to Mr. Hicks, to whom he had sent to arrange his burial? that his sentiments in reference to the Christian religion were precisely the same as when he wrote the "Age of Reason." On the 8th of June, (in the words of Clio Rickman) 1809. about nine in the morning, he placidly, and almost without a struggle, died as he had lived, a Deist, aged seventy-two years and five months. He was interred at New Rochelle, upon his own farm; a handsome monument being now erected where he was buried.

It has been the object in the present sketch rather to give, in a brief manner, an account of Paine's life and services, than an elucidation of his writings. His works are well known, and *they* will speak for themselves but much wrong is done to his memory by the perversions and misrepresentations of the religious publications. No doubt had his views been different on "religious" subjects, he would have been held up as a model of genius, perseverance, courage, disinterestedness of purpose, and purity of life, by the men who now find him no better name than the "Blasphemer." We hope that those not previously acquainted with the facts of his life, will find in the present sketch sufficient reason to think and speak otherwise of a man who made the world his country, and the doing good his religion.

> *"As Euclid near his various writings shone,*
>
> *His pen inspired by glorious truth alone,*
>
> *O'er all the earth diffusing light and life,*
>
> *Subduing error, ignorance, and strife;*
>
> *Raised man to just pursuits, to thinking right,*
>
> *And yet will free the world from woe and falsehood's night;*
>
> *To this immortal man, to Paine 'twas given,*
>
> *To metamorphose earth from hell to heaven."*

J. W.

BAPTISTE DE MIRABAUD

Jean Baptiste de Mirabaud was born at Paris, in the year 1675. Of his early life we can glean but very scanty information. He appears first to have embraced the military profession, but it not being consonant with his general character, he soon quitted the army, and devoted himself to literature. He was, however, nearly forty-nine years of age before he became known in the literary world. He then published a French translation of Tasso's "Jerusalem," which brought him much fame; and many of the contributors to the French Encyclopaedia appear to have associated with him, and courted his friendship. He was afterwards elected a member of the French Academy of which he became the Secretary in 1742. Mirabaud was a constant visitor at the house of his friend, the Baron d'Holbach, down to the period of his death. He wrote "The World: its Origin and its Antiquity," "Opinions of the Ancients upon the Jews," "Sentiments of the Philosophers upon the Nature of the Soul," and other minor works. The "System of Nature" was also for many years attributed to Mirabaud, but it appears now to be extremely doubtful whether he ever wrote a single line of the work. The Abbe Galiani was one of the first who pointed out D'Holbach as the author. In the memoirs of M. Suard, edited by M. Garat, the same hypothesis is supported with additional firmness. Dugald Stewart seems to put much faith in the latter authority, as fixing the authorship of the "System of Nature" upon D'Holbach. Voltaire attributes the work to Damilaville, in a somewhat positive manner, for which he is sharply criticised in the "Biographie Universelle," published in 1817. The "System of Nature" is a book of which Dugald Stewart speaks, as "the boldest, if not the ablest work of the Parisian Atheists," and it has undoubtedly obtained great popularity. Voltaire, who has written against the "System of Nature" in a tone of bitter sarcasm, and who complains of its general dullness and prolixity, yet admits that it is "often humorous, sometimes eloquent." It certainly is not written in that lively, but rather superficial style, which has characterized many of the French writers, but it speaks in plain yet powerful language, evincing an extensive acquaintance with the works of previous philosophers, and much thought in relation to the subjects treated upon. Some of its pages exhibiting more vivacity than the rest of the book, have been attributed to Diderot, who (it is alleged by Marmontel and others) aided, by his pen and counsel, many of the Freethinking works issued during his life.

The "System of Nature" was not published during the life-time of Mirabaud, and it is therefore impossible to use any argument which might have been based upon Mirabaud's conduct in relation to it.

Mirabaud died in Paris in 1760, at the advanced age of nearly eighty-six years. Contemporary with him were D'Alembert, D'Holbach, Voltaire, Diderot, Helvetius, Condorcet, Buffon, Rousseau, Frederick II. of Prussia, Montesquieu, Grimm, Sir William Tempte, Toland, Tindel, Edmund Halley, Hume, Gibbon, Adam Smith, Franklin, and Darwin, forming a *role* of names, whose fame will be handed down to posterity for centuries to come, as workers in the cause of man's redemption from mental slavery. If (as it appears very probably) it be the fact that Mirabaud had but little part in the authorship of "La Système de la Nature," D'Holbach, in using the name of his deceased friend, only associated him with a work which (judging from his other writings, the tenor of his life, and the noble character of his associates) Mirabaud would have issued with pride himself, had the book been really written by him.

BARON D'HOLBACH

Paul Thyry, Baron D'Holbach, was born at Heidesheim, in the Palatinate, in the month of January, 1723. His father appears to have been a very wealthy man, and brought his son to Paris, for the purpose of superintending his education, but died white he was still a child. In his youth, D'Holbach appears to have been noted for his studious habits and retentive faculties, and ultimately attained to some eminence in chemistry and mineralogy. He married when very young, and he had not been married one year when his wife died. He afterwards obtained a dispensation from the Pope, and married his deceased wife's sister, by whom he had four children, two sons and two daughters.

D'Holbach appeared to have spent the greater part of his life in Paris, and for forty years he assembled around his table, every Sunday, the *elite* of the literary world, including nearly the whole of those who took part in the first Encyclopedia. If that table were only in the hands of some of our spirit friends of the present day, what brilliant anecdotes might it not rap out—the sparkling wit of Diderot, the good humor of out host, the hospitable and generous D'Holbach, the occasional bitterness of Jean Jacques Rousseau, the cautious expression of opinion by D'Alembert, the agreeable variety of Montesquieu, and the bold enthusiasm of the youthful but hardworking Naigeon! If ever a table were inclined to turn, this table should have been; but perhaps it may be that tables never turn when reason is the ruler of those who sit around.

It seems more than probable that D'Holbach at first held opinions differing widely from those entertained by him during the later periods of his life, and it is asserted that Diderot contributed much to this change of opinion. D'Holbach was an amiable man of the world, fond of amusement, and without pretension; he was, notwithstanding, well versed in Roman and Grecian literature, mathematics, chemistry, botany, and modern languages. He was generous to every one. "I content myself," he said, "with performing the disagreeable character of benefactor, when I am forced to it. I do not wish to be repaid my money; but I am pleased when I meet with some little gratitude, if it be only as proving that the persons I have assisted were such sort of men as I desired."

Although about forty-five works are now ascribed to D'Holbach, not one of them was published during his life-time in his own name. The manuscripts were taken to Amsterdam by Naigeon, and there printed by Michael Rey. D'Holbach never talked publicly of his literary productions himself and his secrets seem to have been well kept by his friends. Several of the works were condemned and suppressed by the government; but D'Holbach lived unsuspected and unmolested. The expression used by the Avocat, General Seguier, in his réquisitoire against the "System of Nature" is worthy of notice. The Avocat General said—"The restless spirit of Infidelity, inimical to all dependence, endeavors to overthrow all political constitutions. Its wishes will not be satisfied until it has destroyed the *necessary* inequality of rank and condition, and until it has degraded the majesty of kings, and rendered their authority subordinate to the *caprices* of the *mob*." Note the three words we have italicised. For the first read unnecessary; for the second, voice; for the third, peoples. We trust that Free-thought never will be satisfied until it has destroyed the unnecessary inequalities of rank and condition, and rendered it impossible for the authority of kings to be enforced in opposition to the voice of the people.

The following description of D'Holbach is given in a little sketch, published by Mr. Watson in 1834, as taken from Grimm's "Correspondence:"— "D'Hol-bach's features were, taken separately, regular, and even handsome, yet he was not a handsome man. His forehead, large and open, like that of Diderot, indicated a vast and capacious mind; but his forehead having fewer sinuosities, less roundness than Diderot's, announced less warmth, less energy, and less fecundity of ideas. A craniologist would say that in both D'Holbach and Diderot, the philosophical organs were largely developed, but that Diderot excelled in ideality; D'Holbach's countenance only indicated mildness, and the habitual sincerity of his mind. He was incapable of personal hatred. Though he detested priests and Jesuits, and all other supporters of despotism and superstition; and though when speaking of such people, his mildness and good temper were sometimes transformed into bitterness and irritability; yet it is affirmed that when the Jesuits were expelled from France, D'Holbach regarded them as objects of commiseration and of pity, and afforded them pecuniary assistance."

The titles of D'Holbach's works may be found in Barbier's "Dictionary of Anonymous Works," and in St. Surins's article in the "Biographie Universelle," so in the little tract before mentioned as published by J.

Watson. D'Holbach contributed largely to the first French Encyclopaedia, and other works of a like character. Of the "System of Nature" we have already spoken, and shall rather leave our readers to the work itself than take up more space in discussing its authorship.

After having lived a life of comfort, in affluent circumstances, and always surrounded by a large circle of the best men of the day, D'Holbach died on January the 21st, 1789, being, then sixty-six years of age. The priests have never pictured to us any scene of horror in relation to his dying moments. The good old man died cheered and supported in his last struggle by those men whom he had many times assisted in the hard fighting of the battle of life. J. A. Naigeon, who had been his friend for thirty years; paid an eloquent tribute to D'Holbach's memory, in an article which appeared in the "Journal de Paris" of February the 9th, 1789, and we are not aware that any man has ever written anything against D'Hol-bach's personal character.

EXTRACTS FROM "THE SYSTEM OF NATURE."

Although we may not attempt to express a decided opinion as to the authorship of "Le Système de la Nature," we feel it our duty to present some of its principal arguments to the consideration of our readers. The author opens his work with this passage:—

"Man always deceives himself when he abandons experience to follow imaginary systems. He is the work of nature. He exists in nature. He is submitted to her laws. He cannot deliver himself from them. He cannot step beyond them even in thought. It is in vain his mind would spring forward beyond the visible world: an imperious necessity ever compels his return—for a being formed by Nature, who is circumscribed by her laws, there exists nothing beyond the great whole of which he forms a part, of which be experiences the influence. The beings his imagination pictures as above Nature, or distinguished from her, are always chimeras formed after that which he has, already seen, but of which it is utterly impossible he should ever form any correct idea, either as to the place they occupy, or their manner of acting—for him there is not, there can be nothing out of that nature which includes all beings. Instead, therefore, of seeking out of the world he inhabits for beings who can procure him a happiness denied by Nature, let him study this nature, learn her laws, contemplate her energies, observe the immutable rules by which she acts."

Speaking of the theological delusions under which many men labor, and of the mode in which man has been surrounded by those delusions, he says:—

"His ignorance made him credulous: his curiosity made him swallow large draughts of the marvellous: time confirmed him in his opinions, and he passed his conjectures from race to race, for realities; a tyrannical power maintained him in his notions, because by those alone could society be enslaved. It was in vain, that some faint glimmerings of Nature occasionally attempted, the recall of his reason; that slight corruscations of experience sometimes threw his darkness into light; the interest of the few was bottomed on his enthusiasm; their pre-eminence depended on his love of the wonderful; their very existence rested on the solidity of his ignorance they consequently suffered no opportunity to escape, of smothering even the lambent flame. The many were thus first deceived into credulity, then coerced into submission. At length, the whole science of man became a confused mass of darkness, falsehood, and contradictions, with here and there a feeble ray of truth, furnished by that Nature of which he can never entirely divest himself, because, without his knowledge, his necessities are continually bringing him back to her resources."

Having stated that by "nature" he means the "great whole," our author complains of those who assert that matter is senseless, inanimate, unintelligent, etc., and says, "Experience proves to us that the matter which we regard as inert or dead, assumes action, intelligence, and life, when it is combined in a certain way:" —

"If flour be wetted with water, and the mixture closed up, it will be found, after some little lapse of time, by the aid of a microscope, to have produced organized beings that enjoy life, of which the water and the flour were believed incapable: it is thus that inanimate matter can pass into life, or animate matter, which is in itself only an assemblage of motion. Reasoning from analogy, which the philosophers of the present day hold perfectly compatible, the production of a man, independent of the ordinary means, would not be more marvellous than that of an insect with flour and water. Fermentation and putrefaction evidently produce living animals. We have here the principle; with proper materials, principles can always be brought into action. That generation which is styled *equivocal* is only so for those who do not reflect, or who do not permit themselves, attentively, to observe the operations of Nature."

This passage is much ridiculed by Voltaire, who asserts that it is founded on some experiments made by one Needham, who placed some rye-meal in well-corked bottles, and some boiled mutton gravy in other bottles, and found that eels were produced in each. We do not know sufficient of the history of Needham's experiments, either to affirm or deny their authenticity, but we feel bound to remind our readers of the much-decried experiments conducted by Mr. Crosse, and which were afterwards verified by Mr. Weekes, of Sandwich. In these cases, insects were produced by the action of a powerful voltaic battery upon a saturated solution of silicate of potash, and upon ferro cyanuret of potassium. The insects were a species of acarus, minute and semi-transparent, and furnished with long bristles, which could only be seen by the aid of the microscope. The sixth chapter treats of man, and the author thus answers the question, "What is man?":—

"We say he is a material being, organized after a peculiar manner, conformed to a certain mode of thinking, of feeling, capable of modification in certain modes peculiar to himself, to his organization, to that particular combination of matter which is found assembled in him. If again it be asked, What origin we give to beings of the human species? We reply, that like all other beings, man is a production of nature, who resembles them in some respects, and finds himself submitted to the same laws; who differs from them in other respects, and follows particular laws determined by the diversity of his conformation. If then it be demanded, Whence came man? We answer, our experience on this head does not capacitate us to resolve the question; but that it cannot interest us, as it suffices for us to know that man exists, that he is so constituted as to be competent to the effects we witness."

In the seventh chapter the author, treating of the soul and spirit says:—

"The doctrine of spirituality, such as it now exists, offers nothing but vague ideas, or, rather, is the absence of all ideas. What does it present to the mind but a substance which possesses nothing of which our senses enable us to have a knowledge? Can it be truth, that man is able to figure to himself a being not material, having neither extent nor parts; which, nevertheless, acts upon matter without having any point of contact, any kind of analogy with it; and which itself receives the impulse of matter by means of material organs, which announce to it the presence of other beings? Is it possible to conceive the union of the soul with the body; to comprehend how this material body can bind, enclose, constrain, determine a fugitive being, which escapes all our senses? Is it honest, is it plain dealing, to solve these difficulties, by saying there is a mystery in them, that they are the effects of a power more inconceivable than the human soul, than its mode of acting, however concealed from our view? When to resolve these problems, man is obliged to have recourse to miracles, to make the Divinity interfere, does he not avow his own ignorance? When notwithstanding the ignorance he is thus obliged to avow by availing himself of the divine agency, he tells us, this immaterial substance, this soul, shall experience the action of the element of fire, which he allows to be material; when he confidently says, this soul shall be burnt; shall suffer in purgatory—have we not a right to believe, that either he has a design to deceive us, or else that he does not himself understand that which he is so anxious we shall take upon his word?"

The ninth chapter, after treating of the diversity of the intellectual faculties, proceeds, "Man at his birth brings with him into the world nothing but the necessity of conserving himself, of rendering his existence happy; instruction, examples, the custom of the world, present him with the means, either real or imaginary, of achieving it; habit procures for him the facility of employing these means:"—

"In order that man may become virtuous, it is absolutely requisite that he should have an interest, that he should find advantages in practicing virtue. For this end, it is necessary that education should implant in him reasonable ideas; that public opinion should lean towards virtue, as the most desirable good; that example should point it out as the object most worthy of esteem; that government should faithfully recompense, should regularly reward it; that honor should always accompany its practice; that vice should constantly be despised; that crime should invariably be punished. Is virtue in this situation amongst men! Does the education of man infuse into him just, faithful ideas of happiness—true notions of virtue—- dispositions really favorable to the beings with whom he is to live? The examples spread before him, are they suitable to innocence of manners? Are they calculated to make him respect decency, to cause him to love probity, to practice honesty, to value good faith, to esteem equity, to revere conjugal fidelity, to observe exactitude in fulfilling his duties? Religion, which alone pretends to regulate his manners, does it render him sociable? does it make him pacific? does it teach him to be humane? The arbiters, the sovereigns of society, are they faithful in recompensing punctual in rewarding, those who have best served their country, in punishing those who have pillaged, who have robbed, who have plundered, who have divided, who have ruined it? Justice, does she hold her scales with a firm, with an even hand, between all the citizens of the state? The laws, do they never support the strong against the weak, favor the rich against the poor, uphold the happy against the miserable? In short, is it an uncommon spectacle to behold crime frequently justified, often applauded, sometimes crowned with success, insolently triumphing, arrogantly striding over that merit which it disdains, over that virtue which it outrages? Well, then, in societies thus constituted, virtue can only be heard by a very small number of peaceable citizens, a few generous souls, who know how to estimate its value, who enjoy it in secret. For the others, it is only a disgusting object; they see in it nothing but the supposed enemy to their happiness, or the censor of their individual conduct."

In the tenth chapter, which is upon the soul, the author says:—

"The diversity in the temperament of man, is natural, the necessary source of the diversity of passions, of his taste, of his ideas of happiness, of his opinions of every kind. Thus this same diversity will be the fatal source of his disputes—of his hatreds—of his injustice—every time he shall reason upon unknown objects, but to which he shall attach the greatest importance. He will never understand either himself or others, in speaking of a spiritual soul, or of immaterial substances distinguished from nature; he will, from that moment, cease to speak the same language, and he will never attach the same ideas to the same words. What then shall be the common standard that shall decide which is the man that thinks with the greatest justice?

"Propose to a man to change his religion for yours, he will believe you a madman; you will only excite his indignation, elicit his contempt; he will propose to you, in his turn, to adopt his own peculiar opinions; after much reasoning, you will treat each other as absurd beings, ridiculously opinionated, pertinaciously stubborn; and he will display the least folly who shall first yield. But if the adversaries become heated in the dispute, which always happens, when they suppose the matter important, or when they would defend the cause of their own self-love, from thence their passions sharpen, they grow angry, quarrels are provoked, they hate each other, and end by reciprocal injury. It is thus that for opinions, which no man can demonstrate, we see the Brachman despised; the Mahomedan hated; the Pagan held in contempt; that they oppress and disdain each with the most raucorous animosity: the Christian burns the Jew at what is called an *Auto-da-fe*, because he clings to the faith of his fathers; the Roman Catholic condemns the Protestant to the flames, and makes a conscience of massacreing(sp.) him in cold blood; this re-acts in his turn; sometimes the various sects of Christians league together against the incredulous Turk, and for a moment suspend their own bloody disputes that they may chastise the enemies to the true faith: then, having glutted their revenge, return with redoubied fury, to wreak over again their infuriated vengeance on each other."

The thirteenth chapter argues as follows, against the doctrine of the immortality of the soul and a future state:—

"In old age, man extinguishes entirely, his fibres become rigid, his nerves lose their elasticity, his senses are obtunded, his sight grows dim, his ears lose their quickness, his ideas become unconnected, his memory fails, his imagination cools,—what, then, becomes of his soul. Alas! it sinks down with the body, it gets benumbed as this loses its feeling, becomes sluggish as this decays in activity; like it, when enfeebled by years, it fulfils its functions with pain; this substance, which is deemed spiritual, which is considered immaterial, which it is endeavored to distinguish from matter, undergoes the same revolutions, experiences the same vicissitudes, submits to the name modifications as does the body itself. In despite of this proof of the materiality of the soul, of its identity with the body so convincing to the unprejudiced, some thinkers have supposed that although the latter is perishable, the former does not perish; that this portion of man enjoys the especial privilege of immortality; that it is exempt from dissolution; free from those changes of form all the beings in nature undergo: in consequence of this, man is persuaded himself that this privileged soul does not die.

"It will be asked, perhaps, by what road has man been conducted to form to himself gratuitous ideas of another world. I reply, that it is a truth man has no idea of a future life; they are the ideas of the past and the present, that furnish his imagination with the materials of which he constructs the edifice of the regions of futurity. Hobbes says, 'We believe that, that which is will always be, and that the same causes will have the same effects.' Man in his actual state has two modes of feeling—one, that he approves; another, that he disapproves: thus persuaded that these two modes of feeling must accompany him even beyond his present existence, he placed in the regions of eternity two distinguished abodes; one destined to felicity; the other to misery: the one must contain those who obey the calls of superstition, who believe in its dogmas; the other is a prison, destined to avenge the cause of heaven on all those who shall not faithfully believe the doctrines promulgated by the ministers of a vast variety of superstitions. Has sufficient attention been paid to the fact that results as a necessary consequence from this reasoning; which on examination will be found to have rendered the first place entirely useless, seeing, that by the number and contradiction of these various systems, let man believe whichever he may, let him follow it in the most faithful manner, still he must be ranked as an Infidel, as a rebel to the divinity; because he cannot believe in all; and those from which he dissents, by a consequence of their own creed, condemn him to the prison-house?—Such is the origin of the ideas upon a future life, so diffused among mankind. Everywhere may be seen an Elysium, and a Tartarus, a Paradise and a Hell; in a word, two distinguished abodes, constructed according to the imagination of the enthusiasts who have invented them; who have accommodated them to their own peculiar prejudices, to the hopes, to the fears of the people who believe in them. The Indian figures the first of these abodes as one of inaction, of permanent repose, because, being the inhabitant of a hot climate, he has learned to contemplate rest as the extreme of felicity: the Mussulman promises himself corporeal pleasures, similar to those that actually constitute the object of his research in this life: each figures to himself that on which he has learned to set the greatest value."

"As for the miserable abode of souls, the imagination of fanatics, who were desirous of governing the people, strove to assemble the most frightful images to render it still more terrible; fire is of all things that which produces in man the most pungent sensation; not finding anything more cruel, the enemies to the several dogmas were to be everlastingly punished with this torturing element: fire, therefore, was the point at which their imagination was obliged to stop; the ministers of the various systems agreed pretty generally, that fire would one day avenge their offended divinities; thus, they painted the victims to the anger of the gods, or rather those who questioned their own creeds, as confined in fiery dungeons; as perpetually rolling into a vortex of bituminous flames; as plunged in unfathomable gulfs of liquid sulphur; making the infernal caverns resound with their useless groanings, with their unavailing gnashing of teeth. But it will, perhaps, be inquired, how could man reconcile himself to the belief of an existence accompanied with eternal torments; above all, as many according to their own superstitions had reason to fear it for themselves—Many causes have concurred to make him adopt so revolting an opinion: in the first place, very few thinking men have ever believed such an absurdity, when they have deigned to make use of their reason; or, when they have accredited it, this notion was always counterbalanced by the idea of the goodness, by a reliance on the mercy, which they attributed to their respective divinities: in the second place, those who were blinded by their fears never rendered to themselves any account of these strange doctrines which they either received with awe from their legislators, or which were transmitted to them by their fathers; in the third place, each sees the object of his terrors only at a favorable distance; moreover, superstition promises him the means of escaping the tortures he believes he has merited."

We conclude by quoting the following eloquent passage:—

"Oh! Nature! sovereign of all beings! and ye, her adorable daughters, Virtue, Reason, and Truth! remain forever our reverend protectors. It is to you that belong the praises of the human race; to you appertains the homage of the earth. Show us, then, oh! Nature! that which man ought to do, in order to obtain the happiness which thou makest him desire. — Virtue! animate him with thy beneficent fire! Reason! conduct his uncertain steps through the paths of life. Truth! let thy torch illumine his intellect, dissipate the darkness of his road.... Banish error from our mind, wickedness from our hearts, confusion from our footsteps. Cause knowledge to extend its salubrious reign, goodness to occupy our souls, serenity to dwell in our bosoms.... Let our eyes, so long either dazzled or blindfolded, be at length fixed upon those objects we ought to seek. Dispel forever those mists of ignorance, those hideous phantoms, together with those seducing chimeras, which only serve to lead us astray. Extricate us from that dark abyss into which we are plunged by superstition, overthrow the fatal empire of delusion, crumble the throne of falsehood, wrest from their polluted hands the power they have usurped."

ROBERT TAYLOR

Many of the readers of this number will, from their own memories, be better able to do justice to him, whom Henry Hunt named "The Devil's Chaplain," than we shall in our limited space. Robert Taylor was born at Edmonton, in the county of Middlesex, on the 18th of August, 1784. His family was highly respectable, and his parents were in affluent circumstances; but, being a younger son in a family of eleven children, it was necessary that Robert Taylor should follow some profession. His father died when he was about seven years old, leaving him under the guardianship of a paternal uncle. When seventeen years of age, he was apprenticed to a surgeon, at Birmingham, and studied medicine afterwards under Sir Astley Cooper and Mr. Clive, passing the College of Surgeons with considerable *eclat*. When about twenty-three, he became acquainted with the Rev. Thomas Cotterell, a clergyman of the Established Church, of high evangelical principles, who induced him to quit physic for metaphysics, and in 1809 Robert Taylor entered Saint John's College, Cambridge, and in 1813 took his degree of Bachelor of Arts. He was publicly complimented by the Master of the College as a singular honor to the University in his scholarship, and was ordained on the 14th of March, 1813, by the bishop of Chichester; from that time until 1818, Taylor officiated as curate at Midhurst. Here he became acquainted with a person named Ayling who held Deistical opinions, and who induced Taylor to read various Free-thinking works; this soon resulted in an avowal of Deism on the part of Taylor, who tendered his resignation to his Bishop. His friends and family were much alarmed, and much pressure was brought to bear upon him, and we regret to state that it had the effect of producing a temporary recantation. This, however, brought Taylor no relief; he found himself in distress, and shunned by his family. Through the kindness of an old friend, he obtained the curacy of Yardley, near Birmingham, but his previous apostacy having reached the ears of the Bishop, the necessary license was refused, and the rector received a peremptory notice to dismiss Taylor. This harsh treatment caused a reaction, and while the rector sought another curate, Taylor preached a series of sermons, by means of which he shook the faith of nearly the whole of his congregation. The following is an abstract of his last sermon at Yardley:—

"The text was, 'For as Jonah was three days and three nights in the whale's belly, so shall the son of man be three days and three nights in the heart of the earth.'—Matt, xii., 40. He began, 'Then this glorious miracle of the man having been swallowed alive by a fish, and remaining alive for seventy-two hours, undigested and unhurt, in the fish's bowels, and being vomited up unhurt and safe upon the dry land, was as true as the gospel; and consequently the gospel was as true, but not more true, than this sea-sick miracle. He inferred that no person could have a right to pretend to believe in the death and resurrection of Christ, who had the least doubt as to the reality of the deglutition and evomition of the prophet Jonah. As to the natural improbabilities and physical impossibilities of this very wonderful Bible miracle, these were nothing in the way of a true and lively faith. Where miracles of any sort were concerned, there could be no distinction into the greater and the less, since infinite power was as necessary to the reality of the least as to the greatest. We should never forget that it was the Lord who prepared the fish, and prepared him for the express purpose of swallowing the man, and probably gave him a little opening physic, to cleanse the apartment for the accommodation of its intended tenant; and had the purpose been, that the whole ship and all the crew should have been swallowed as well as he, there's no doubt that they could have been equally well accommodated. But as to what some wicked Infidels objected, about the swallow of the whale being too narrow to admit the passage of the man, it only required a little stretching, and even a herring or a sprat might have gulped him. He enlarged, most copiously, on the circumstance of the Lord speaking to the fish, in order to cause him to vomit; and insisted on the natural efficacy of the Lord, which was quite enough to make anybody sick. He pointed out the many interesting examples of faith and obedience which had been set by the scaly race, who were not only at all times easy to be caught in the gospel net, when thrown over them by the preaching of the word, but were always ready to surrender their existence to the Almighty, whenever he pleased to drop 'em a line. That as the first preachers of the gospel were fishermen, so the preachers of the gospel, to this day, might truly be said to be looking after the loaves and fishes, and they who, as the Scripture says, are 'wise to catch soles,' speak to them for no other purpose than that for which the Lord spake unto the whale—that is, to ascertain how much they can swallow. The moral of this pungent persiflage, aimed to admonish the proud and uncharitable believer, who expected his acceptance with the deity on the score of his credulity, that when his credulity was fairly put to trial, it might be found that he was in reality as far from believing what he did not take to be true as the most honest and avowed Infidel. 'Thou then who wouldst put a trick upon infinite wisdom, and preferest the imagined merit of a weak understanding to the real utility of an honest heart—thou who wouldst

> 'Compound for sins thou art inclined to,
> By damning those thou hast no mind to;'

hast thou no fears for thy presumptuous self? Thou believest only that which seemeth to thee to be true; what does the Atheist less? And that which appeareth to be a lie thou rejectest; what does the Atheist more? Can we think that God has given us reason only to betray us, and made us so much superior to the brute creation, only to deal with us so much worse than they, to punish us for making the best use we could of the faculties he has given us, and to make the very excellence of our nature the cause of our damnation?'"

This concluded his connection with the Church of England, and his brother having consented to make him an allowance of one pound per week if he would quit England, he retired to the Isle of Man. After nine weeks his brother ceased to remit; and to support himself, Taylor wrote for the two newspapers then published in the island, but his articles attracting attention, he was summoned before the Bishop, and compelled to quit the island under a threat of imprisonment. In deep distress, he went to Dublin, where he lectured on Deism until 1824, when he came to London, and founded the Christian Evidence Society.

Many of the discourses delivered by him were printed in "The Lion." which was first published in 1828. In 1827 Mr. Taylor was tried at Guildhall for blasphemy, and was sentenced to imprisonment in Oakham gaol for one year. In Oakham he wrote "The Diegesis" and "Syntagma." After his release from prison in 1829, he, together with Richard Carlile, made a tour through England on an Infidel mission, commencing with a challenge to the Cambridge University. In 1830 and 1831 he delivered a series of discourses, which are printed together under the title of "The Devil's Pulpit." On the 4th July, 1831, he was again tried for blasphemy and sentenced to two years' imprisonment In 1833 he delivered a number of discourses, which were printed in the "Philalethean." He was the friend and companion of Richard Carlile for several years. It is difficult to quote from Robert Taylor's works, unless at the risk of doing him great injustice, and we must therefore refer our readers to the works we have named. The following is from "The Devil's Pulpit:" —

"The gentlemen who distribute religious tracts, the general body of dissenting preachers, and almost all persons engaged in the trade of religion, imagine themselves to have a mighty advantage against Infidels, upon the strength of that last and reckless argument—that whether the Christian religion be true or false, there can be no harm in believing; and that belief is, at any rate, the safe side. Now, to say nothing of this old Popish argument, which a sensible man must see is the very essence of Popery, and would oblige us to believe all the absurdities and nonsense in the world: inasmuch as if there be no harm in believing, and there be some harm and danger in not believing, the more we believe the better: and all the argument necessary for any religion whatever would be, that it should frighten us out of our wits: the more terrible, the more true: and it would be our duty to become the converts of that religion whatever it might be, whose priests could swear the loudest, and damn and curse the fiercest. But I am here to grapple with this Popery in disguise, this wolfish argument in sheepish clothing, upon Scriptural ground, and on Scriptural ground only; taking the Scriptures of the Old and New Testament, for this argument's sake, to be divine authority. The question proposed is, 'Whether is the believer or the unbeliever the more likely to be saved, taking the Scriptures to be of divine authority!' And I stand here, on this divine authority, to prove that the unbeliever is the more likely to be saved: that unbelief, and not belief, is the safe side, and that a man is more likely to be damned for believing the gospel, and because of his having believed it, than for rejecting and despising it, as I do.... But, if a patient hearing be more than good Christians be minded to give us, when thus advance to meet them on their own ground, their impatience and intolerance itself will supply the evidence and demonstration of the fact, that, after all, they dare not stand to the text of their own book, that it is not the Bible that they go by, nor God whom they regard: but that they want to be God-a'-mighties themselves, and would have us take their words for God's words; you must read it as they read it, and understand it as they understand it: you must 'skip, and go on,' just where a hard word comes in the way of the sense they choose to put upon it: you must believe what the book contains, what you see with your own eyes that it does not contain: you must shut your eyes, and not see what it does contain; or you'll be none the nearer the mark of their liking.... Taking the authority of Scripture, for this argument's sake, to be decisive, I address the believer who would give himself airs of superiority, would chuckle in an imaginary safety in believing, and presume to threaten the unbeliever as being in a worse case, or more dangerous plight, than he. 'Hast thou no fears for thy presumptuous self?' when on the showing of thine own book, the safety (if safety there be) is all on the unbelieving side? When for any one text that can be produced, seeming to hold out any advantage or safety in believing, we can produce two in which the better hope is held out to the unbeliever? For any one apparent exhortation to believe, we can produce two forbiddances to believe, and many threaten-ings of God's vengeance to, and for the crime and folly of, believing. To this proof I proceed, by showing you:—1st. What the denunciations of God's vengeance are: with no comment of mine, but in the words of the text itself. 2d. That these dreadful denunciations are threatened to believers: and that they are not threatened to unbelievers. And 3d. That all possible advantages and safety, which believing could confer on any man, are likely, and more likely to be conferred on the unbeliever than on the believer. That the danger of the believer is so extreme, that no greater danger can possibly be. 1st. What are the denunciations of God's vengeance! 'There are' (says the holy Revelation, xiv. 10,) 'who shall drink of the wine of the wrath of God, which is poured out without mixture into the cup of his indignation, and shall be tormented with fire and brimstone, and the smoke of their torment ascendeth up forever and ever: and they have no rest day or night.' There's 'glad tidings of great joy' for you! The Christian may get, over the terror of this denunciation by the selfish and ungenerous chuckle of his 'Ah! well, these were very wicked people, and must have deserved their doom; it need not alarm us: it doesn't apply to us.' But good-hearted men would rather say, 'It does apply. We cannot be indifferent to the misery of our fellow-creatures. The self-same Heaven that frowns on them, looks lowering upon us.' And who were they? and what was their offence? Was it Atheism! was it Deism' was it Infidelity? No! It was for church and chapel-going; it was for adoring, believing, and worshipping. They worshipped the beast: I know not what beast they worshipped; but I know that if you go into any of our churches and chapels at this day, you will find them worshipping the Lamb; and if worshipping a lamb be not most suspiciously like worshiping a beast, you may keep the color in your cheeks, while mine are blanched with fear. The unbeliever only can be absolutely safe from this danger. He only who has no religion at all, is sure not to be of the wrong religion. He who worships neither God nor Devil, is sure not to mistake one of those gentlemen for the other. But will it be pretended, that these are only metaphors of speech, that the thing said is not the thing that's meant? Why, then, they are very ugly metaphors. And what is saying that which you don't mean, and meaning the contrary to what you say, but lying? And what worse can become of the Infidel, who makes it the rule of his life 'to hear and speak the plain and simple truth,' than of the Christian, whose religion itself is a system of metaphors and allegories, of double meanings, of quirk and quiddities in dread defiance of the text that warns him, that 'All liars shall have their part in the lake which burneth with fire and brimstone?' Rev. xxi. 8.

"Is it a parable that a man may merely entertain his imagination withal, and think no more on't,—though not a word be hinted about a parabolical signification, and the text stands in the mouth of him who, we are told, was the truth itself? And he it is who brought life and immortality to light, that hath described in the 16th of Luke, such an immortality as that of one who was a sincere believer, a son of Abraham, who took the Bible for the rule of his life, and was anxious to promote the salvation of his brethren, yet found for himself no Saviour, no salvation; but, 'In Hell he lifted up his eyes being in torment: and saith Father Abraham, have mercy on me, and send Lazarus, that he may dip the tip of his finger in water, and cool my tongue, for I am tormented in this flame.' But that request was refused. 'Then he said, I pray thee, therefore, Father, that thou wouldst send him to my father's house; for I have five brethren, that he may testify unto them, lest they also come to this place of torment.' But that request was refused. There's 'glad tidings of great joy' for you! That the believer's danger of coming or going into that place of torment is so great, that greater cannot possibly be: and that his belief will stand him in no stead at all, but make his plight a thousand times worse than if he had not been a believer; and that unbelief is the safer side—Christ himself being judge—I quote no words but his to prove. Is the believer concerned to save his soul, then shall he most assuredly be damned for being so concerned: for Christ hath said, 'Whosoever will save his soul shall lose it.' Matthew xvi. 25. Is the believer a complete beggar? If he be not so, if he hath a rag that he doth call his own, he will be damned to all eternity. For Christ hath said, 'Whosoever he be of you who forsaketh not all that he hath, he cannot be my disciple.' Luke xiv. 33. Is the believer a rich man? and dreams he of going to Heaven? It is easier for a camel to go through the eye of a needle.' Matthew xix. 24. Is he a man at all, then he cannot be saved, for Christ hath said, 'Thou believest that there is one God;' saith St. James, 'Thou dost well, the Devils also believe and tremble.' 2 James xix. And so much good, and no more, than comes to damned spirits in the flames of Hell, is all the good that ever did and can come of believing. 'For though thou hadst all faith, so that thou couldst remove mountains,' saith St. Paul, 'It should profit thee nothing.' 1 Cor. xiii. 2. Well, then! let the good Christian try what saving his prayers will do for him: this is the good that they'!! do for him; and he hath Christ's own word to comfort him in't, 'He shall receive the greater damnation.' Luke xx. 47. Well, then, since believing will not save him, since faith will not save him, since prayer will not save him, but all so positively make things all the worse, and none the better, there's one other chance for him. Let him go and receive the Sacrament, the most comfortable Sacrament, you know, 'of the body and blood of Christ,' remembering, as all good communicants should, 'that he is not worthy so much as to gather up the crumbs that fall from that table.' 'Truth, Lord! But the dogs eat of the crumbs that fall from their master's table!' O what happy dogs! But let those dogs remember, that it is also truth, that 'He that eateth and drinketh unworthily, eateth and drinketh damnation to himself.' 1 Cor. xvi. 29. O what precious eating and drinking!

> "'My God! and is thy table spread;
> And doth thy cup with love o'erflow?
> Thither be all the children led,
> And let them all thy sweetness know.'

"That table is a snare, that cup is deadly poison that bread shall send thy soul to Hell. Well, then! try again, believer: perhaps you had better join the Missionary Society, and subscribe to send these glad tidings of these blessed privileges, and this jolly eating and drinking, to the Heathen. Why, then; you have Christ's own assurance, that when you shall have made one proselyte, you shall just have done him the kindness of making him twofold more the child of Hell than yourself. Mat. xxiii. 15. Is the believer liable to the ordinary gusts of passion, and in a passion shall he drop the hasty word, 'thou fool!' for that one word 'he shall be in danger of Hell fire.' Mat. v. 22. Nay, Sirs! this isn't the worst of the believer's danger. Would he but keep his legs and arms together, and spare his own eyes and limbs; he doth by that very mercy to himself damn his eyes and limbs—and hath Christ's assurance that it would have been profitable for him rather to have plucked out his eyes, and chopt off his limbs, and so to have wriggled and groped his way through the 'Straight gate and the narrow way that leadeth unto life,' than having two eyes and two arms, or two legs, to be cast into Hell, into the fire that never shall be quenched, where their 'worm dieth not, and the fire is not quenched.' Mark ix. 43. Well, then! will the believer say, what were all the miracles and prophecies of both the Old and the New Testament for those unquestionable miracles, and clearly-accomplished prophecies, if it were not that men should believe? Why, absolutely, they were the very arguments appointed by God himself to show us that men should not believe, but that damnation should be their punishment if they did believe. 'To the law and the testimony.'" Sirs! These are the very words:—'Of miracles, saith God's word, 'They are the spirits of devils, that work miracles.' Rev. xvi. 14. And it is the Devil who 'deceiveih them which dwell on the earth, by means of those miracles which he hath power to do.' Rev. xiii. 14. So much for miracles. Is it on the score of prophets and of prophecies, then, that you will take believing to be the safe side? Then 'thus saith the Lord of Hosts, the God of Israel, the prophets prophesy falsely and the priests bear rule by their means.' Jer. v. 31. 'The prophet is a fool: the spiritual man is mad.' Hosea i. 7. 'Thus saith the Lord of Hosts: hearken not unto the prophets.' Jer. xxiii. 15. 'O Israel, thy prophets are like the foxes of the desert.' Ezekiel xiii. 4. 'They lie unto thee.' Jerem. xiv. 14. 'And they shall be tormented day and night forever and ever.' Rev. xx. 10. 'And the punishment of the prophet shall be even as the punishment of him that seeketh unto him.' Ezekiel xiv. 10. Nay more, then, it is, when God hath determined to damn men, that he, in every instance, causeth them to become believers, and to have faith in divine Revelation, in order that they may be damned. Believers, and none but believers, becoming liable to damnation; believers and none but believers, being capable of committing that unpardonable sin against the Holy Ghost, which hath never forgiveness, neither in this world nor in that which is to come. 'Whereas all other kinds of blasphemy shall be forgiven unto men, and all sorts of blasphemy wherewith soever they shall blaspheme. But there is no forgiveness for believers.' Mark iii. 28. For it is written, 'For this cause God shall send them strong delusion, that they should believe a lie: that they all might be damned.' 2 Thessal. ii. 11. So when it was determined by God that the wicked Ahab should perish, the means to bring him to destruction, both of body and soul, was to make him become a believer.

"I offer no comment of my own on words so sacred; but these are the words: 'Hear thou, therefore, the word of the Lord. I saw the Lord sitting upon his throne, and all the hosts of Heaven standing by him on his right hand and on his left. And the Lord said, who shall persuade Ahab that he may go up and fall at Ramoth Gilead? and one said on this manner, and another said on that manner. And there stood forth a spirit, and stood before the Lord, and said: I will persuade him. And the Lord said unto him wherewith? And he said, I will go forth, and I will be a lying spirit in the mouth of all his prophets. And he said, thou shalt persuade him, and prevail also. Go forth and do so. Now, therefore, behold the Lord hath put a lying spirit in the mouth of all thy prophets.' 1 kings xxii. 22. There were 400 of 'em; they were 'the goodly-fellowship of the prophets for you; all of them inspired by the spirit from on high, and all of them lying as fast as they could lie.' So much for getting on the safe side by believing. Had Ahab been an Infidel, he would have saved his soul alive. As it was, we may address him in the words of St. Paul to just such another fool, 'King Ahab, believest thou the prophets? I know that thou believest: but no better than I know, that for that very belief, fell slaughter on thy soul: and where thou soughtest to be saved by believing, it was by believing thou wert damned.' So when Elijah had succeeded in converting the 450 worshippers of Baal, who had been safe enough while they were Infidels, and they began crying, 'the Lord He is God, the Lord He is God:' the moment they got into the right faith, they found themselves in the wrong box; and the prophet, by the command of God, put a stop to their Lord-Godding, by cutting their throats for 'em, 'Elijah brought them down to the brook of Kishon, and slew them there.' 1 Kings xviii. 40. Oh! what a blessed thing, you see, to be converted to the true faith! Thus all the sins and crimes that have been committed in the world, and all God's judgments upon sin and sinners have been the consequence of religion, and faith, and believing. What was the first sin committed in the world? It was believing. Had our great mother Eve not been a believing credulous fool, she would not have been in the transgression. Who was the first reverend divine that began preaching about God and immortality? It was the Devil. What was the first lie that was ever told, the very damning and damnable lie? It was the lie told to make folks believe that they would not be dead when they were dead, that they should not surely die, but that they should be as gods, and live in a future state of existence. 'When God himself hath declared, that there is no future state of existence: that 'Dust thou art, and unto dust shalt thou return.' Who is it, then, that prefers believing in the Devil rather than in God, but the believer? — And from whom is the hope of a future state derived, but from the father of lies — the Devil? But if in defiance of so positive a declaration of Almighty God, men will have it that there is a future state of existence after death, who are they who shall sit down with Abraham, Isaac, and Jacob, in the kingdom of Heaven, but unbelievers, let them come from the north, from the south, from the east, or from the west? And who are they that shall be cast out, but believers, 'the children of the kingdom?' As St. Peter very charitably calls them, 'cursed children.' 2 Peter ii. 14. That is, I suppose, children with beards, children that never grew to sense enough to put away childish things, but did in gawky manhood, like new-born babes, desire the pure milk and lollipop of the gospel. 'For of such is the kingdom of Heaven.' And who are they whom Christ will set upon his right hand, and to whom he will say, 'Come ye blessed of my father!' but unbelievers, who never troubled their minds about religion, and never darkened the doors of a gospel shop? But who are they to whom he will say, 'Depart ye cursed into everlasting fire, prepared for the Devil and his angels,' but believers, every one of them believers, chapel-going folks, Christ's blood men, and incorrigible bigots, that had been bothering him all their days with their 'Lord! Lord!' to come off at last with no better reward of their faith than that he will protest unto them, I never knew ye.

"One text there is, and only one, against ten thousand of a contrary significancy: which, being garbled and torn from its context, seems, for a moment, to give the advantage to the believer; the celebrated 19th chapter of Mark, v. 16:—'He that believeth, and is baptized, shall be saved; but he that believeth not, shall be damned.' But little will this serve the deceitful hope of the Christian, for it is immediately added. And these signs shall follow them that believe; in my name shall they cast out devils; they shall speak with new tongues; they shall take up serpents; and if they drink any deadly thing, it shall not hurt them; they shall lay hands on the sick, and they shall recover.' Can the Christian show these signs, or any of them? Will he dare to take-up a serpent, or drink prussic acid? If he hesitate, he is not a believer, and his profession of belief is a falsehood. Let belief confer what privilege it may, he hath no part nor lot in the matter; the threat which he denounces against Infidels hangs over himself, and he hath no sign of salvation to show. Believing the gospel, then, (or rather, I should say, professing to believe it, for I need not tell you that there's a great deal more professing to believe, than believing,) instead of making a man the more likely to be saved, doubles his danger of damnation, inasmuch as Christ hath said, that 'the last state of that man shall be worse than the first.' Luke xi. 26. And his holy apostle Peter addeth, 'It would have been better for them not to have known the way (2 Peter ii. 21) of righteousness.' The sin of believing makes all other sins that a man can commit so much the more heinous and offensive in the sight of God, inasmuch as they are sins against light and knowledge: and 'the servant who knew his Lord's will, and did it not, he shall be beaten with many stripes.' Luke xii. 47. While unbelief is not only innocent in itself, but so highly pleasing to Almighty God, that it is represented as the cause of his forgiveness of things which otherwise would not be forgiven. Thus St. Paul, who had been a blasphemer, a persecutor, and injurious, assures us that it was for this cause he obtained mercy, 'because he did it ignorantly in unbelief.' 1 Tim. i. 13. Had he been a believer, he would as surely have been damned as his name was Paul. And 'tis the gist of his whole argument, and the express words of the 11th of the Epistle to the Romans, that 'God included them all in unbelief, that he might have mercy upon all.' Unbelief being the essential qualification and recommendation to God's mercy: not without good reason was it that the pious father of the boy that had the devil in him, when he had need of Christ's mercy, and knew that unbelief would be the best title to it, cried out and said with tears, 'Lord, I believe, help thou mine unbelief!' Mark ix. 24. While the Apostles themselves, who were most immediately near and dear to Christ, no more believed the Gospel than I do; and for all they have said and preached about it, they never believed it themselves, as Christ told 'em that they hadn't so much faith as a grain of mustard seed. And the evangelist John bears them record, to their immortal honor; that 'though Christ had done so many miracles among them, yet believed they not.' John xii. 37. And the same divine authority assures us that 'neither did his brethren believe in him.' John vii. 5. Which then is 'the safe side.' Sirs, on the showing of the record itself? On the unbelieving side, the Infidel stands in the glorious company of the Apostles, in the immediate family of Christ, and hath no fear; while the believer doth as well and no better than the devils in hell, who believe and tremble."

"I."

JOSEPH BARKER

In any work, purporting to be a true record of Freethinkers, the name of Joseph Barker cannot be omitted. We find in him, from the commencement of his public life till the present time, an ardent desire for, and a determination to achieve, freedom of thought and ex-pression on all subjects appertaining to theology, politics, and sociology. Possessing a vigorous intellect, a constitution naturally strong, great oratorical ability, and an unrivalled command oi the Saxon language, he has made himself a power among each party with whom the transitory state of his mind has brought him in contact. It is seldom we find men with equal boldness, when once connected with Wesleyan Methodism, rising superior in thought to its narrow, selfish, dogmatic, unnatural, and humiliating views, and claiming for human nature a more dignified and exalted position; gradually advancing to Unitarianism; ultimately to land safely on the shore of Materialism. Joseph Barker has passed, amid persecution and privation, through these different phases of theology, to arrive at "Infidelity," to be, he states, a better, wiser, and happier man. In his autobiography, we read that he was born in Bramley, an old country town in the West Riding of Yorkshire, in 1806, the *day* of his birth being forgotten. His parents, and his ancestors, so far as is known of them, were of humble means. His grandfather was addicted to drinking freely of those beverages which meet with so much opposition from Mr. Barker himself. His aunt also was unfortunate, having married a man who was a minister, a drunkard, and a cock-fighter. His parents appear to have been uneducated and pious; belonging to the old school of Methodists, those who look on this life merely as a state of trial and probation; always looking forward to enjoy their mansion in the skies—the house not made with hands eternal in the heavens, thinking nothing

> .... *Worth a thought beneath,*
> *But how they may escape the death*
> *That never, never dies.*

Although living *in* this world, they were not *of* it. It was to them, all vanity and vexation of spirit. They attended their chapel, their love feasts, their class-meetings, their prayer meetings, and their revival meetings, where they would lament over the wickedness and depravity of human nature, where they would "speak their experience," tell of their temptations, pray for the conversion of the world, and sing their hymns, such as the following, which was a favorite with Mr. Barker's family:—

> "Refining fire, go through my heart,
> Illuminate my soul;
> Scatter my life through every part,
> And sanctify the whole."

Such being the character of Mr. Barker's parents, it is no wonder that *he* was "brought up" under the same influence, with the same false notions of life, of humanity, and of the world; and we cannot prize too highly the man who had the industry to investigate, the ability to discern, and the courage to expose the falsity of such doctrines and the disastrous effects of such teaching.

In the extracts we shall give from Mr. Barker's works will be found that simplicity of style and force of argument peculiar to himself. The first extract we take shows the falsity of the orthodox doctrine of the total depravity of human nature:—

"On looking back on the earlier periods of my life, I first see proofs that the orthodox doctrine of original sin, or of natural total depravity, is a falsehood. I was *not* born totally depraved. I never recollect the time, since I began to think and feel at all, when I had not good thoughts, and good feelings. I never recollect the time since I began to think and feel at all, when I had not many good thoughts, and strong inclinations to goodness. So far was my heart from being utterly depraved or hardened, that I sympathised, even in my childhood, with the humblest of God's creatures, and was filled to overflowing with sorrow at the sight of distress. I recollect one Sunday, while I was searching about for something in one of the windows upstairs, I found a butterfly that had been starved to death, as I supposed. When I laid hold of it, it crumbled to pieces. My feelings were such at the thought of the poor butterfly's sufferings, that I wept. And for all that day I could scarcely open my lips to say a word to any one without bursting into tears.... And I recollect well what a struggle I had when I first told a lie. A school in the neighborhood had a feast, ours had not, so I played the truant, after a serious struggle, to have an opportunity of seeing the scholars walk. I had a miserable afternoon; for I felt that I was doing wrong, and I was afraid lest my mother should find me out. My sister found me out and told my mother, but my mother was loth to believe her till she had asked me myself. When I went home my mother asked me if I had been to school, and I said yes, and my mother, as she had never found me out in a lie before, believed me. But I was sadly distressed afterwards when I thought of what I had done. That lie caused me days of remorse, and my sufferings were all the severer in consequence of my mother having so readily believed what I said."

The unhappy and unnatural effects of theology on the minds of earnest, truth-seeking men—the total prostration of manly dignity, the perversion of the mental faculties, and the debasement of human nature, is truly stated by Mr. Barker in the following extract:—

"I also recollect being very much troubled with dreadful and indescribably awful dreams, and for several months during certain parts of the year I was accustomed to rise during my sleep, and walk about the house in a state of sleep for hours together. I say in a state of sleep: but I cannot exactly describe the state in which I was. It was not *perfect* sleep, and yet I was not properly awake. My eyes were open, and I saw, as far as I can remember, the things around me, and 1 could hear what was said to me. But neither what I saw nor what I heard seemed to have power to penetrate far enough into my soul to awake me properly. During those occasions, I was frequently very unhappy, dreadfully unhappy, most horribly miserable. Sometimes I fancied I had been doing something wrong, and my fancied offence seemed horrible beyond all expression, and alarmed and overwhelmed me with unutterable terrors and distress. On one occasion I fancied that both I and my father had both been doing something wrong, and this seemed most horrible and distressing of all; and as I wandered about in my mysterious state, I howled most piteously, and cried and wept as if my heart would break. I never recollect being roused from that dismal state while I was walking about the house, except twice. Once when I struck my shins violently against a large earthenware bowl and hurt myself sadly; and another was when I was attempting to go up the chimney: I put my foot upon fire and burnt myself, and that awoke me. I suffered in this way for several years. After I went to bed at night I soon fell asleep, and slept perhaps an hour or nearly two. I would then begin to cry, or moan, or howl, and at times to sing. One night I sang a whole hymn of eight verses through; the hymn in Wesley's Hymn Book, beginning

> With glorious clouds encompassed round
> Whom angels dimly see,
> Will the unsearchable be found
> Or God appear to me?'"

Few persons who have not attended the "class-meetings" of the Wesleyan Methodists can form an adequate idea of the stereotyped phrases and absurd sayings indulged in by those who "speak their experience," etc., at those meetings. Certain sentences are learned, and uttered indiscriminately, without reference to time, place, or other conditions. Mr. Barker, after speaking of the recklessness of speech thus indulged in, says:—

"In many cases this false way of speaking is the result of mere thoughtlessness perhaps, or of ignorance, joined with the notion that it is their duty to pray, or to say something in public. The parties have no *intention* to deceive: but being called on to speak, or invited to pray, they begin, and catch hold of such words as they can find, whether right or wrong, whether true or false. And their words are oftener foolish or false, than wise or true. Their talk is at times most foolish and ridiculous. I will give an example or two. It is customary for people, when praying for preachers, to say, 'Lord, bless thy servants when they stand up to declare thy word: be thou *mouth matter, and wisdom* to them.' This has some meaning in it when offered in reference to a preacher, especially a preacher about to preach. In other cases it would be most foolish and ridiculous. Yet I once heard a person in a prayer-meeting at Chester use this same form of expression in behalf of the sick and the dying. 'O Lord,' said he, 'bless the sick and the afflicted, and those that are in the article of death;—be thou mouth, matter, and wisdom to them.' At another prayer-meeting at Chester, on a *Friday* evening, one of the leaders gave out the following lines:—

'*Another six days' work is done;*
Another Sabbath is begun.' etc.

I once heard a woman say in class, 'I do thank God that he ever gave me a desire to see that *death* that never, never *dies.*'"

Soon after Mr. Barker became "religious" and attended his class-meetings, he awaited the usual "call" to preach the gospel. Accordingly, having received the "call," he became a Methodist preacher, belonging to the Old Connexion, the New Connexion, and then advancing to Unitarianism, ultimately arriving at the climax of Freethought, in which cause he is now so distinguished an advocate. While a Methodist preacher, he was induced by a neighbor, an Atheist, to read Carlile's "Republican." We can readily understand why Christians are taught not to read "Infidel" works. The effect the "Republican" produced on Mr. Barker's mind would be augmented, did those Christians investigate what they so often ignorantly denounce. In reference to the "Republican," Mr. Barker says:—

"I was very much struck in reading some portions of the work [Carlile's], and agitated and shaken by its arguments on some points. The object of many of its articles was to prove Christianity irrational and false. The principal doctrines which it assailed were such as the trinity—the common notion about the fall of man, and its effects upon the human race—the Calvinistic notions of eternal, universal, and absolute predestination, unconditional election and reprobation—the Calvinistic notion of God's sovereignty or partiality—the utter depravity of every human being born into the world, and yet the obligation of those utterly depraved beings to steer clear of all evil, and to do all that is right and good, on pain of eternal damnation. The doctrine of satisfaction to justice, was also assailed, and the doctrine of the immortality of the human soul, and the notion that because it is immaterial, it must, as a consequence, be immortal.... The consequence was, that my mind was thrown into a state of doubt and suspense. I cannot say that I doubted the truth of the Christian religion exactly, but still I doubted the truth of certain doctrines which I had been taught to regard as parts of that religion. I can briefly describe the doubts I had. I neither saw clearly that those doctrines to which he objected were no part of the Christian religion, nor could I see any way by which these doctrines could be defended and proved to be rational and true. One thing began to seem almost certain, either that Christianity was not true, or that those doctrines as generally laid down, were no parts of the Christian religion. This led to investigation. I was wishful to ascertain whether those doctrines which were assailed as irrational, were parts of Christianity or not. I began to converse on the subject with one of my religious companions, and I began to read on the subject as I had opportunity. My companion was rather troubled and alarmed at the doubts I expressed with respect to the correctness of some of the common doctrines of what was considered orthodoxy; still, what I had said had some influence on his mind, for he told me shortly after, that he wished he had never heard my doubts, for what I had said had spoiled some of his best sermons; he would never be able to preach them with comfort more.... During my residence in that [Newcastle] circuit, my views on many subjects became anti-Methodistical to a very great extent indeed. I now no longer held the prevailing views with respect to the nature of justifying faith, the witness of the Spirit, regeneration, sanctification, and the like. In reading Wesley's works, I was astonished at the great number of unmeaning and inconsistent passages which I met with. In many of his views I perfectly agreed with him? but with a vast amount of what he said on other subjects, I could not help but disagree.... About this time, finding that there was little likelihood that I should be tolerated in the New Connexion unless I could allow my mind to be enslaved, and feeling that I should be obliged sooner or later to break loose from Methodistical restraint, and speak and act with freedom, I thought of visiting Mr. Turner, the Unitarian minister of Newcastle, and seeking an interview with him. I had heard something to the effect that Unitarians were great lovers of freedom—that they did not bind their ministers and members by any human creeds, but left them at liberty to investigate the whole system of Christianity thoroughly, and to judge as to what were its doctrines and duties for themselves, and to preach what they believe to be true without restraint and persecution, and I thought if this was the case, they must be a very happy people. But from other things which I had heard respecting them, I was led to regard them with something of horror—to look, on them as persons who trifled with Scripture authority, as persons who had rushed from the extremes of false orthodoxy into the extremes of Infidelity. I was in consequence prevented from visiting Mr. Turner, and I remained in comparative ignorance of the Unitarian body, in ignorance both of their principles and of their character, still shut up in the dungeons of orthodox slavery."

"The dungeons of orthodox slavery" did not long contain Mr. Barker; for he afterwards became better acquainted with the Unitarians, and formed one of their most energetic preachers. But Unitarianism, appearing to him at first true in its doctrine and free in its advocacy, shortly became insufficient for the cravings of his mind; and, at length, he found himself outside all the churches. The Bible, which at one period of his life seemed to him a perfect revelation from "God" now appeared only the production of erring and half-informed men; and having a thorough knowledge of its contents, he resolved to employ the remainder of his life in confuting the false notions of its "divine authority." America presenting a congenial residence, he resolved to visit that country and purchase some land, upon which he might occupy his leisure from lecturing and writing. Having settled in the country, he considered something should be said on the Bible. Accordingly, in November, 1852, a Bible Convention was held at Salem, Ohio, Mr. Barker being appointed President, he extract the following from his speech, as illustrating the uncertainty of the Bible translations, the character of the translators, and the nature of the manuscripts from which the translations are made:—

"We say, that the Bible bears on its very face the marks of human imperfection and error. This is true of every Bible in existence. We will begin with the Bible in common use, and what do we find! The title-page tells us it is a *translation* from the original tongues, by the special command of one of the kings of England. Does any one pretend that the translators were infallible—men above the possibility of error? Nothing of the kind. Even those who contend that the original *writers* of the Bible were infallible, do not pretend that the king's translators were so. The sects and priesthoods themselves show that they regard the common translation as imperfect. They all take the liberty to alter it. They alter it in thousands and tens of thousands of places. Nothing is more common than for theological disputants to appeal from the common translation of the Bible to what they call the original Greek and Hebrew. Every commentator takes the same liberty. The leaders of the sects and priesthoods of the day have testified their belief that the Bibles in common use are imperfect and erroneous by making *new* translations. There is scarcely an English sect or priesthood of any note in existence that has not produced a new translation of the Scriptures. John Wesley translated both the Old and New Testament. His translation of the New Testament continues to be used in the Methodist body to this day. Adam Clarke, in his 'Commentary,' translates afresh almost every important passage in the book. Many passages he translates in such a way as to give them meanings quite contrary to the meaning given them in the common Bible. Richard Watson, a Methodist preacher, commenced a new translation of the Bible. Dr. Boothroyd, a Congregationalist minister of England, published another translation. Dr. Conquest, a layman of the same denomination, published another, in which he says he made twenty thousand emendations, or improvements. He must, therefore, have thought the common Bible had twenty thousand imperfections or errors. Mr. Belsham, and other English Unitarians, published a new translation of the New Testament. Mr. Wellbeloved, a Unitarian minister, published a new translation of a great part of the Old testament, intending to publish a new translation of the whole Bible. Even ministers of the Established Church have spoken strongly against the common translation, and some of them have gone so far as to *publish* new translations *of portions* of the Bible. Alexander Campbell, the founder of the denomination which bears his name, has published a new translation of the New Testament. A Mr. Taylor published a new translation of the New Testament from Griesbach's Greek New Testament. A Mr. Sharp published another translation from Griesbach's Greek text. The Baptists have published a new translation of the Bible, I am told.... We are not alone, therefore, in believing that the Bibles in common use bear marks of human imperfection and error. The leading men in all the religious sects and priesthoods of Great Britain and America believe the same. We add, if the translators of the Bible had been the best and wisest men that ever lived, their work would not have been perfect. A translation from Greek and Hebrew cannot be perfect. But the translators employed by King James were not the best or wisest men that ever lived. They were, in some respects, exceedingly ignorant, prejudiced, and immoral.... They were liars and false-swearers. These dignitaries of the Church of England knew, as well as you know, that kings and queens are often vicious, profligate, and godless. They knew that among the kings and queens of England there had been some of the most loathsome lumps of filthiness—some of the most adulterous and lecherous sensualists—some of the most heartless and cruel tyrants—some of the most inhuman and bloody wretches that ever cursed the earth. They knew, too, that English kings and queens generally were under strong temptations to be thus cruel and profligate, and that it was too much to expect any of them to be strictly religious and virtuous. Yet they bound themselves on oath to call their kings and queens, whatever their characters might be, most gracious and religious.' They *did* call the monarch then living, 'most gracious and religious,' and they handed it down as a duty to their successors to give the same high titles to all their future monarchs, though they should be as filthy as that unwieldy, waddling mass of lust and rottenness, King Henry the Eighth, or at false and treacherous as the perjured Charles the First. These translators of the Bible also knew that many who were brought to them to be buried were godless, wicked men. They knew that some of them were drunkards, adulterers, false-swearers. Yet they bound themselves to call them all, as they lowered them into their graves, their 'beloved brethren,' and to declare that they committed them to the dust 'in sure and curtain hope of a resurrection to eternal life,' though they believed in their hearts that they would rise to eternal damnation.... They were the hirelings of the king and government. They regarded the king as the head of the church, and were sworn to obey him in all things. They were sworn to obey him in translating the Bible. The king gave them the rules by which they were to be guided in the work of translation, and they were sworn to follow these rules. These rules were intended to prevent them from putting anything into their translation of the Bible that was at variance with the established priesthoods, and to keep them from leaving out anything that was favorable to the Established Church and government. And they *kept* to their rules, and they were influenced by their interests, their situation, and their prejudices. It would be foolish to think otherwise. To make the Bible agree with their creed, they put into their translation things which were not in the Greek or Hebrew Bibles, and mistranslated vast multitudes of things which were in the Greek and Hebrew Bibles. I will give you an instance or two. Their creed taught that God once died, or laid down his life. There was nothing in the Greek or Hebrew Bibles to uphold this doctrine, so in translating the Bible they so altered a passage as to make it to teach the doctrine. You may find the passage in 1 John, iii. 16. It is as follows:—'Hereby perceive we the love of God, because he laid down his life for us.' Now the word 'God' is not in the Greek; it was put into the passage by the translators. In one place in the Old Testament it is said that Elhanan slew Goliath the Gittite. The translators have altered the passage so as to make it say that it was the *brother* of Goliath that Elhanan slew. See 2 Samuel xxi. 19.... Before a man can give a perfect translation of the Bible, he must have a perfect knowledge of both the Greek and Hebrew Bible, and of the language into which he would translate it. But no man has that knowledge. The Greek and Hebrew languages, from which the Bible has to be translated, are dead languages—languages which are no longer spoken or written by any people—languages which exist only in ancient writings. The meaning of many of the words of those languages is, in consequence, lost. The writings of the Old Testament are the only books remaining in the Hebrew language. There are no Hebrew books to throw light on dark passages, or to settle the meaning of doubtful words and phrases. True, we have Greek and Hebrew dictionaries and grammars, but these dictionaries and grammars are the work of imperfect and erring men, who had no other means oi understanding the meaning of the Greek and Hebrew languages than ourselves. These dictionaries and grammars differ from each other. None of them are perfect. The best abound with errors. We have better means of obtaining a knowledge of the Greek language than of the Hebrew — but the Greek of the New Testament is a peculiar dialect, not to be found in any other book. It is, therefore, as difficult to translate the New Testament as the Old. If, herefore, we would find a Bible that does *not* bear the marks of human imperfection and error, we must look for it in what are called the original Greek and Hebrew. But there is no such Bible. The Greek and Hebrew Bibles are as really imperfect as the English translations. The Greek and Hebrew Bibles are as really the work of imperfect and erring men as the English translations are. Many people imagine that there is only *one* Greek and Hebrew Bible, and that that one was written by Moses and the prophets, and by the evangelists and the apostles. But this is not the case. There are *several* Greek and Hebrew Bibles, and all of them are the compilations of fallible men. We have several Hebrew Old Testaments, and quite a number of Greek New Testaments, all compiled by different persons, but drawn, to some extent, from different sources. It should be understood, that the oldest Greek and Hebrew Bibles are not printed books, but written ones. They were written before the art of printing was known among Jews or Christians. Those written or manuscript Bibles are more numerous than the Greek and Hebrew printed Bibles. They are the work of different men, in different countries, and different ages. And no two of them are alike. They differ from each other almost endlessly. Some contain more, some less. Some have passages in one form, others have them in other forms. John Mills compared a number of those manuscripts of the New Testament, and found that they differed from each other in thirty thousand places. He marked and collated thirty thousand various readings. Other men have compared the Greek manuscripts of the New Testament, and discovered upwards of a hundred thousand various readings—a hundred thousand places or particulars in which they differ from each other. A similar diversity of readings is to be found in the Hebrew manuscripts of the Old Testaments. Now it is from these imperfect and discordant manuscripts that men have to make their Greek and Hebrew Bibles. They have nothing else from which to make them. And those Greek and Hebrew Bible makers have no means of knowing which of the various and contradictory manuscripts are the best.... You must understand that the original writings from which the manuscripts now in existence originated, have perished many ages ago. It is probable that the last of them perished more than sixteen hundred years ago. We have, therefore, no opportunity of comparing existing manuscripts with the original writings, in order to and out which are the true, the original readings. The discordant and contradictory manuscripts, therefore, can never be corrected.... It is not only of the common English Bible, therefore, that the words of the resolution are true, but of every Bible known, whether printed or written, whether in Greek and Hebrew, or in modern languages."

Since Mr. Baker has resided in America, he has visited England, and lectured for the Secular and Freethought Societies in England and Scotland; the total number of lectures he delivered during his visit amounted to 153, besides engaging in several debates, the principal one being with the Rey. Brewin Grant, at Halifax, during ten nights, on the "Divine Authority of the Bible," which is now published. The views now held by Mr. Barker on "God" and Secularism may be seen from the following extract of a letter addressed to the Editor of the Reasoner, written by Mr. Barker from America, on February 22, 1853:—

"I confess I know nothing of God, but as he is revealed in his works. With me, the word God stands for the unseen cause of all natural phenomena. I attribute to God no quality but what seems necessary to account for what I see in nature. My Jewish and Christian notions of God are all gone, except so far as they appear to be the utterances of nature.... As to Secularism, I think our business is with the seen, the worldly, the physical, the secular. Our whole duty seems to me to be truly and fully to unfold ourselves, and truly and fully to unfold others: to secure the greatest possible perfection of being and condition, and the largest possible share of life and enjoyment to all mankind in this present world. The machinery of sects and priesthoods for saving souls and fitting men for heaven, I regard as wasteful and injurious folly, except so far as it may tend to better men and improve their condition here. I have a hope of future life, but whatever is best for this life must be best for another life; whatever is best for the present, must be best for the eternal future. To reveal to men the laws of their own being, and to unfold to them the laws of nature generally, and to bring them into harmony with those laws, is, therefore, with me, the whole business of man. If there be another world, as 1 hope, it will, I suppose, be governed by the same laws as this. If men live on for ever, they will have all the better start in a future life, for having got well on in this. As an *art*, therefore, I believe in Secularism."

J. W.

Note by the American Publisher.—Soon after Mr. Barker's return from England, he resumed his lecturing in various towns and cities in the United States, giving great satisfaction, by his able addresses, to large and intelligent audiences. He still labors occasionally in the same pursuit, though at present he is residing on his farm at Omaha City, in the Territory of Nebraska. Much might be said in praise of his efforts to promote Liberalism in this country; but his greatest triumph, as we consider it, was his public debate with the Rev. Dr. Berg of Philadelphia. This took place on the 9th of January, 1854, and continued no less than *eight evenings*. The question was on "the origin, authority, and tendency of the Bible"—Dr. Berg affirming, and Mr. Barker opposing. This famous discussion was attended by thousands, and was probably the greatest affair of the kind that ever occurred. The speeches on both sides were published, making a large pamphlet of 190 pages. Of course, each of the debaters was victorious, in the opinion of his friends; but the trick played by the Christian party, in the closing scene, showed a determination on their part to claim the victory whether or no! For, as soon as Dr. Berg (who made the last speech) had finished, one of his friends took the platform, and, while the audience were separating, read some resolutions in favor of the Doctor and the Bible. "Less than one fourth of the audience," says the Philadelphia Register, "voted for them. The more serious part of the audience did not vote at all. The great majority seemed to take the thing as a farce. The result of the vote made a good many long faces on the stage and front seats. A short silence ensued, followed by a burst of obstreporous laughter, and cries of '*the Infidels have it!*' And so ended the most remarkable debate ever held in America."

The following correct and candid report of the above discussion, appeared at the time in the columns of the Pennsylvania Freeman:—

The Bible Discussion.—The discussion on the authority of the Bible, at Concert Hall, between Rev. J. F. Berg, of this city and Joseph Barker, of Ohio, closed on Thursday evening last, after a continuance of eight evenings. During the whole time, the vast hall was crowded with an eager multitude—numbering from 2000 to 2500 persons—each paying an admittance of 12 1-2 cents every evening, and on some evenings it is said that hundreds went away, unable to approach the door; nor did the interest appear to flag among the hearers to the last.

Of the merits of the question or the argument, it does not come within the scope of a strictly anti-slavery paper to speak, but we cannot forbear to notice the contrast in the manner and bearing of the two debaters, and the two parties among the audience. Mr. Barker uniformly bore himself as a gentleman, courteously and respectfully towards his opponent, and with the dignity becoming his position, and the solemnity and importance of the question. We regret that we cannot say the same of Dr. Berg, who at times seemed to forget the obligations of the gentleman in his zeal as a controversialist. He is an able and skillful debater, though less logical than Mr. Barker, but he wasted his time and strength too often on personalities and irrelevant matters. His personal inuendoes and epithets, his coarse witticisms, and a bearing that seemed to us more arrogant than Christian, may have suited the vulgar and the intolerant among his party, but we believe these things won him no respect from the calm and thinking portion of the audience, while we know that they grieved and offended some intelligent and candid men who thoroughly agreed with his views. It is surely time that all Christians and clergymen had learned that men whom they regard as heretics and Infidels have not forfeited their claims to the respect and courtesies of social life, by their errors of opinion, and that insolence and arrogance, contemptuous sneers and impeachment of motives and character, toward such men, are not effective means of grace for their enlightenment and conversion.

Among the audience, there was a large number of men, who also lost their self-control in their dislike to Mr. Barker's views, and he was often interrupted, and sometimes checked in his argument, by hisses, groans, sneers, vulgar cries, and clamor, though through all these annoyances and repeated provocations, he maintained his wonted composure of manner and clearness of thought. On the other hand, Dr. Berg was heard with general quiet by his opponents, and greeted with clamorous applause by his friends, who seemed to constitute a large majority of the audience, and to feel that the triumph of their cause, like the capture of Jericho of old, depended upon the amount of noise made.

Mr. Barker, in giving an account of the origin of the discussion, says:—

"In December, 1853 in compliance with a request from the Sunday Institute, I began a course of lectures in Philadelphia, on the origin, authority and influence of the Scriptures. The object of the lectures was to show that the Bible is of *human* origin, that its teachings are not of divine authority, and that the doctrine that the Bible is God's word is injurious in its tendency.

"When I sent the Sunday Institute a programme of my lectures, I authorised the Secretary to announce, through the papers, that I was willing to meet any clergyman, of good standing in any of the leading churches, in public discussion on the Bible question."

[The Rev. Mr. McCalla, a Presbyterian clergyman, accepted the offer, and arrangements were made for a six nights debate; but, on the fifth evening, after trying to raise a mob, he withdrew from the contest.]

"The clergy, or a portion of the clergy, of Philadelphia, unwilling to leave their cause in this plight, demanded that I should discuss the question with Dr. Berg, a minister in whom they had fuller confidence. Being assured that Dr. Berg was a gentleman and a scholar, and that he was the ablest debater the clergy of Philadelphia could boast, I agreed to meet him, and the discussion was fixed for the 9th, 10th, 12th, 13th, 16th, 17th, 18th and 19th of January."....

"Though the Doctor did not prove himself so much of a gentleman as I had been encouraged to expect, I was sorry he declined to continue the discussion four nights longer, as we had not got more than half through the question when the eighth night closed. I wished for an opportunity of laying the whole subject before the public. Perhaps some other clergyman will take the matter in hand—one disposed and able to discuss the subject thoroughly."